MW01618500

**Rare Birds   Amanda de Cadenet**

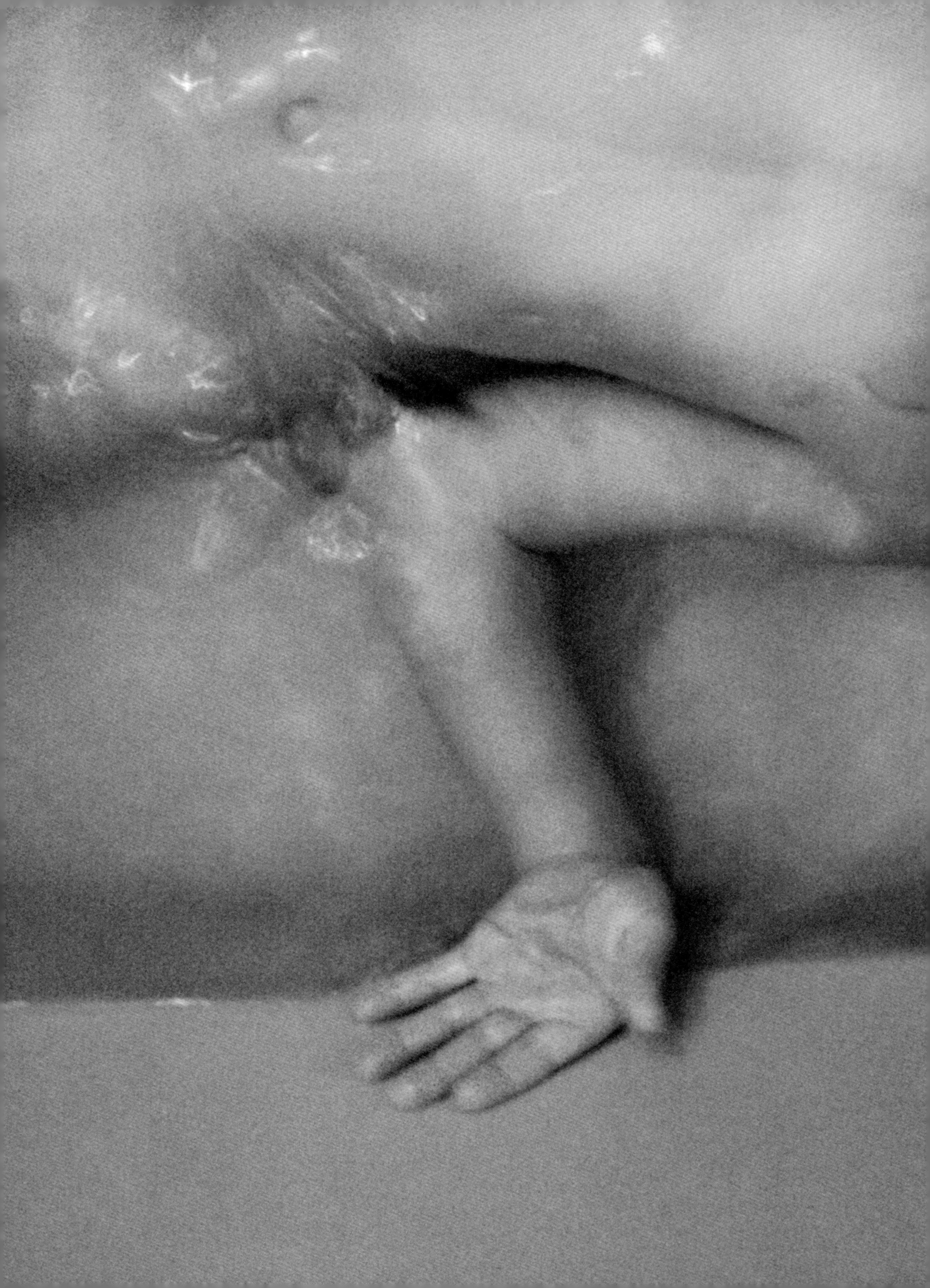

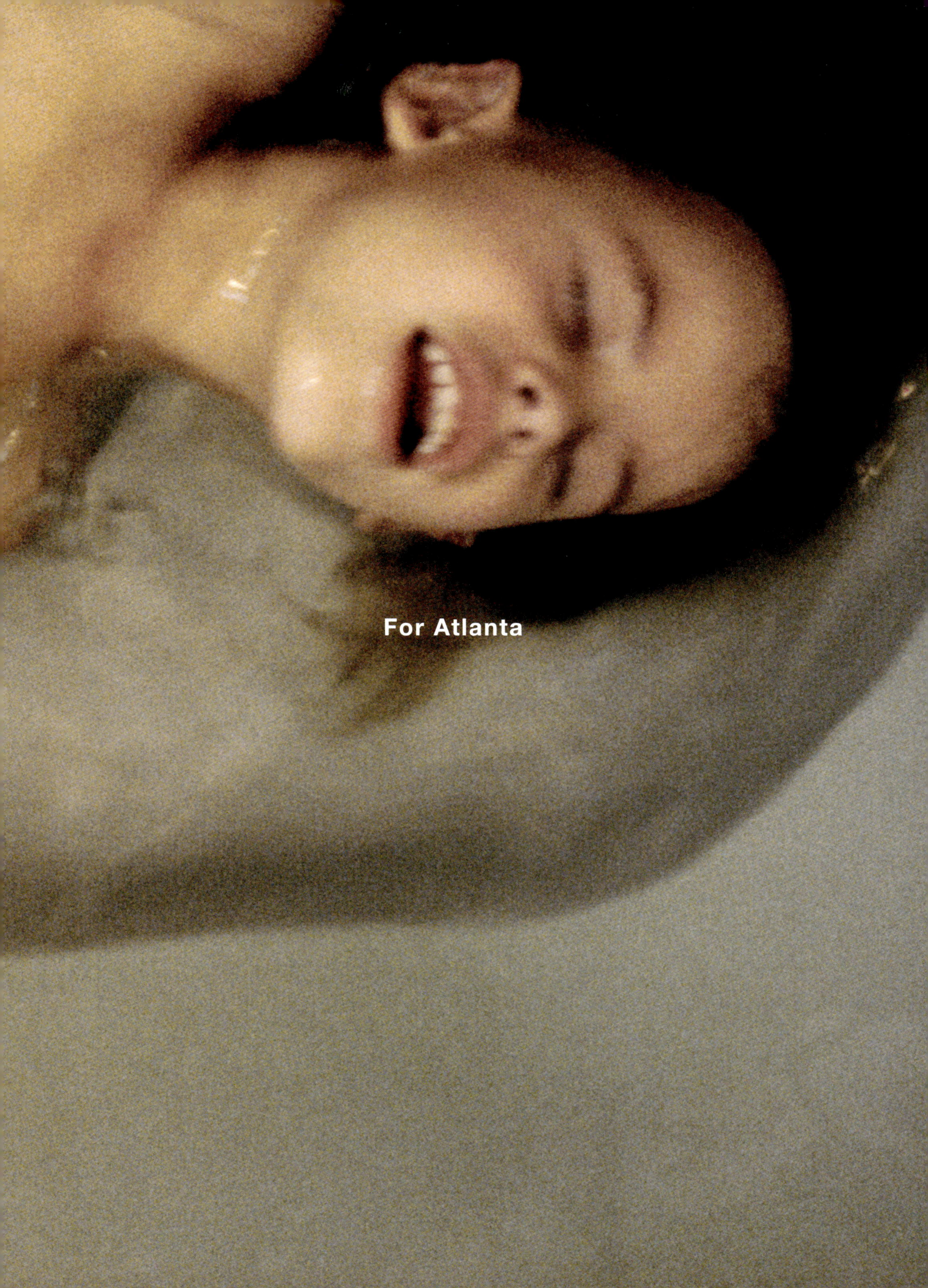

For Atlanta

pH powerHouse Books New York, NY

# Rare Birds Amanda de Cadenet

Conversation with Sophie Dahl + Marc Jacobs

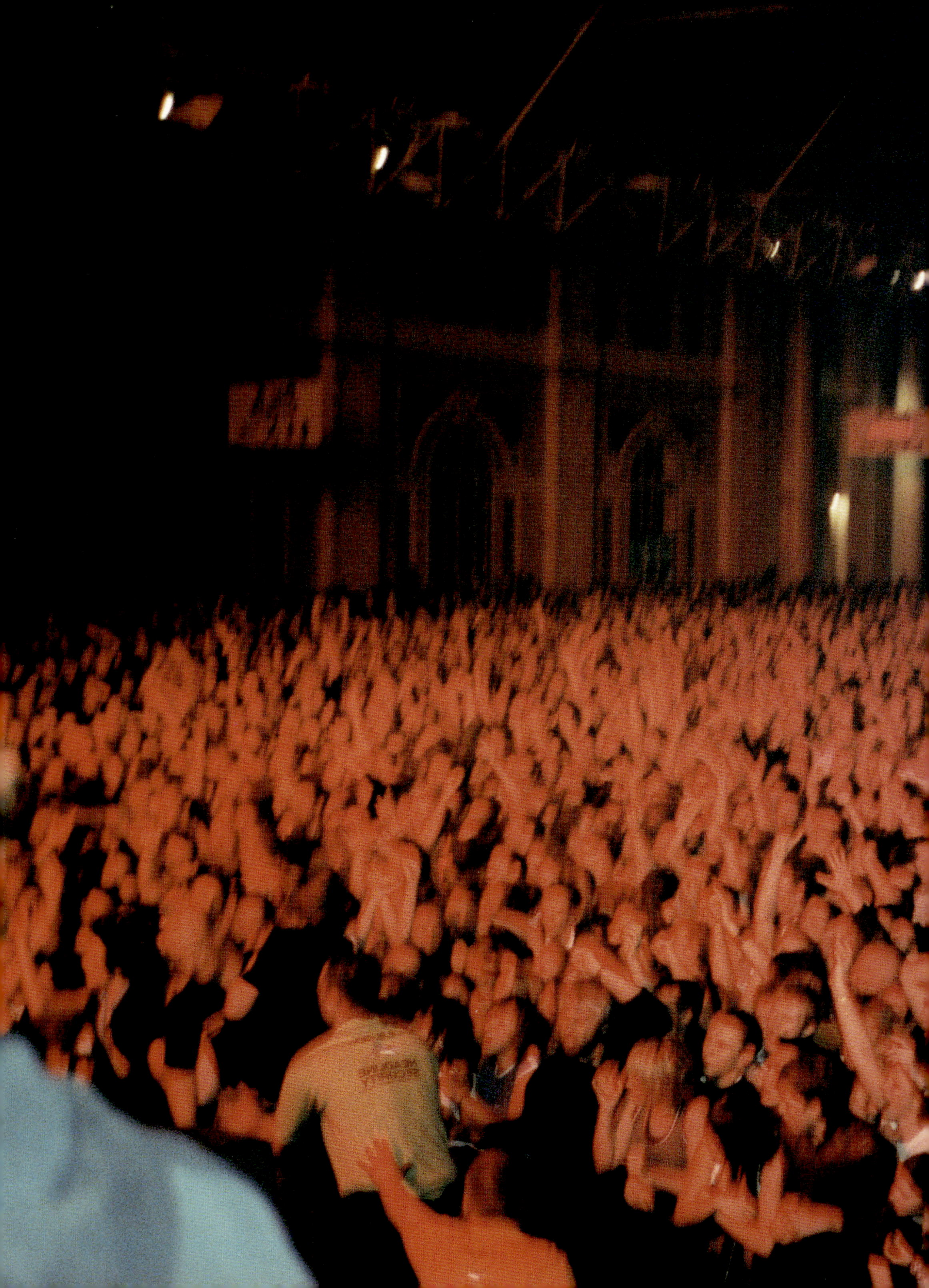

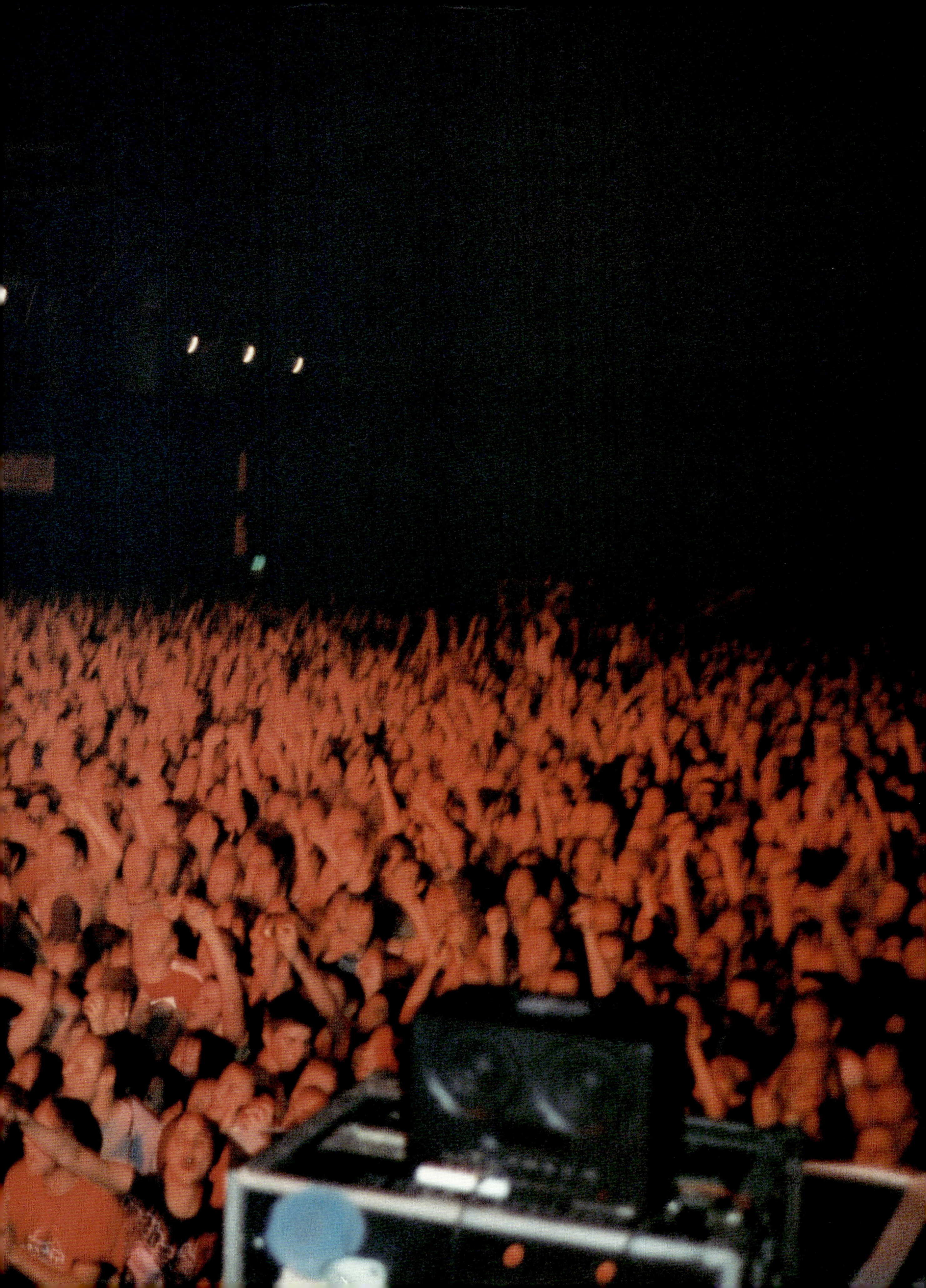

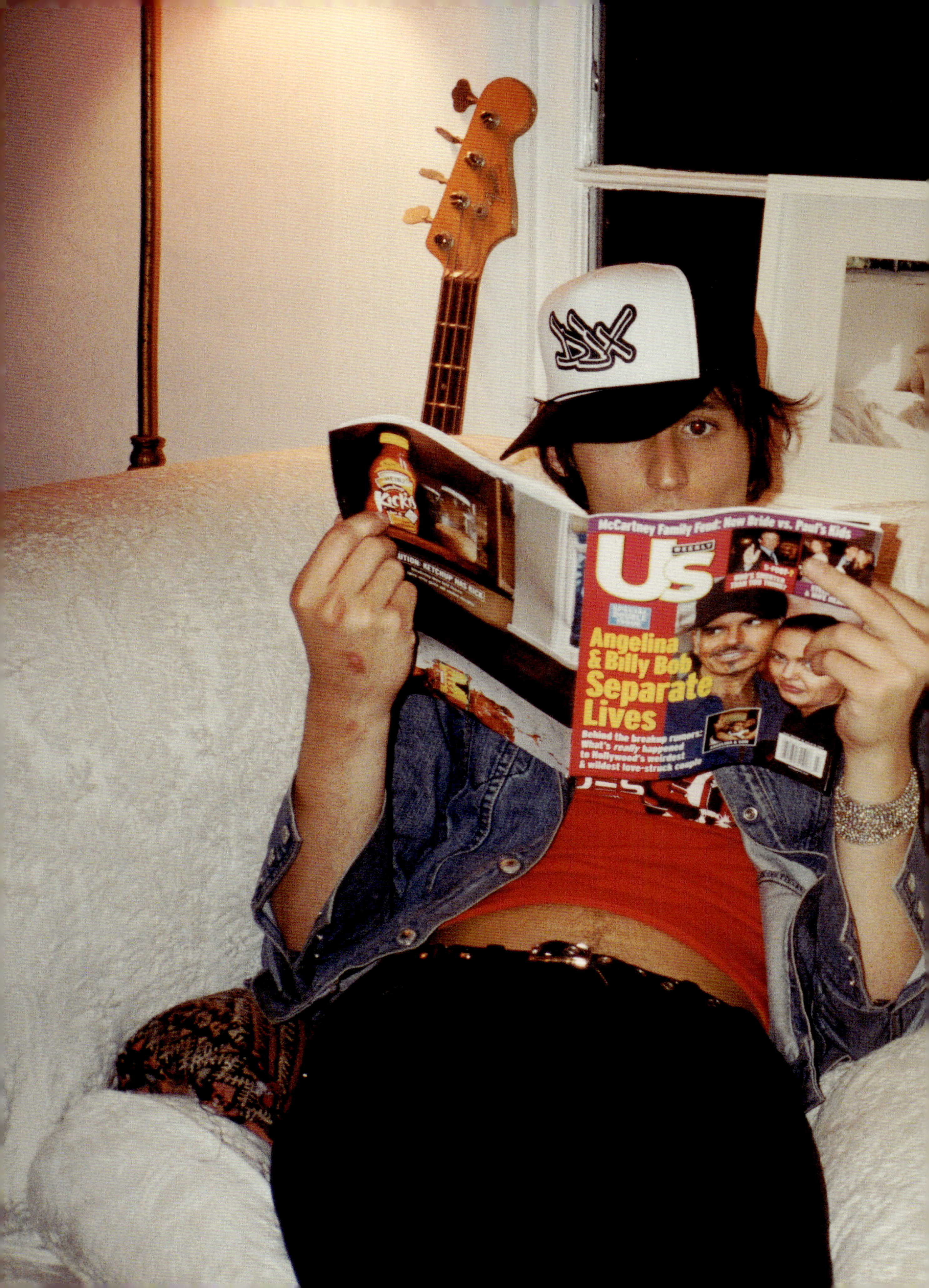
McCartney Family Feud: New Bride vs. Paul's Kids
Us
WEEKLY
Angelina & Billy Bob Separate Lives
Behind the breakup rumors: What's really happened to Hollywood's weirdest & wildest love-struck couple
Kicks

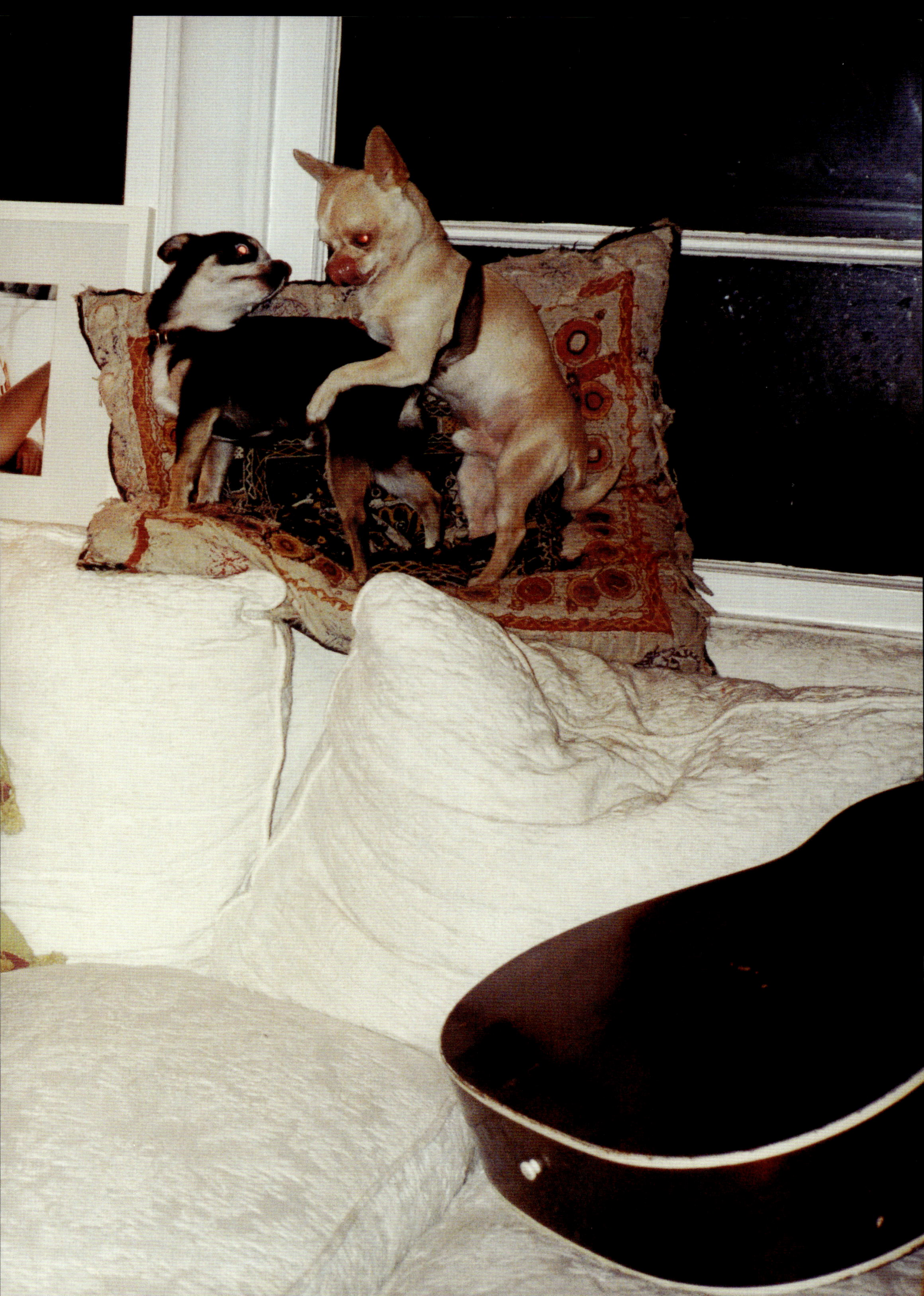

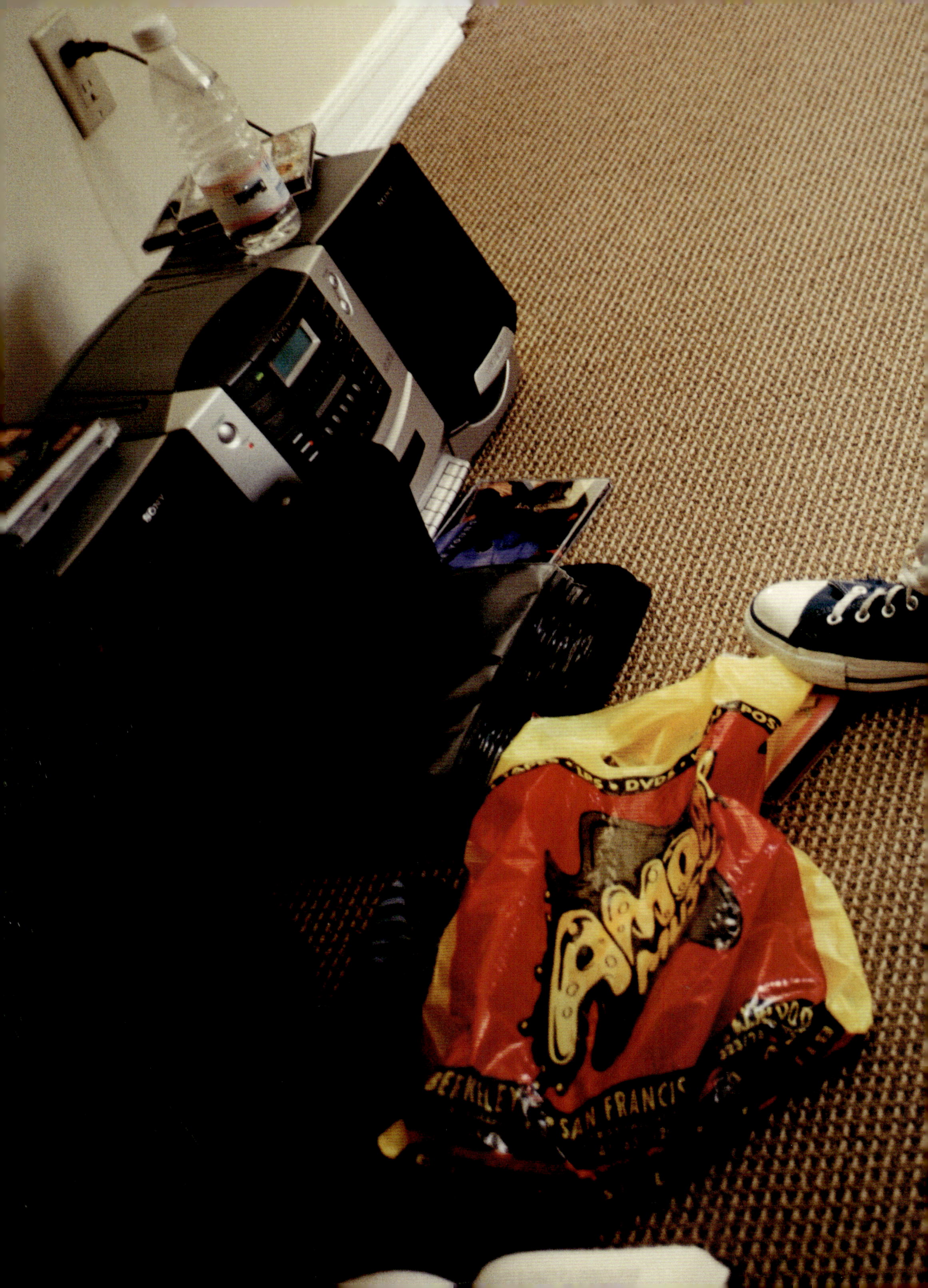
SAN FRANCIS

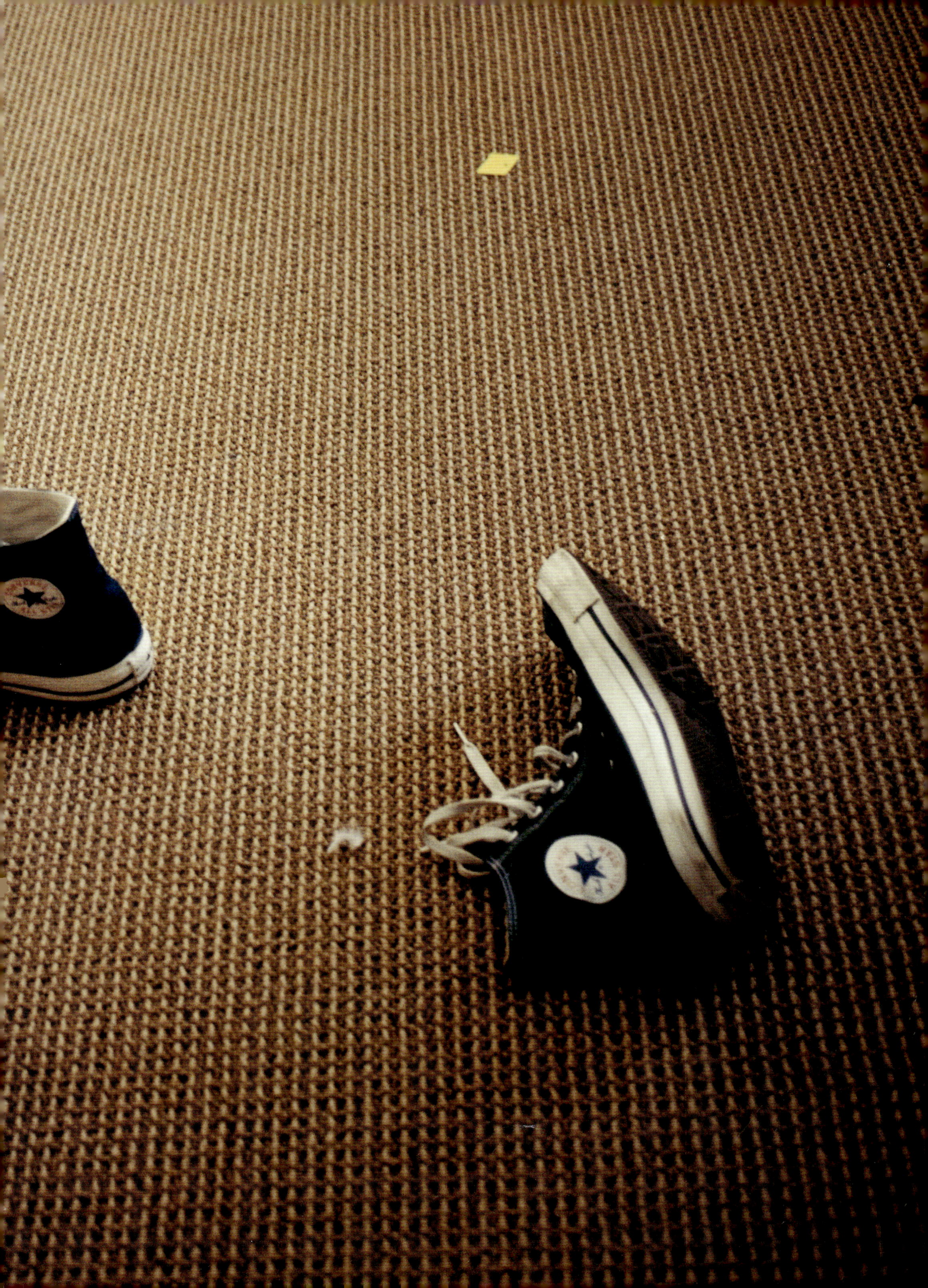

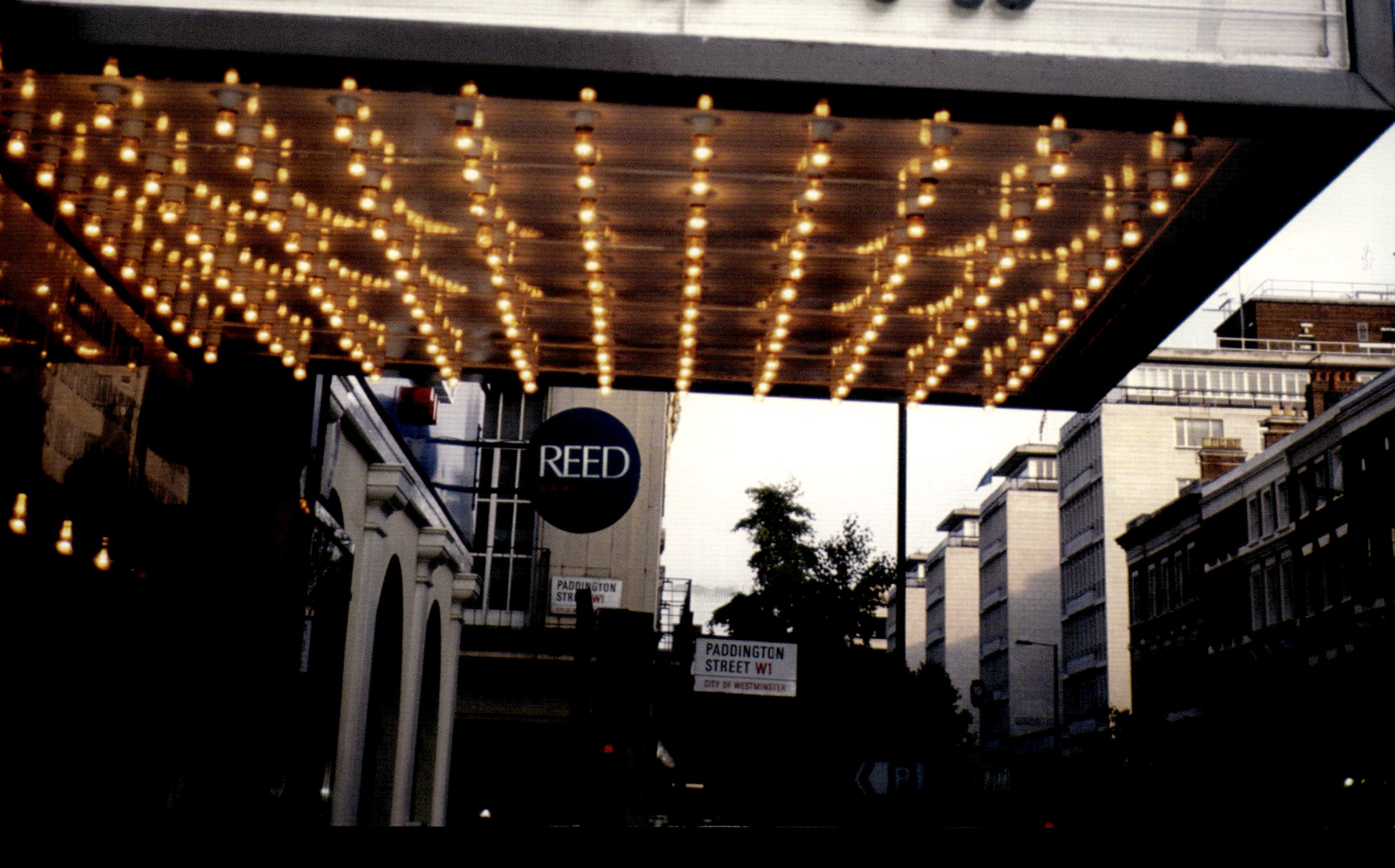
The Screen on Baker St.
KEANU REEVES
THE MATRIX
15
3 10 6 00 8 50
REED
PADDINGTON STREET W1
CITY OF WESTMINSTER

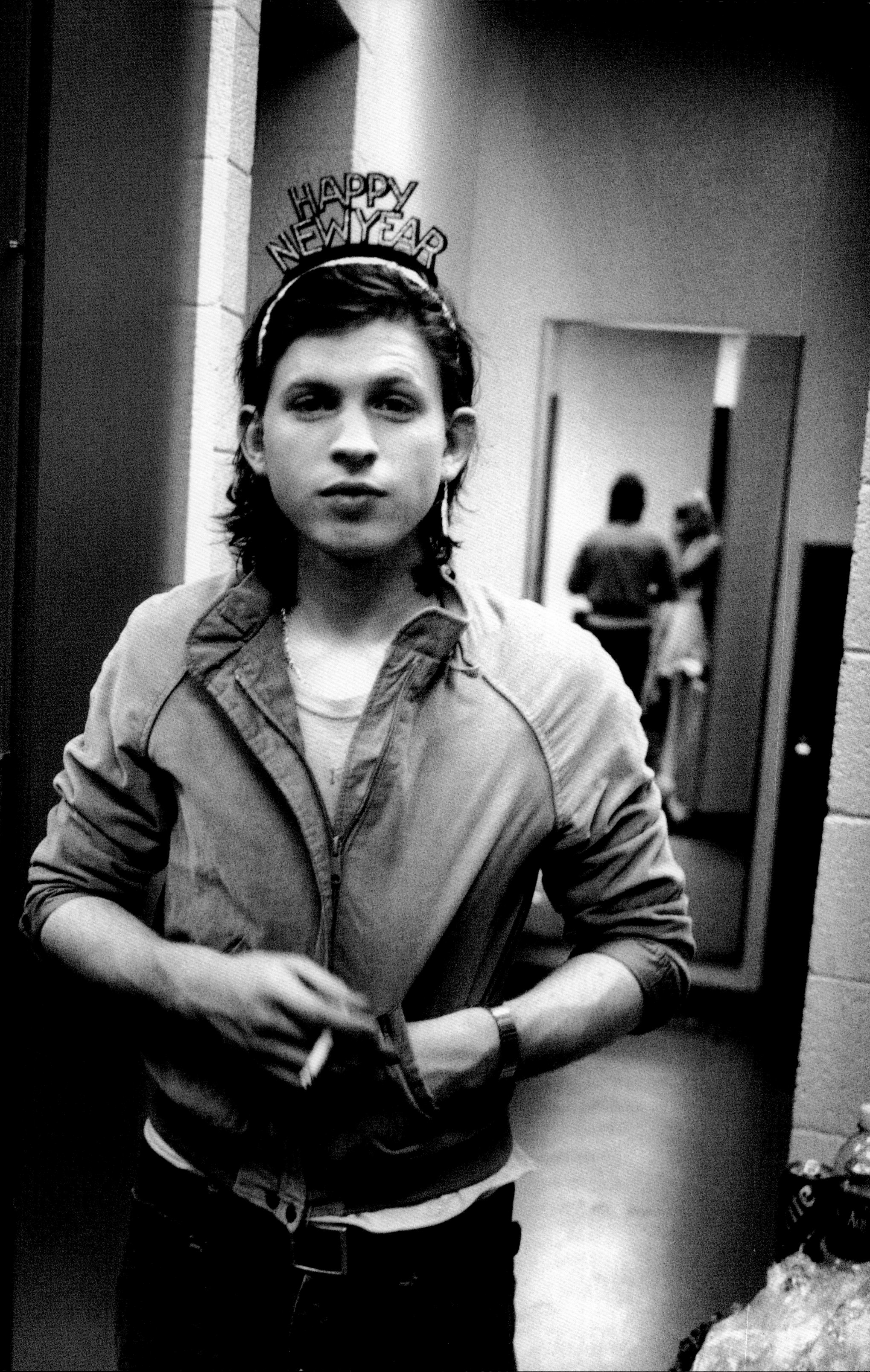
HAPPY
NEW YEAR

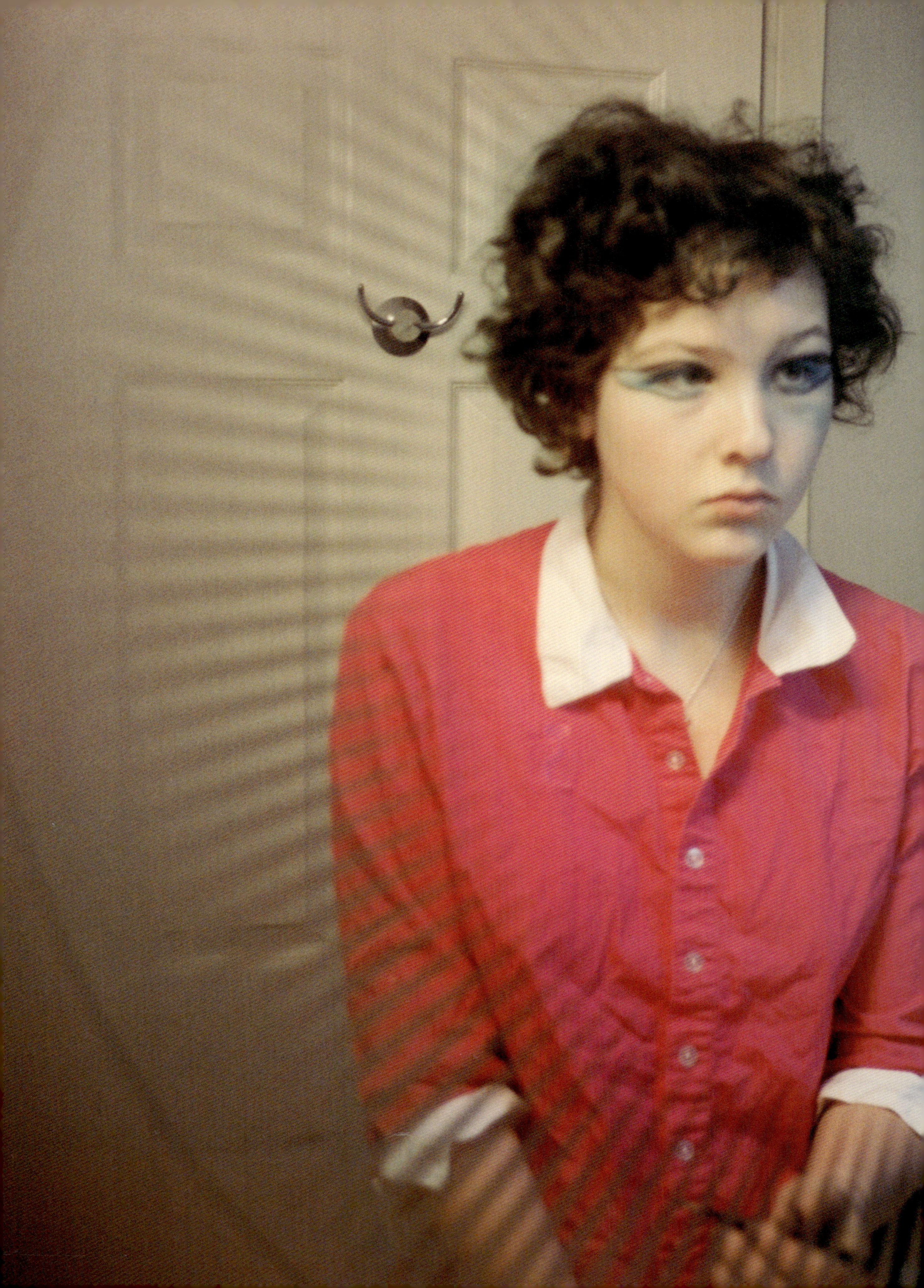

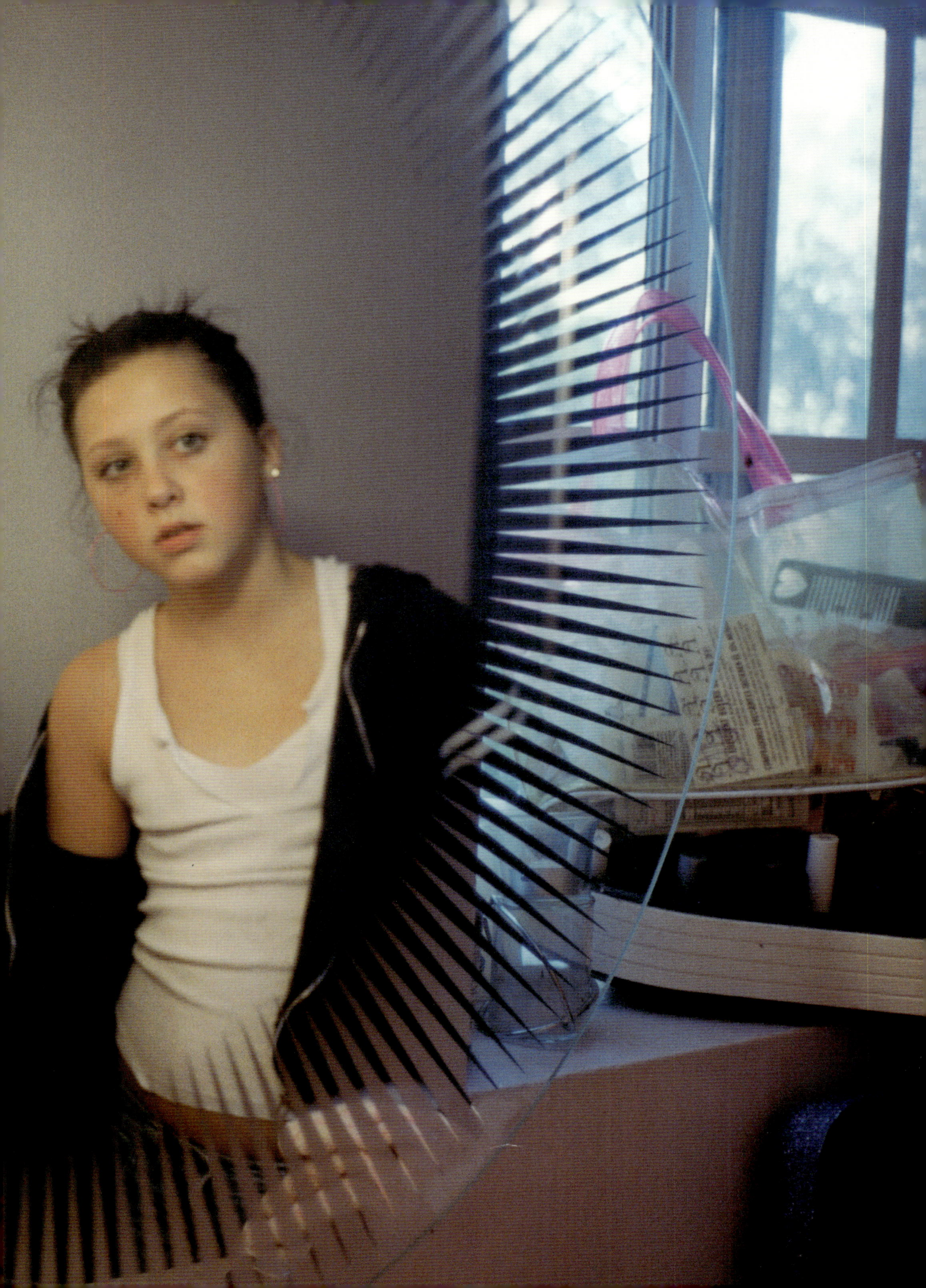

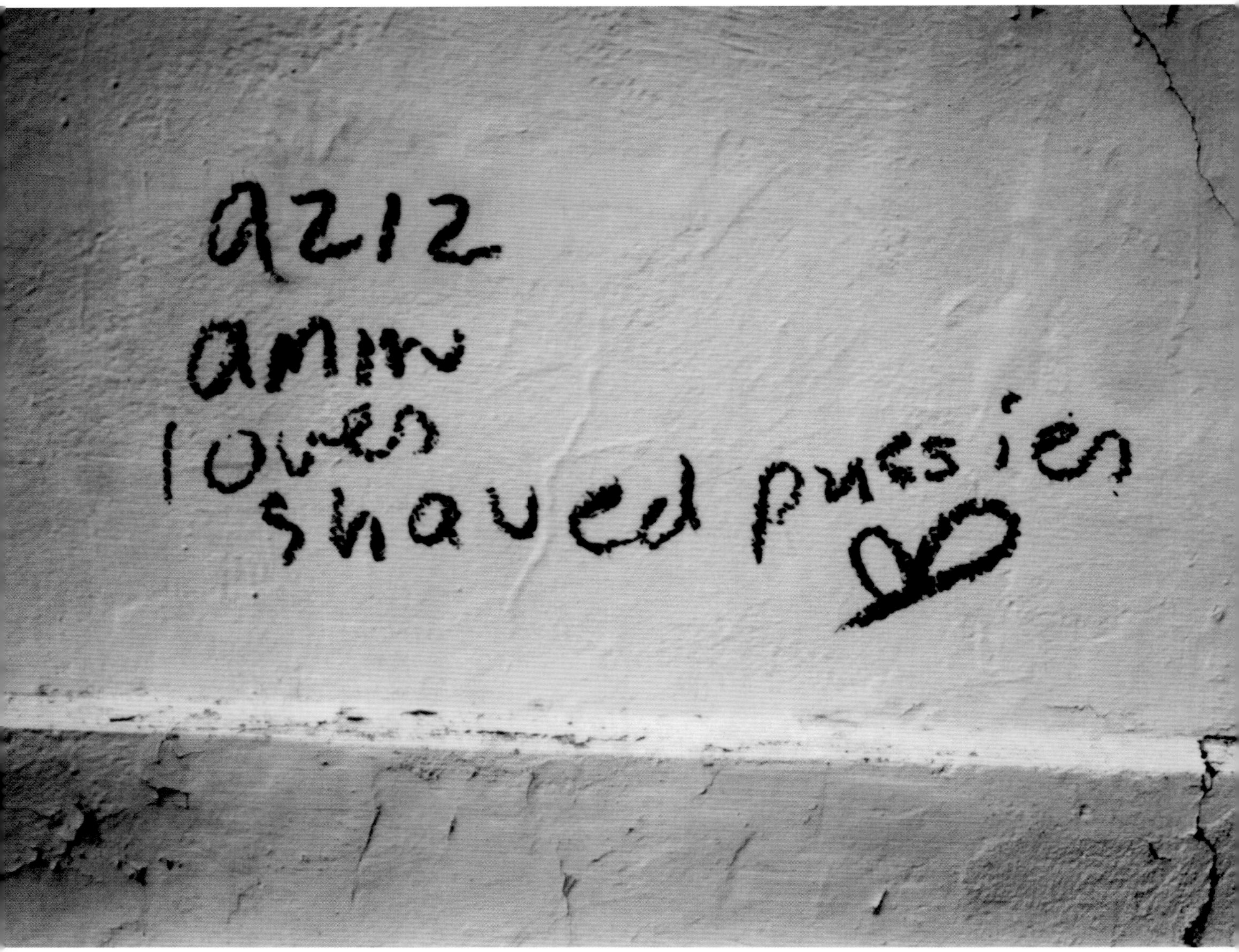

aziz
amin
loves
shaved pussies

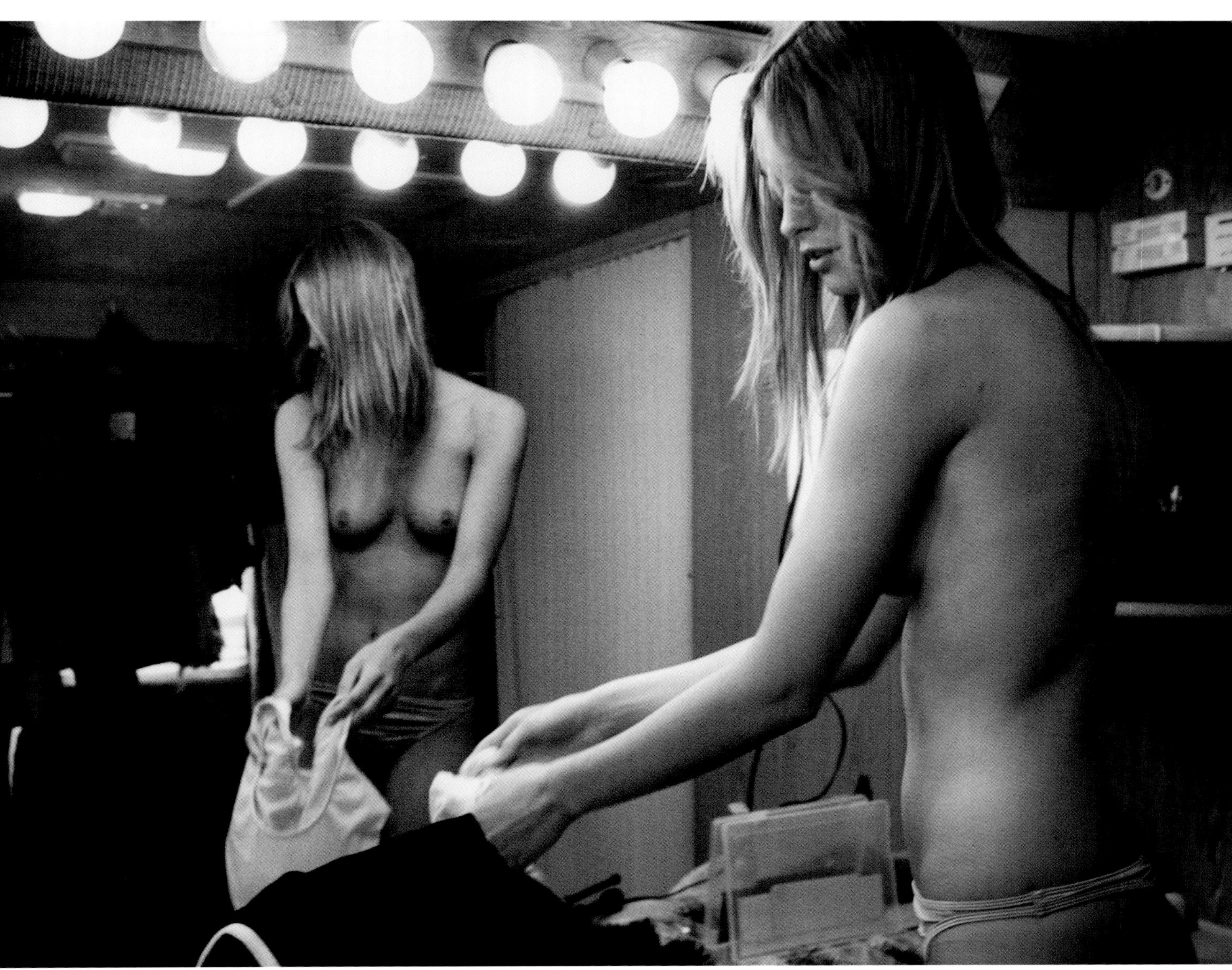

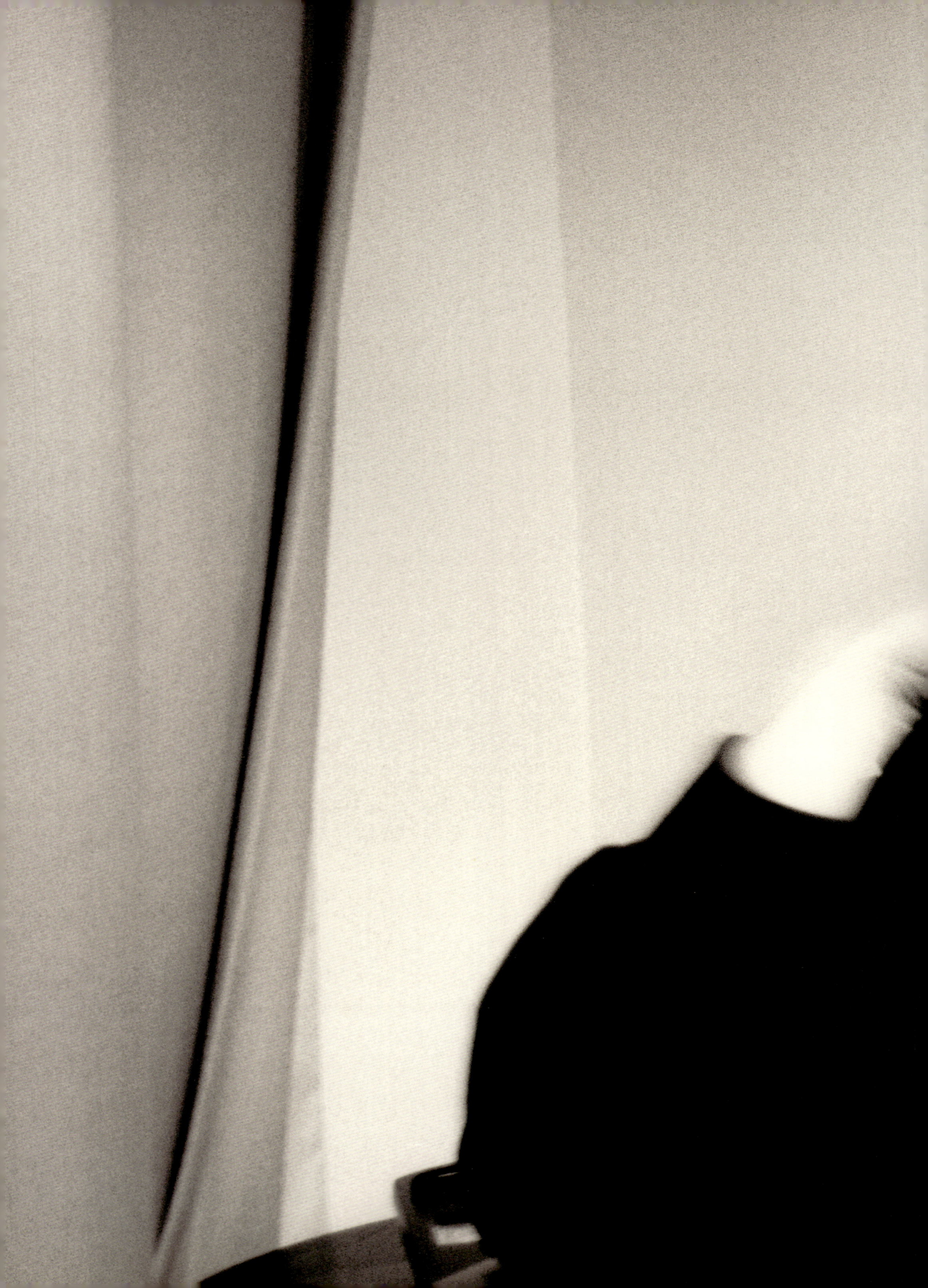

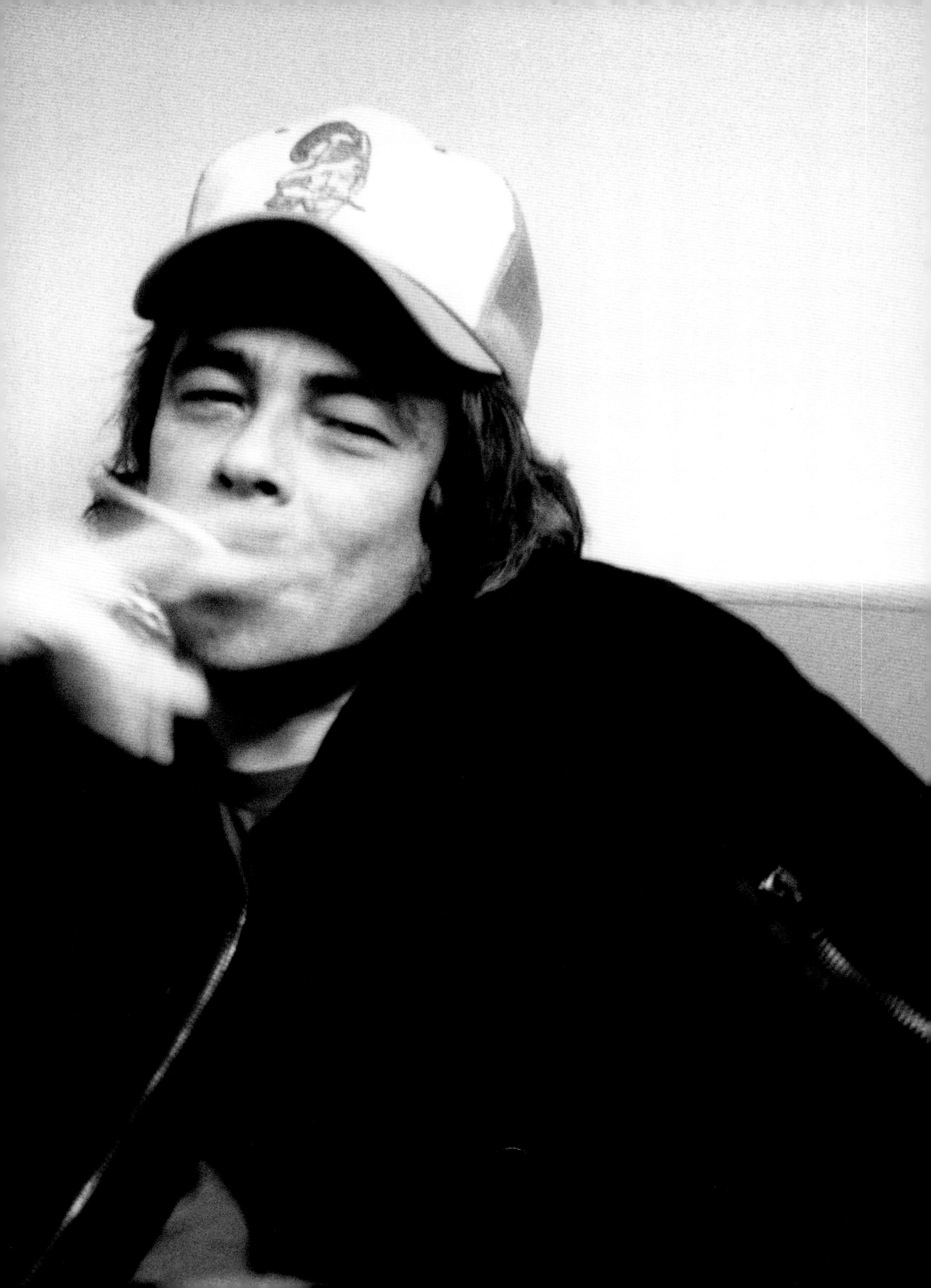

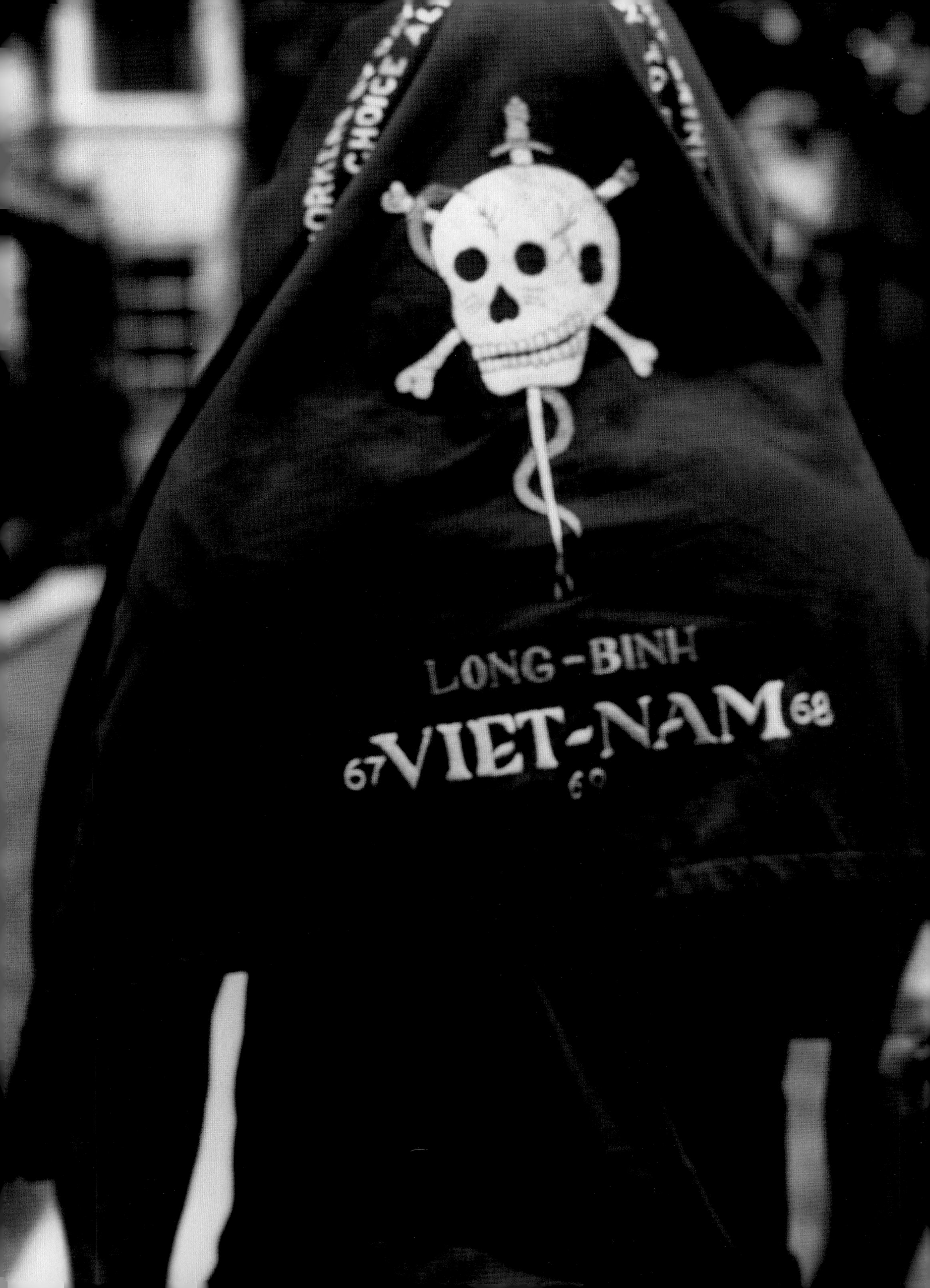

LONG-BINH
67 VIET-NAM 68

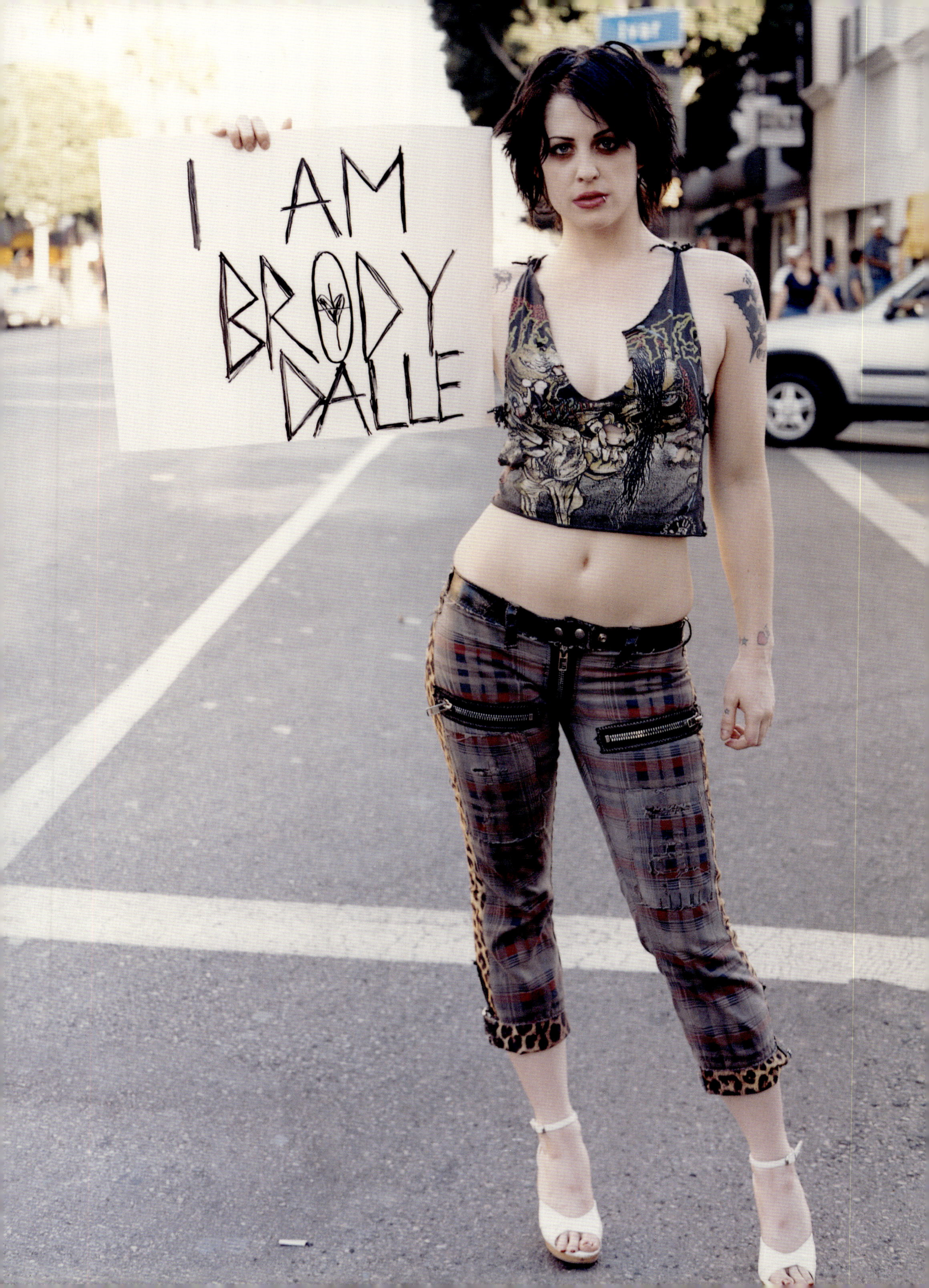
I AM
BRODY
DALLE

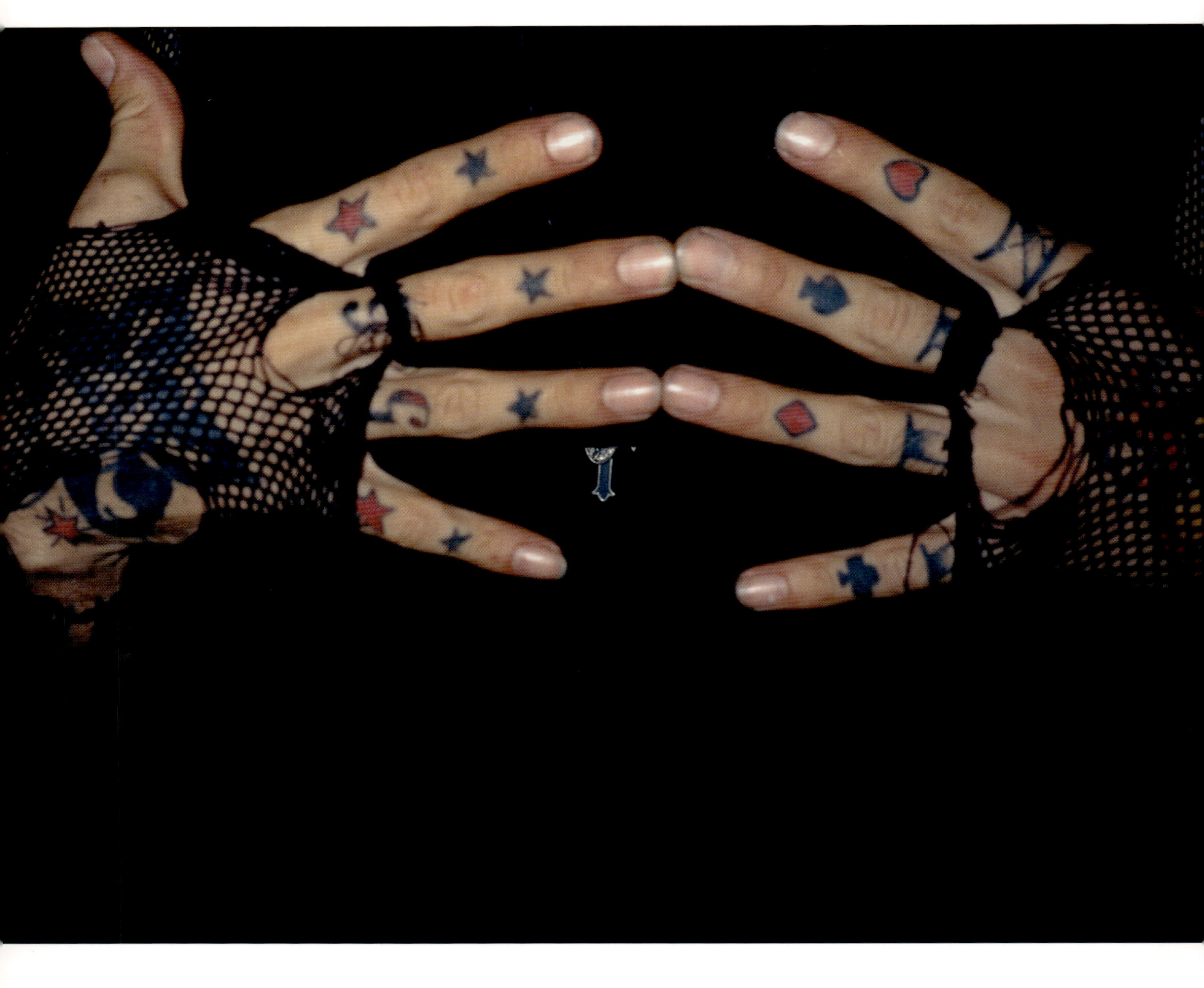

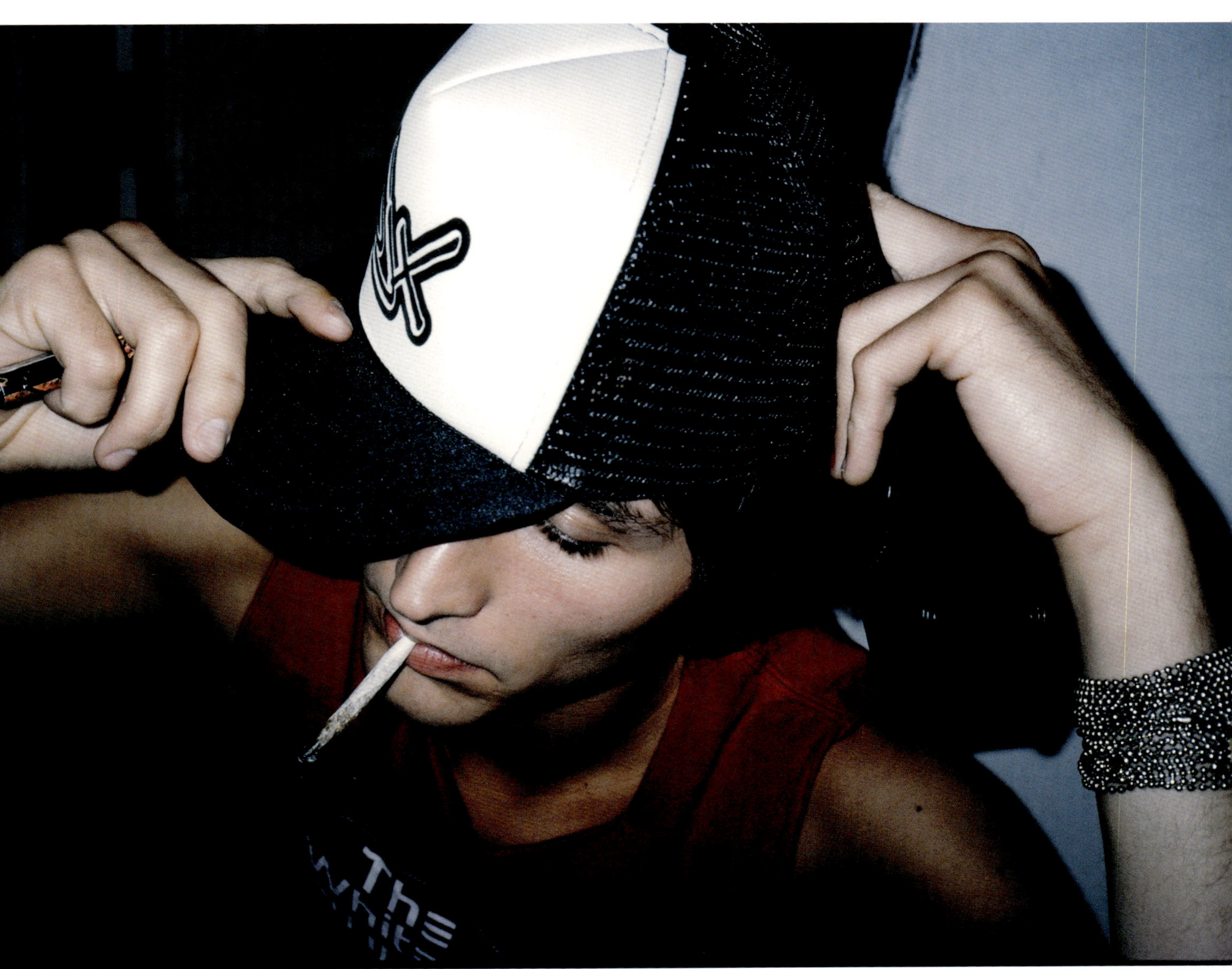
The

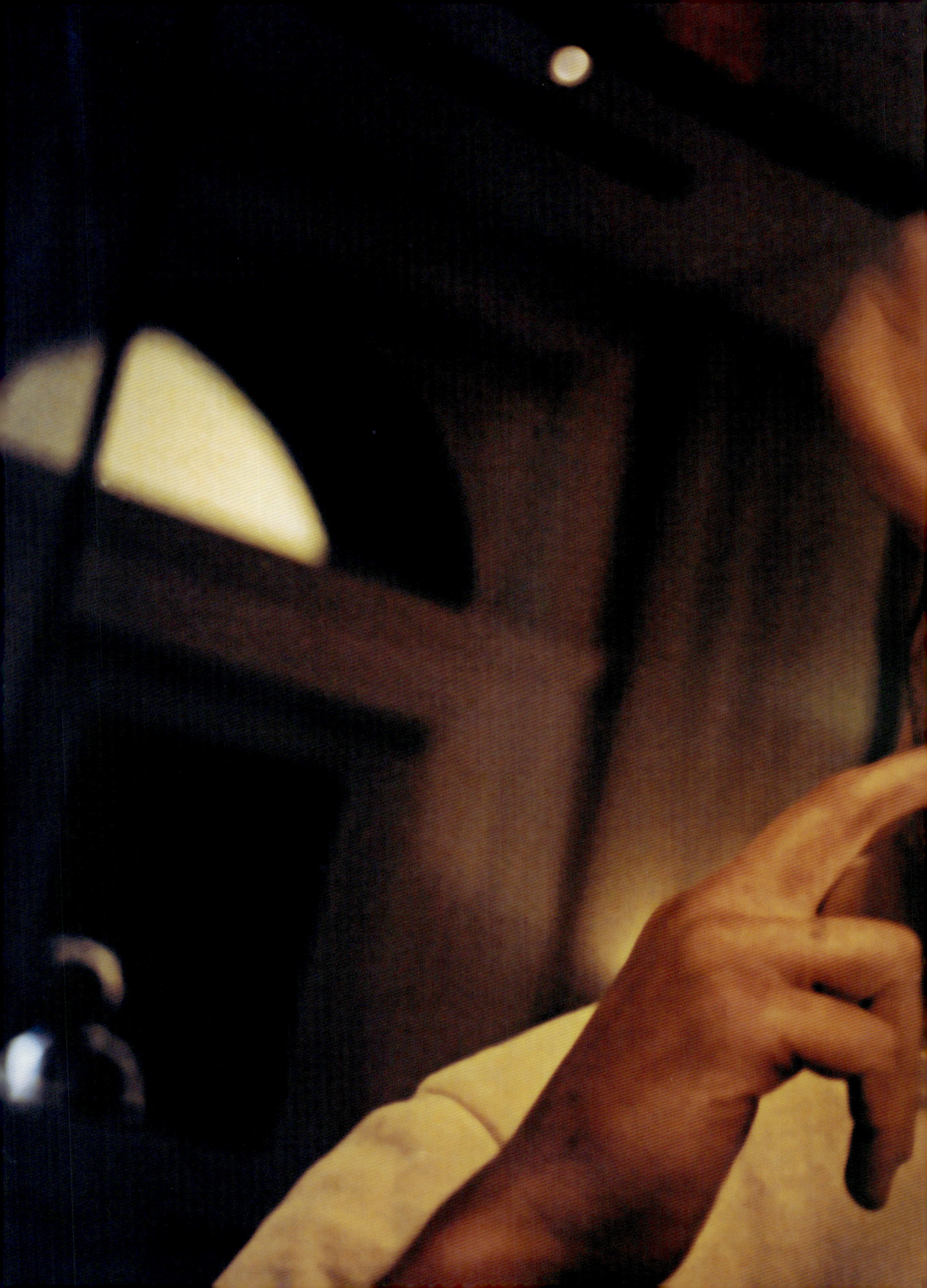

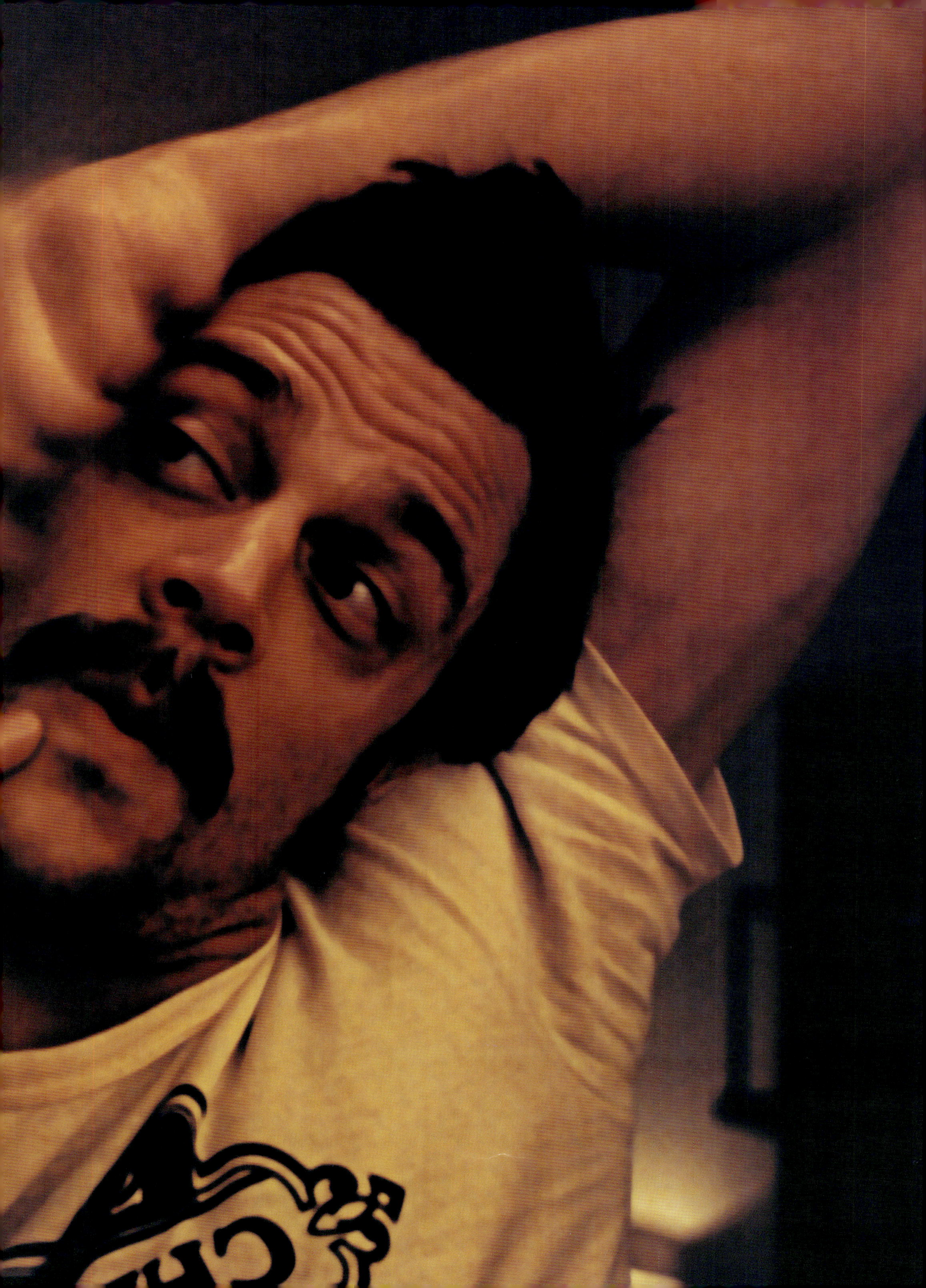

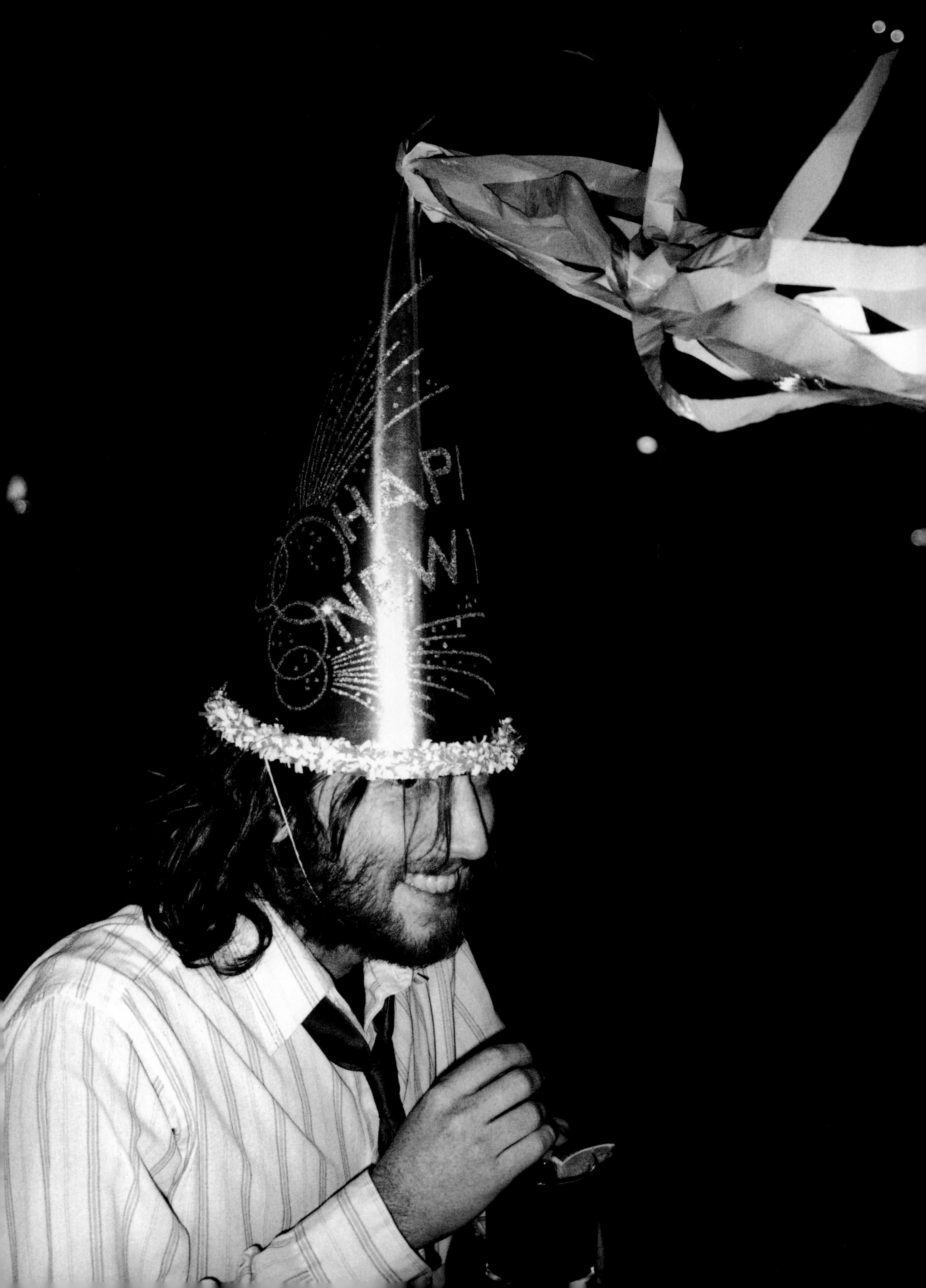
HAP
NEW

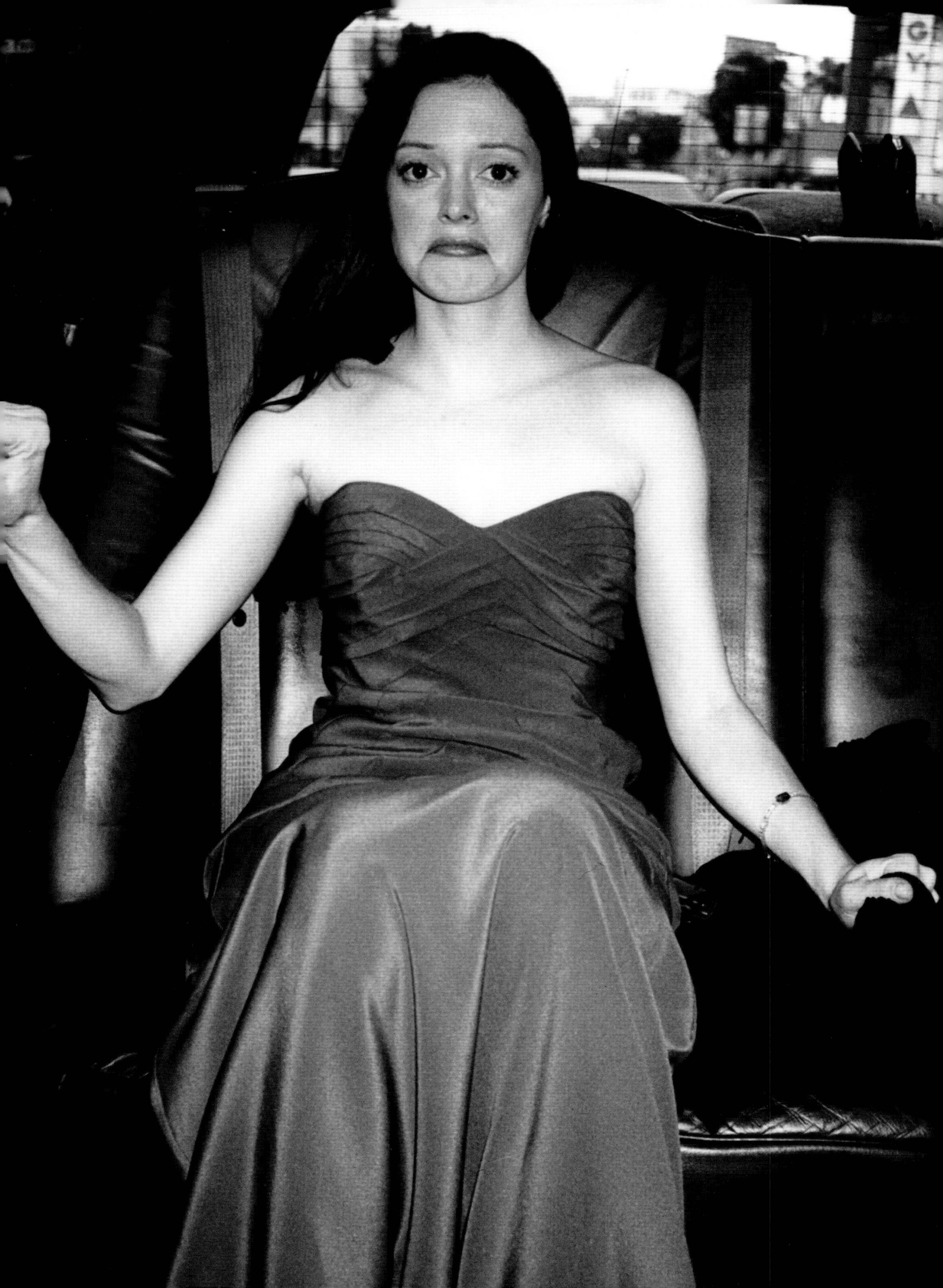

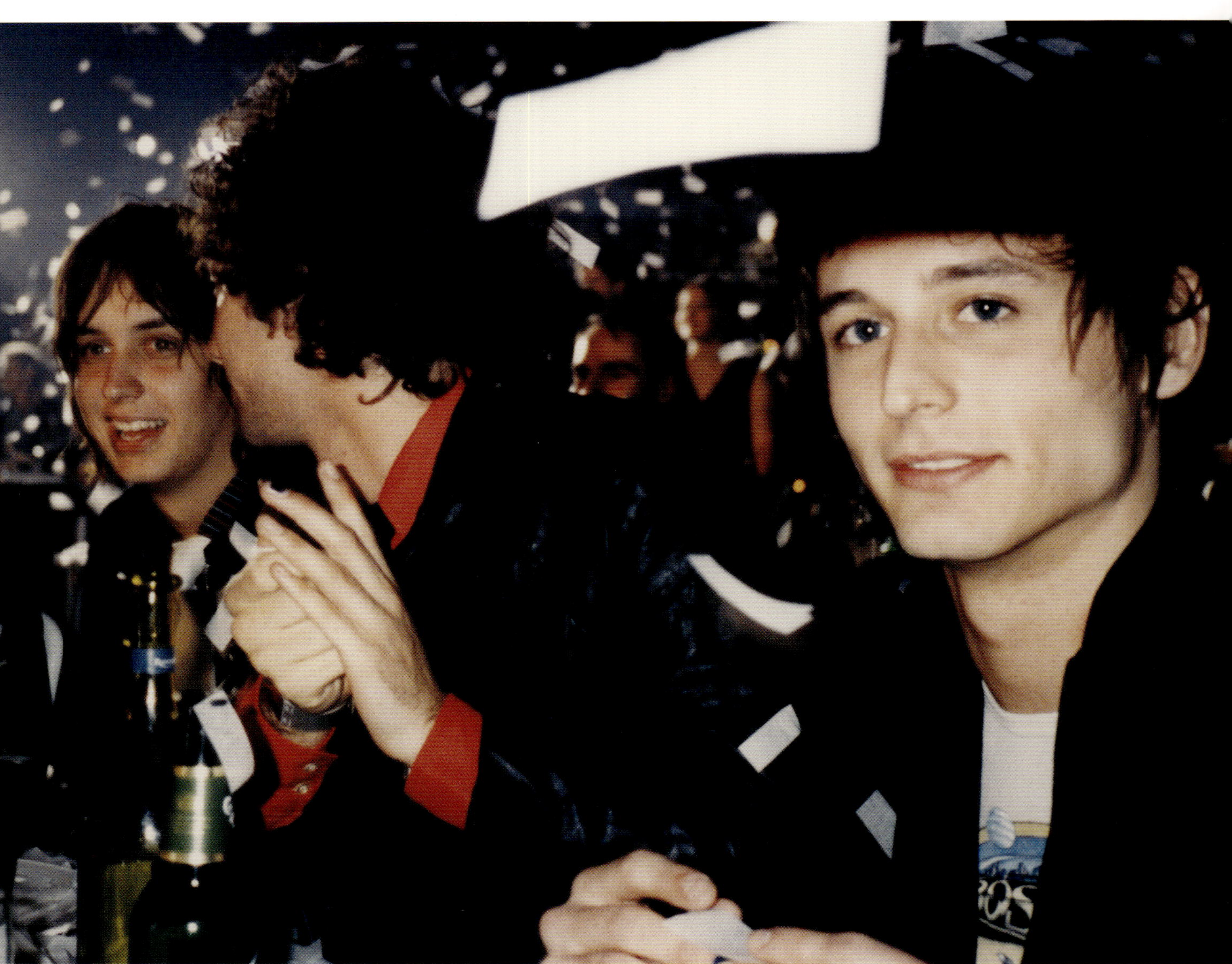

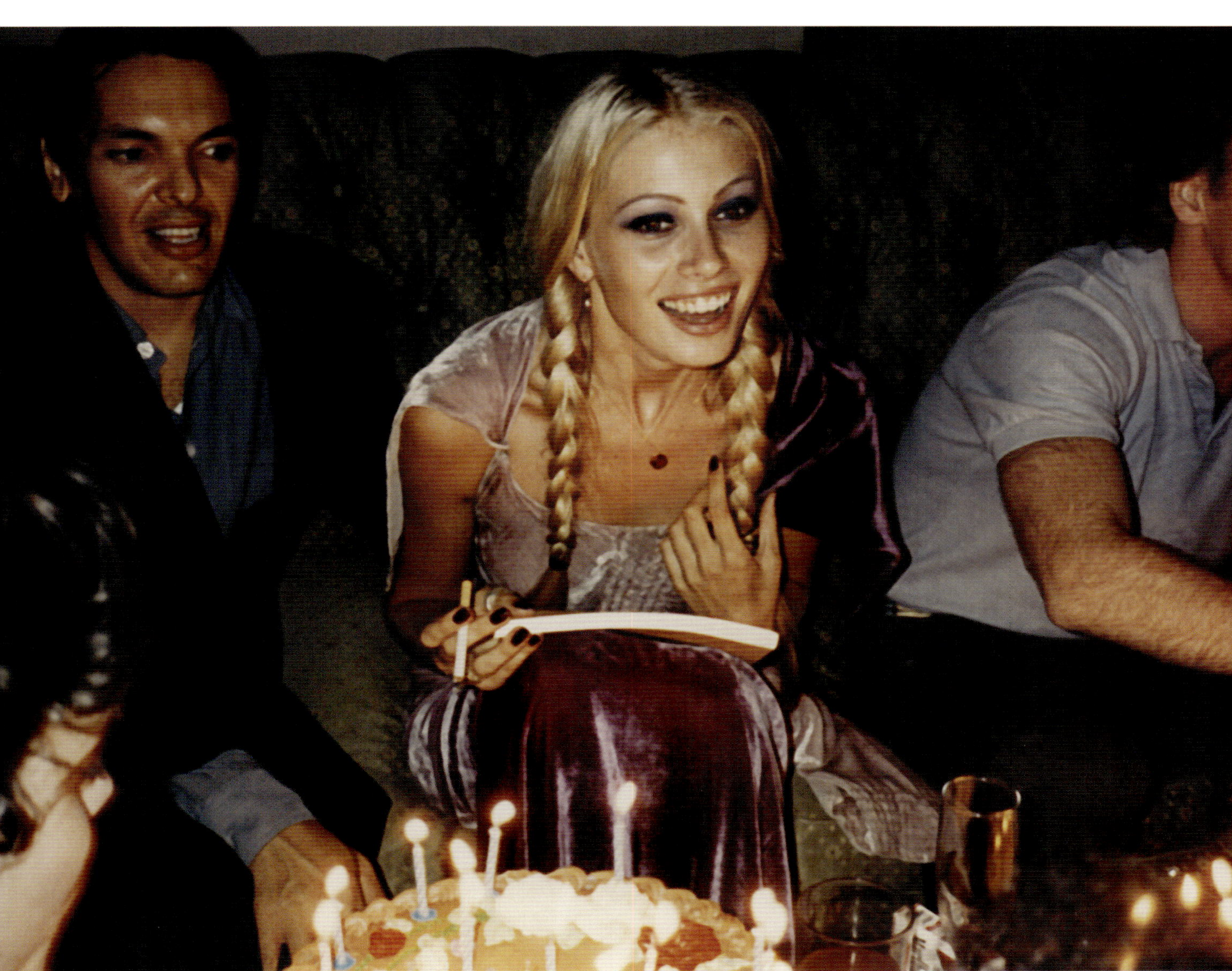

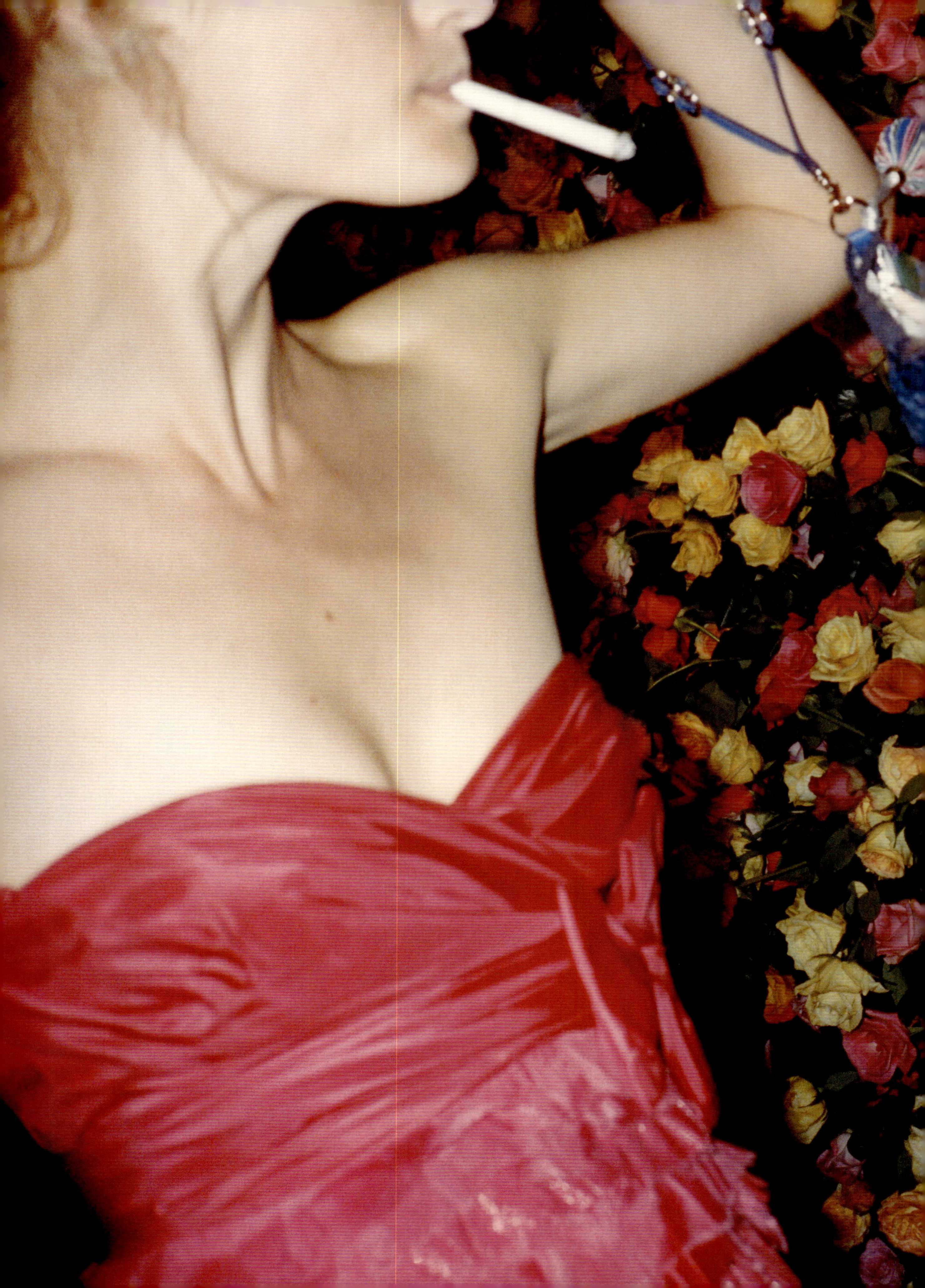

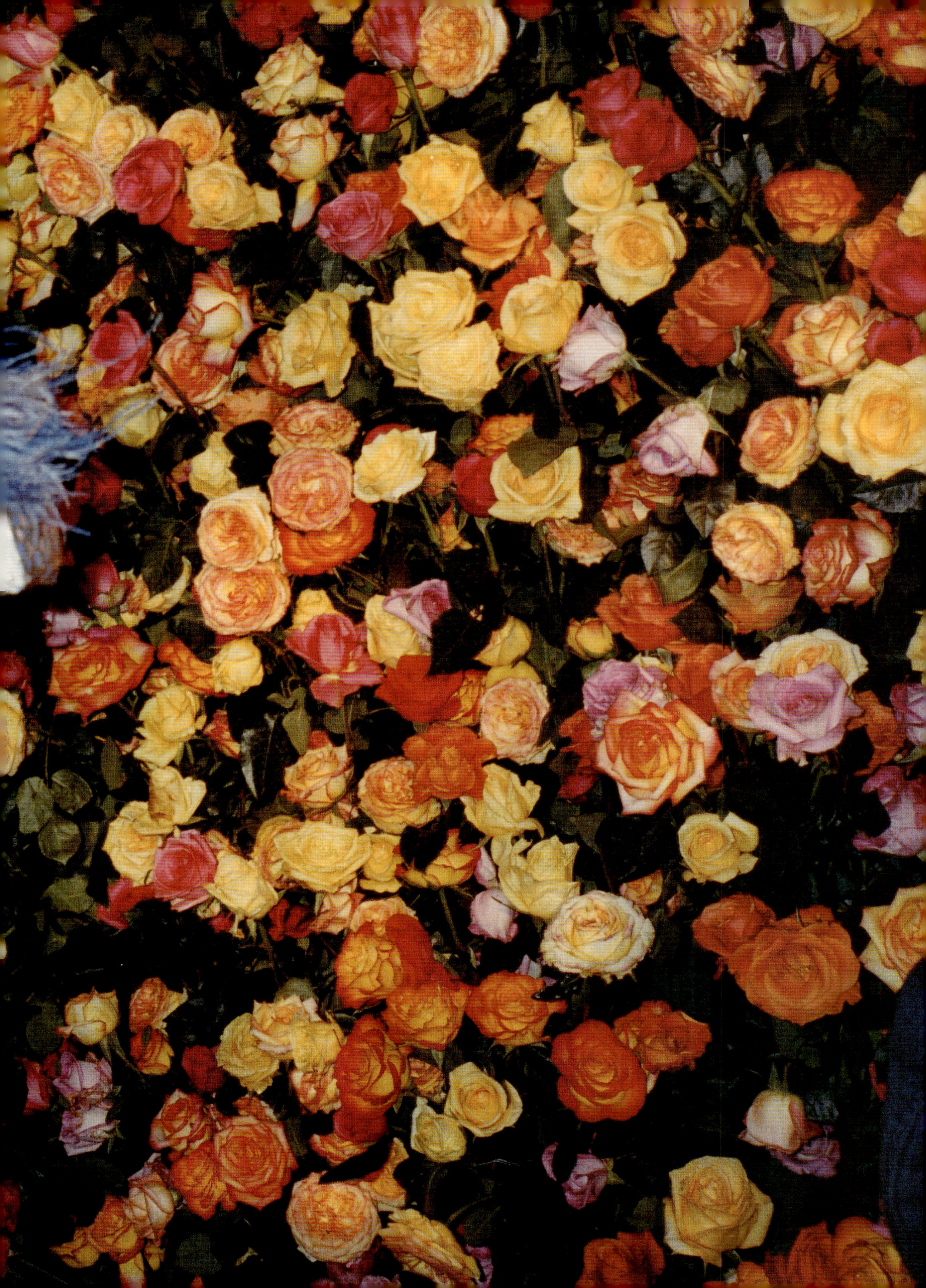

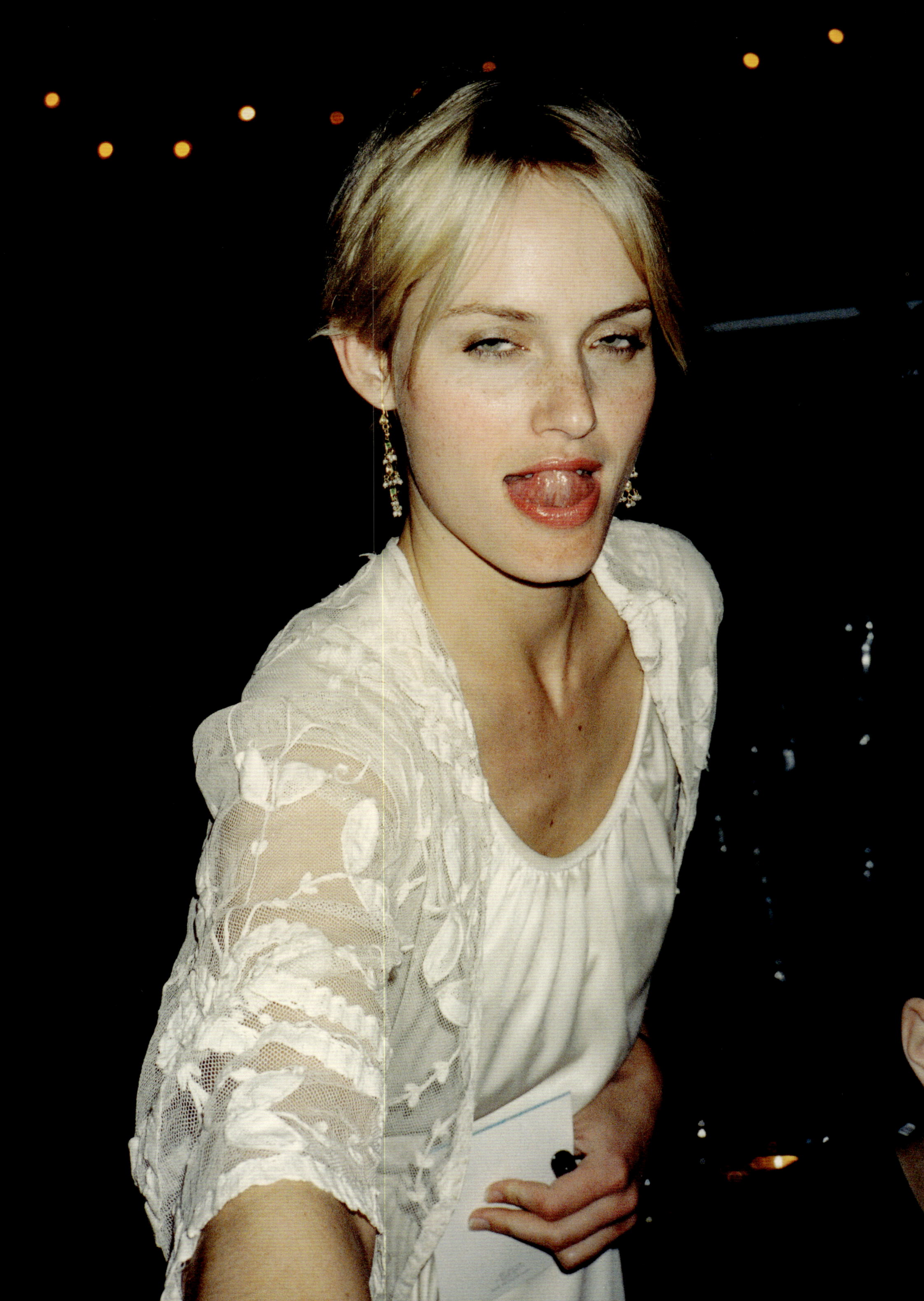

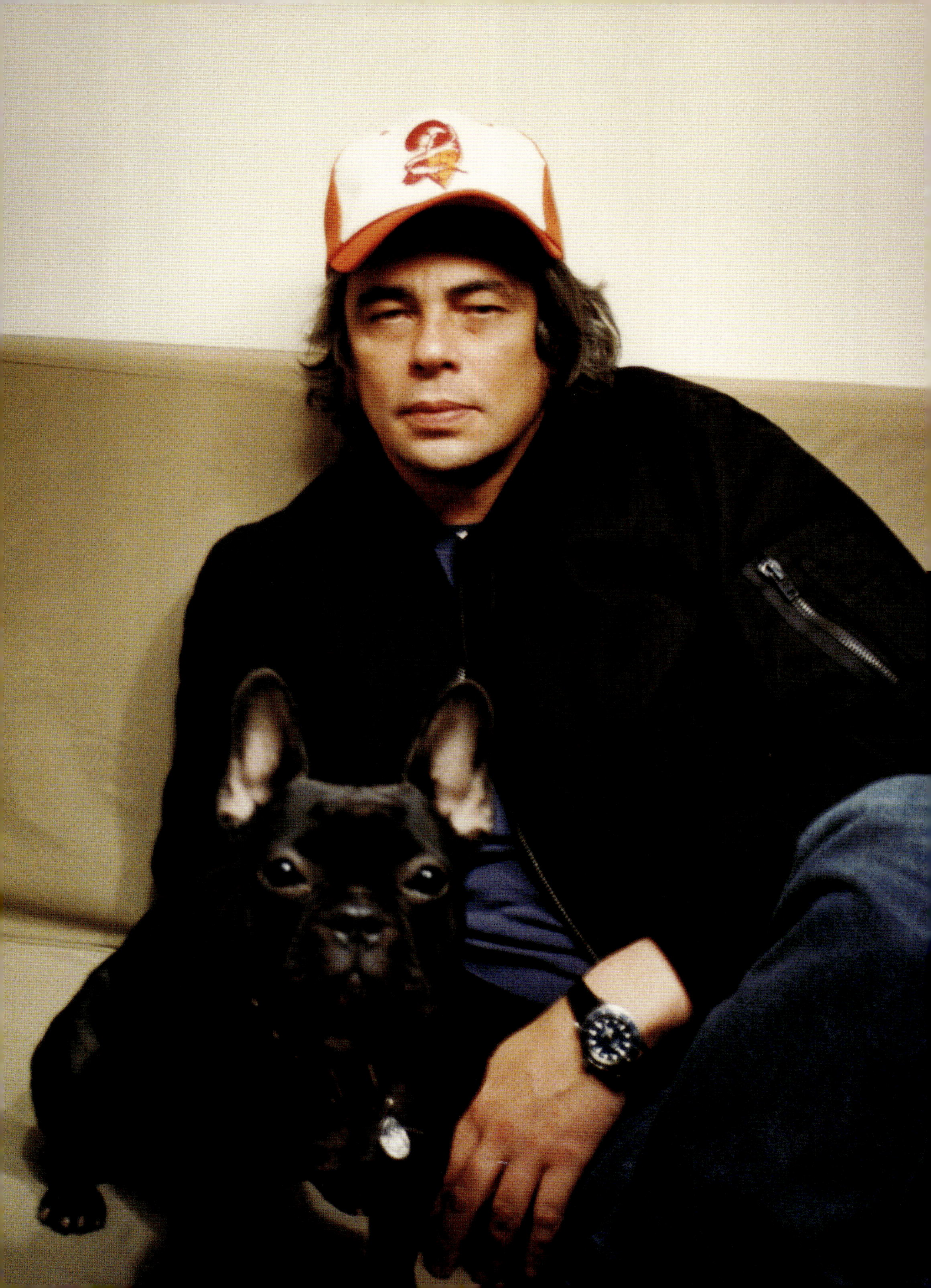

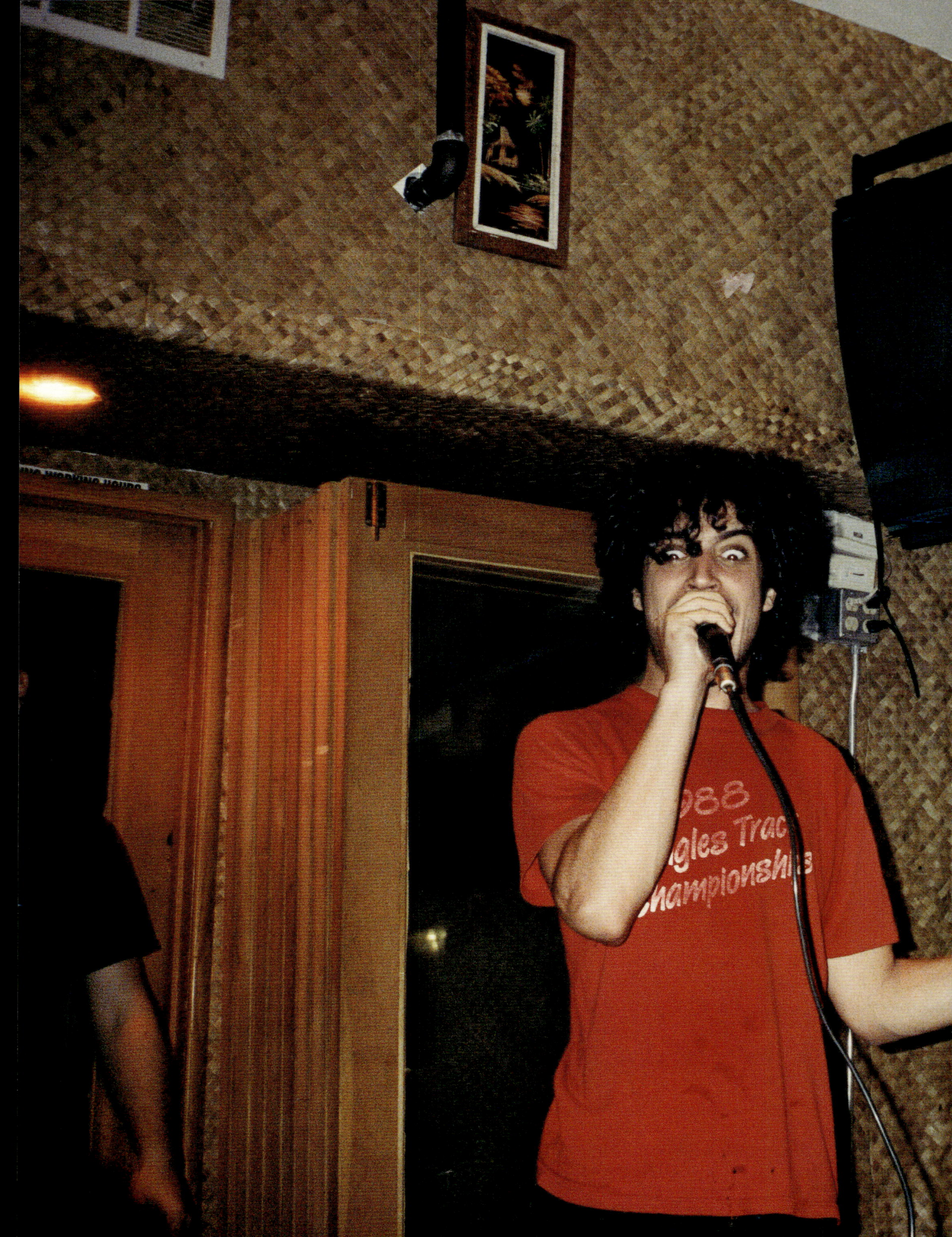

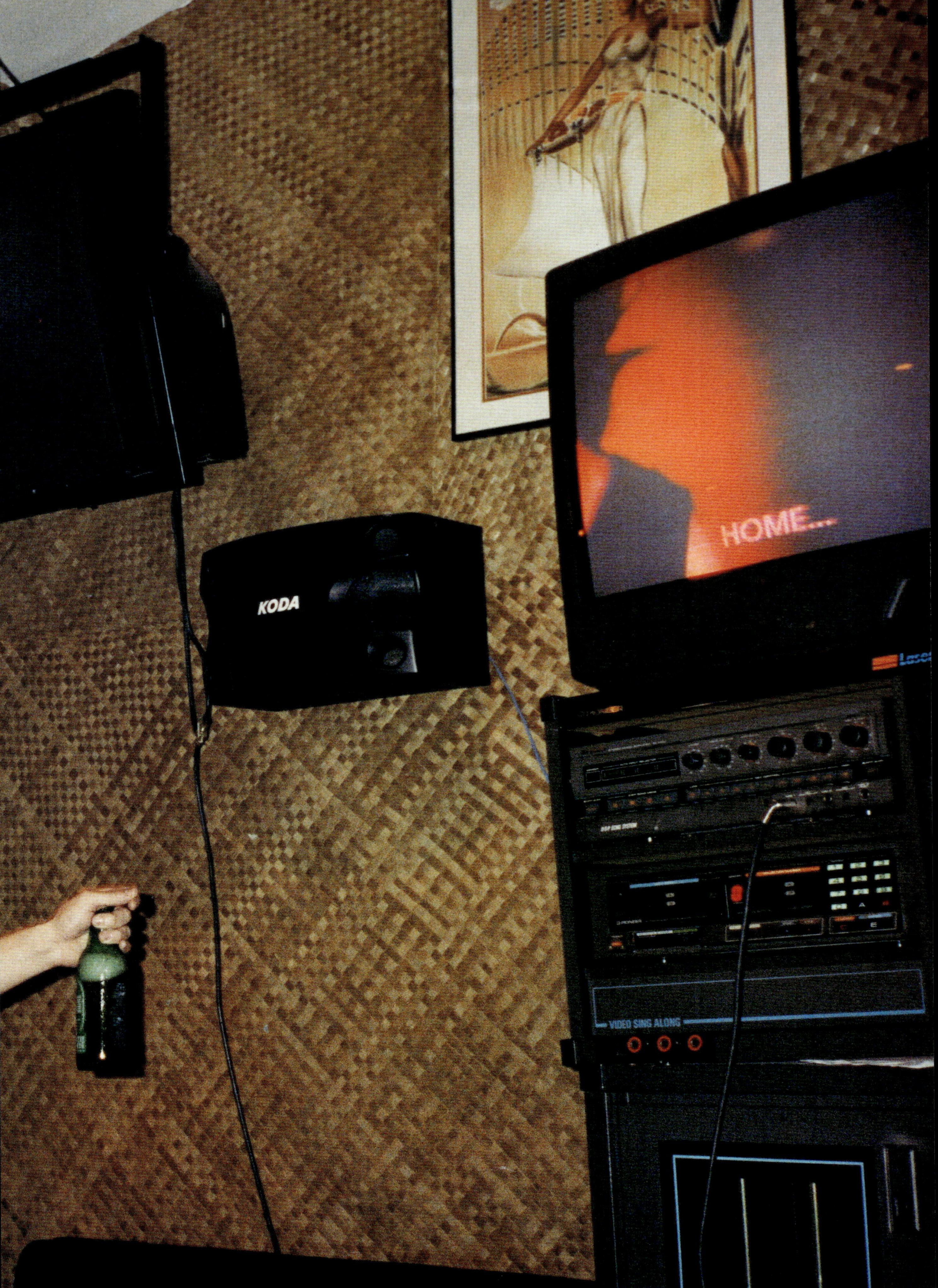
HOME...
KODA
VIDEO SING ALONG

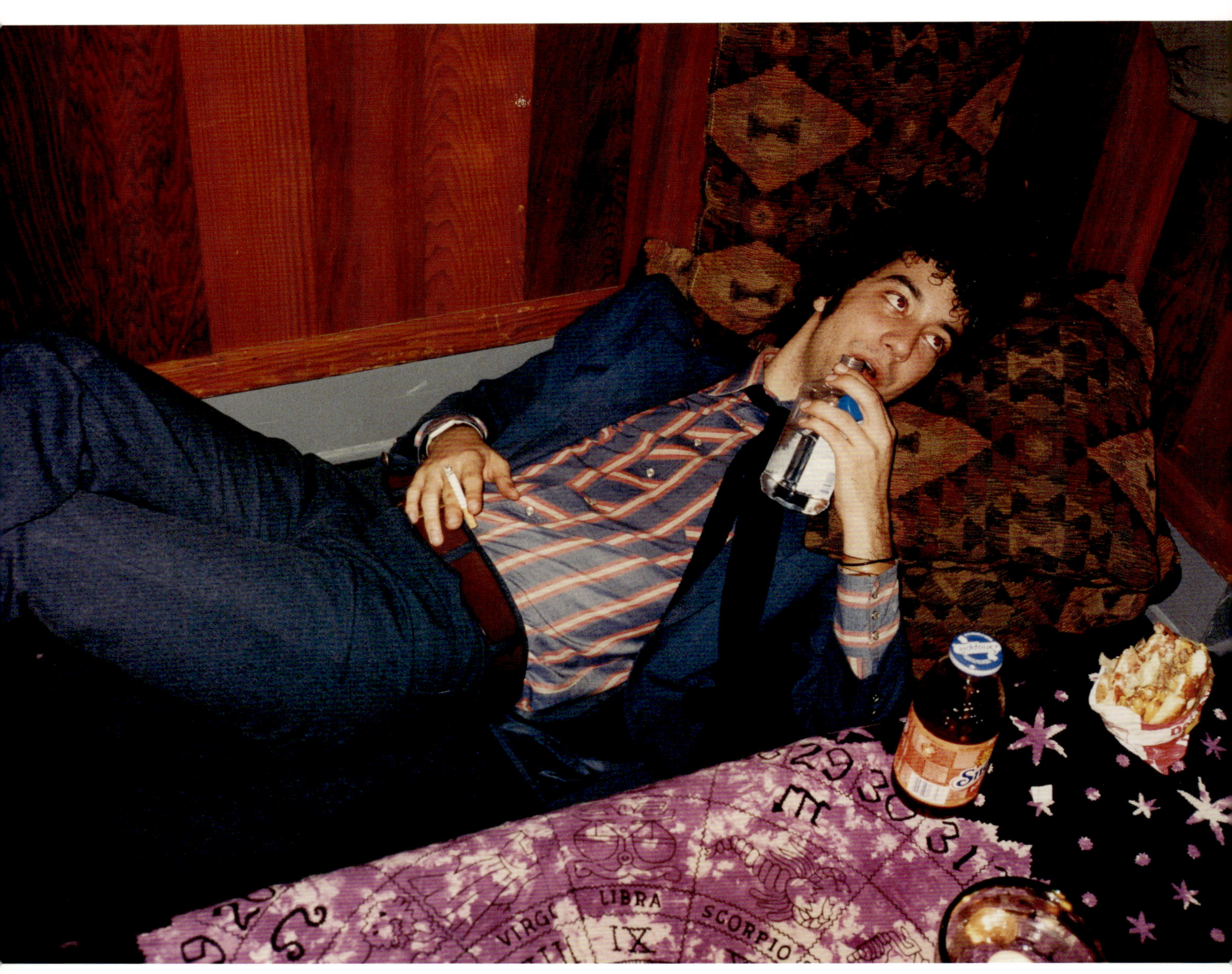
LIBRA
SCORPIO
IX

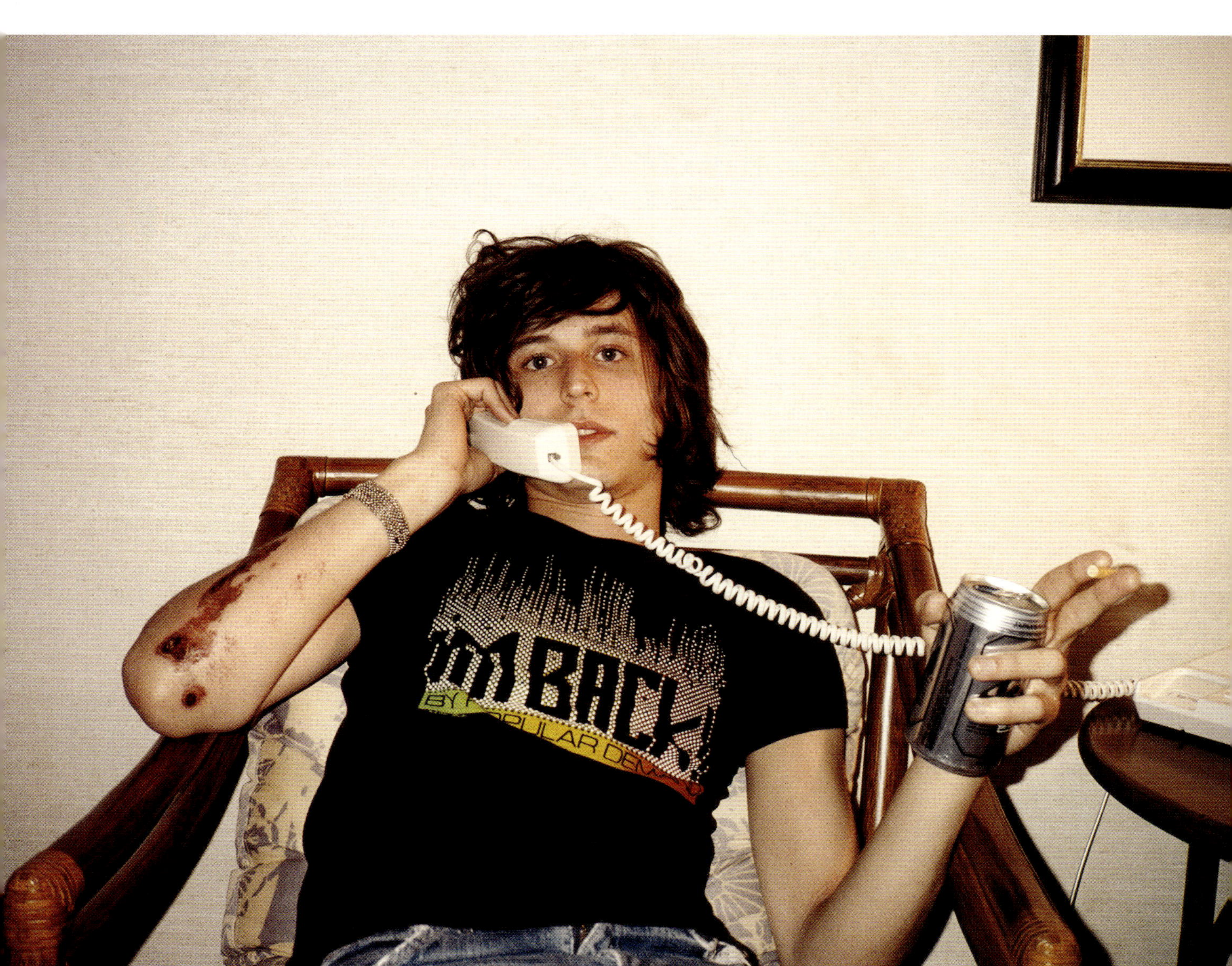
BACK
BY

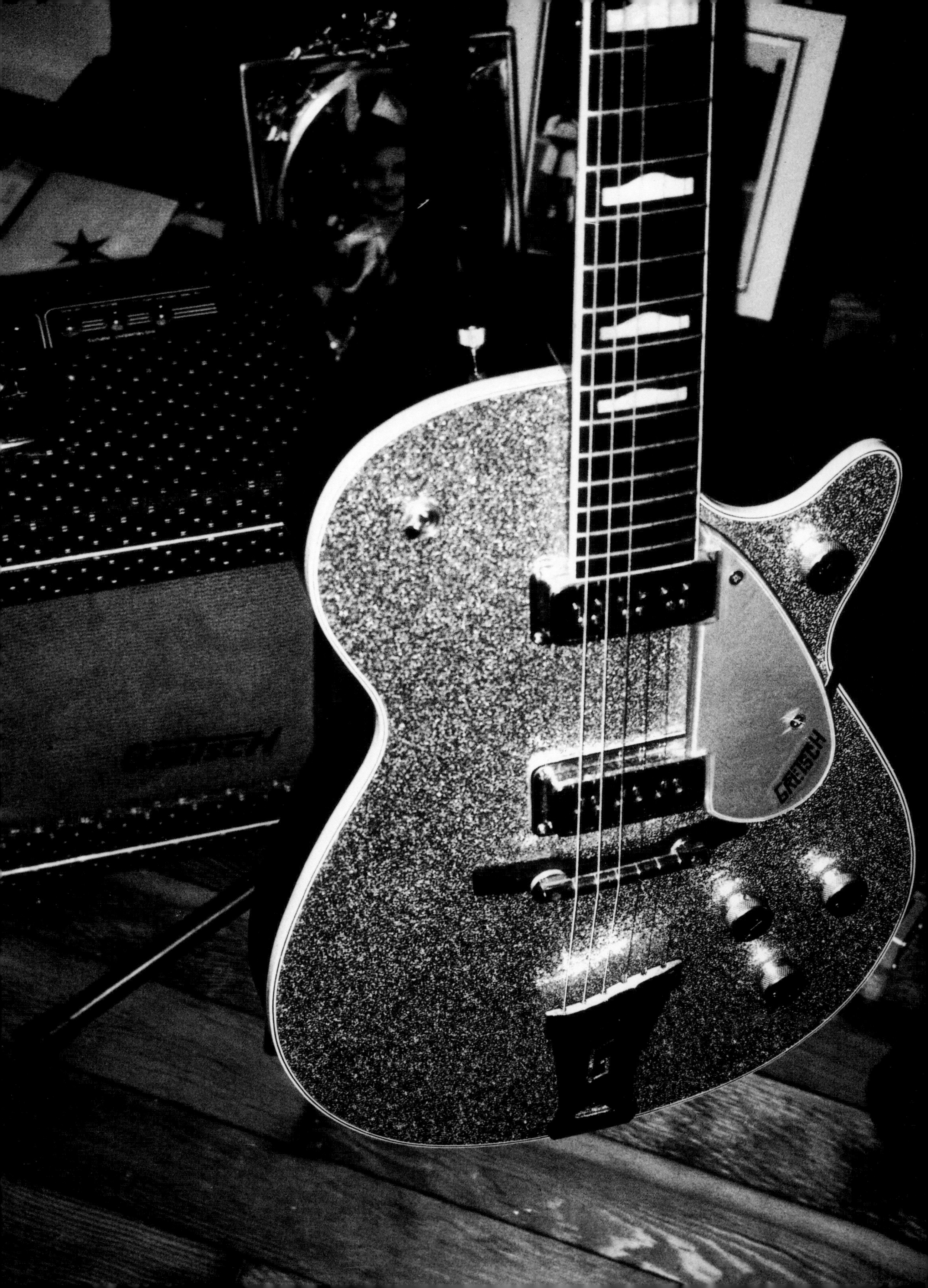
GRETSCH
GRETSCH

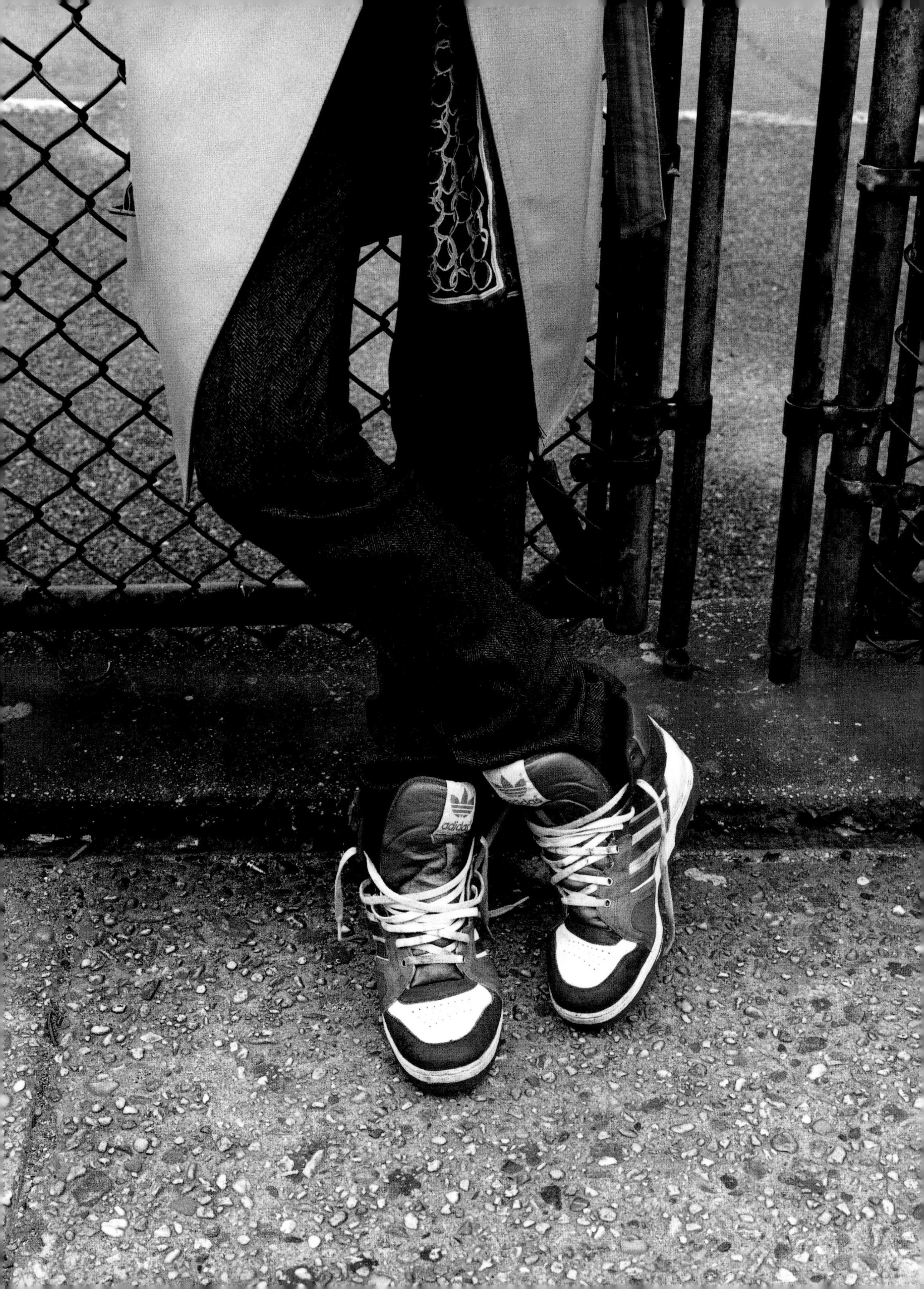
adidas

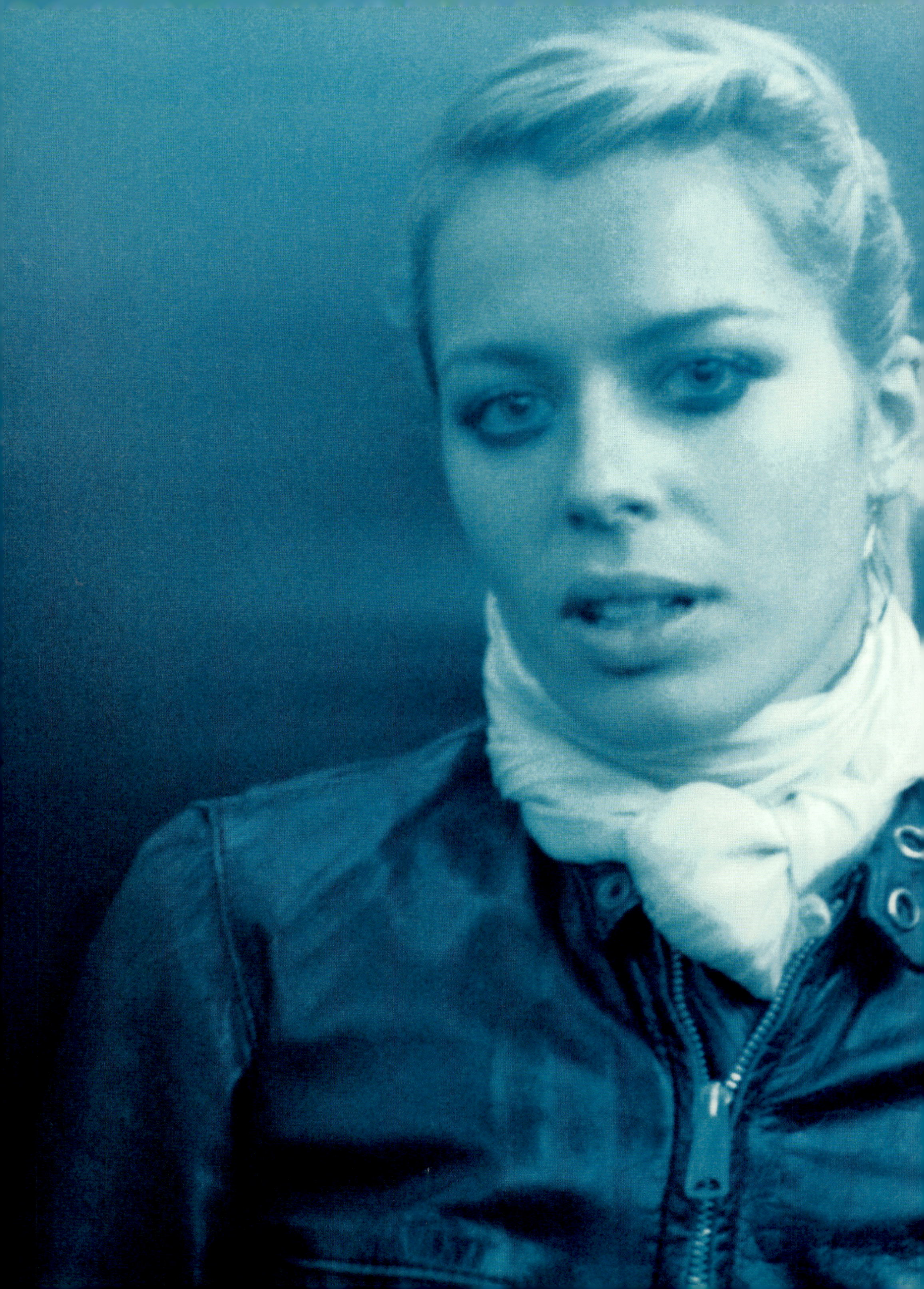

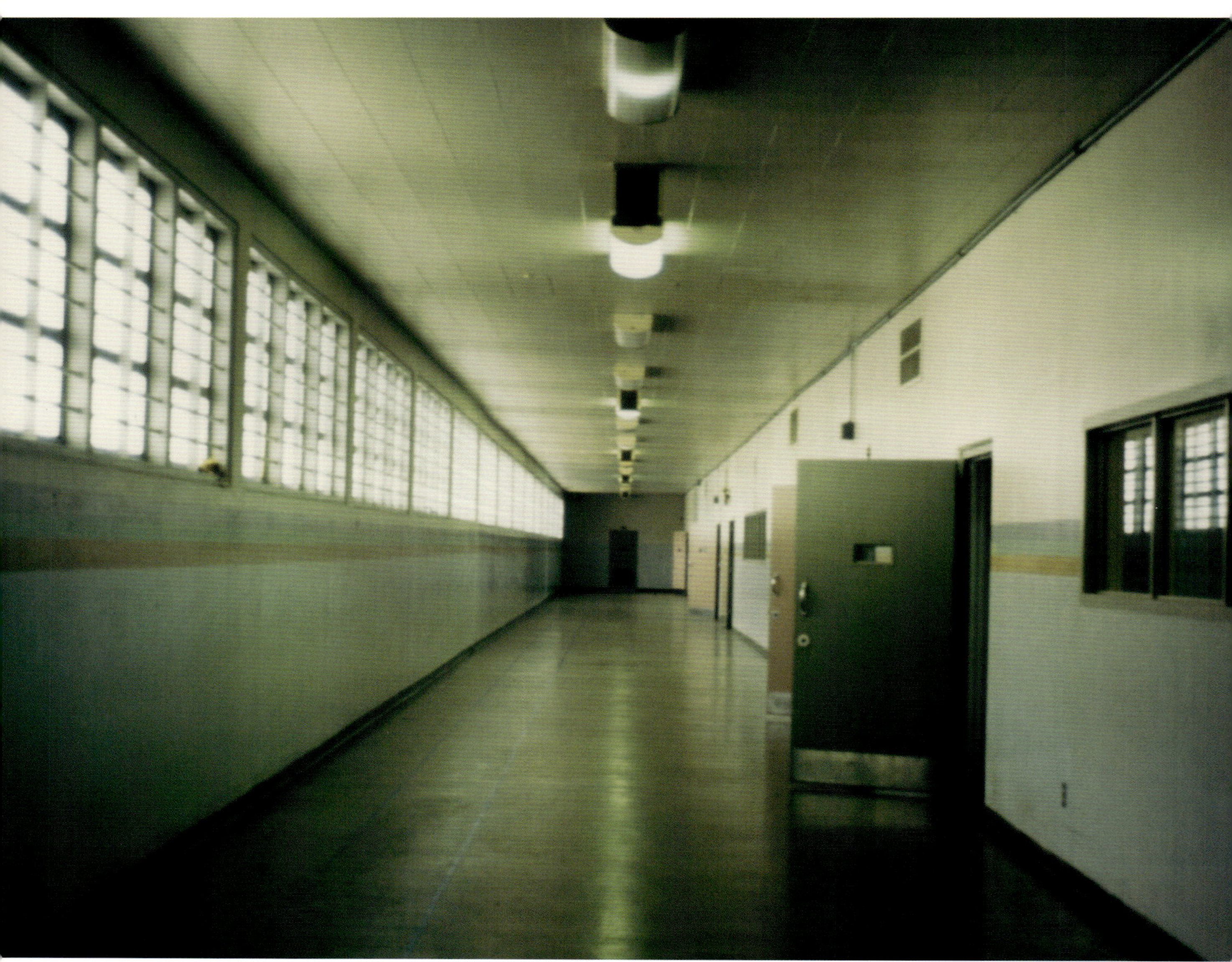

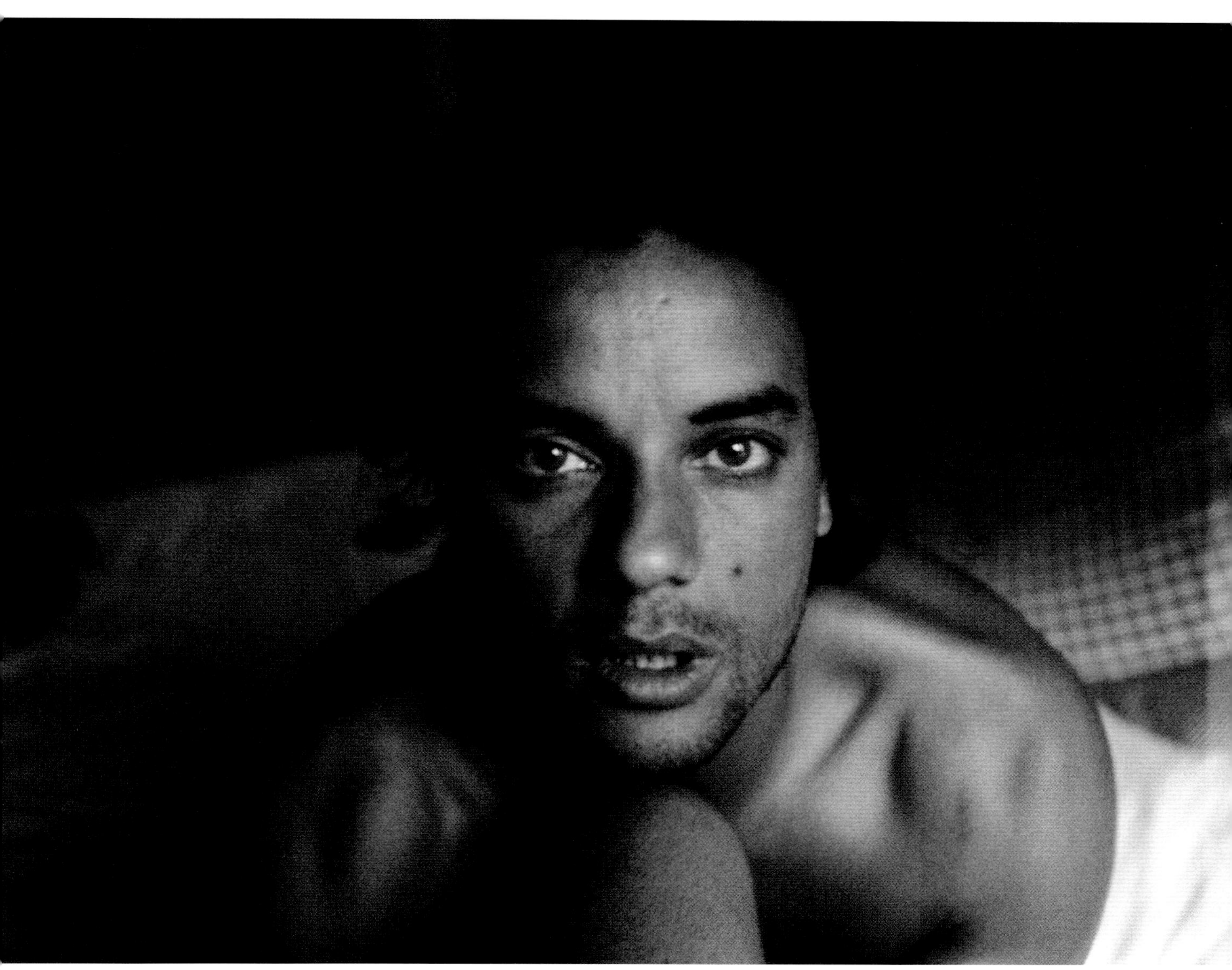

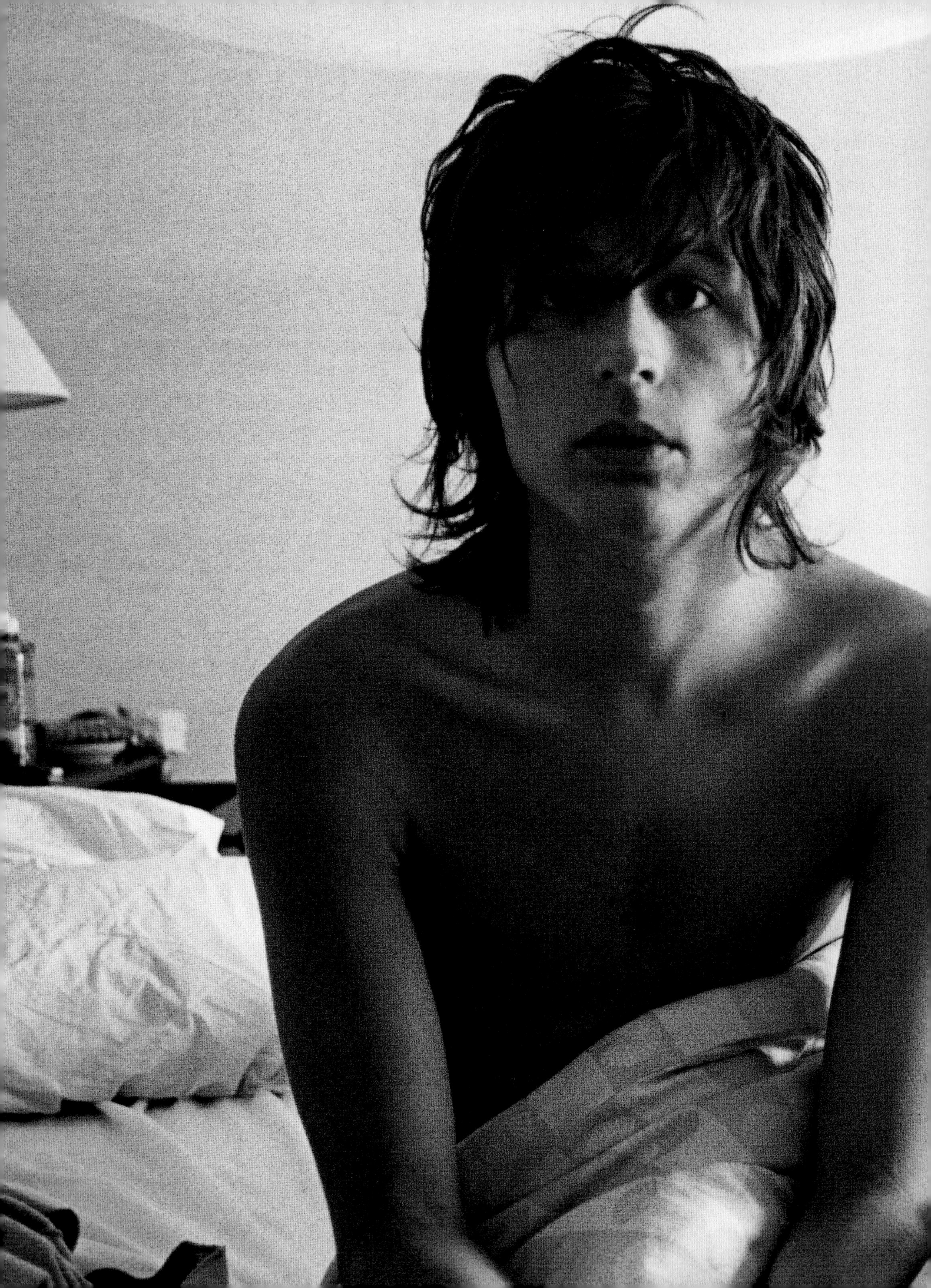

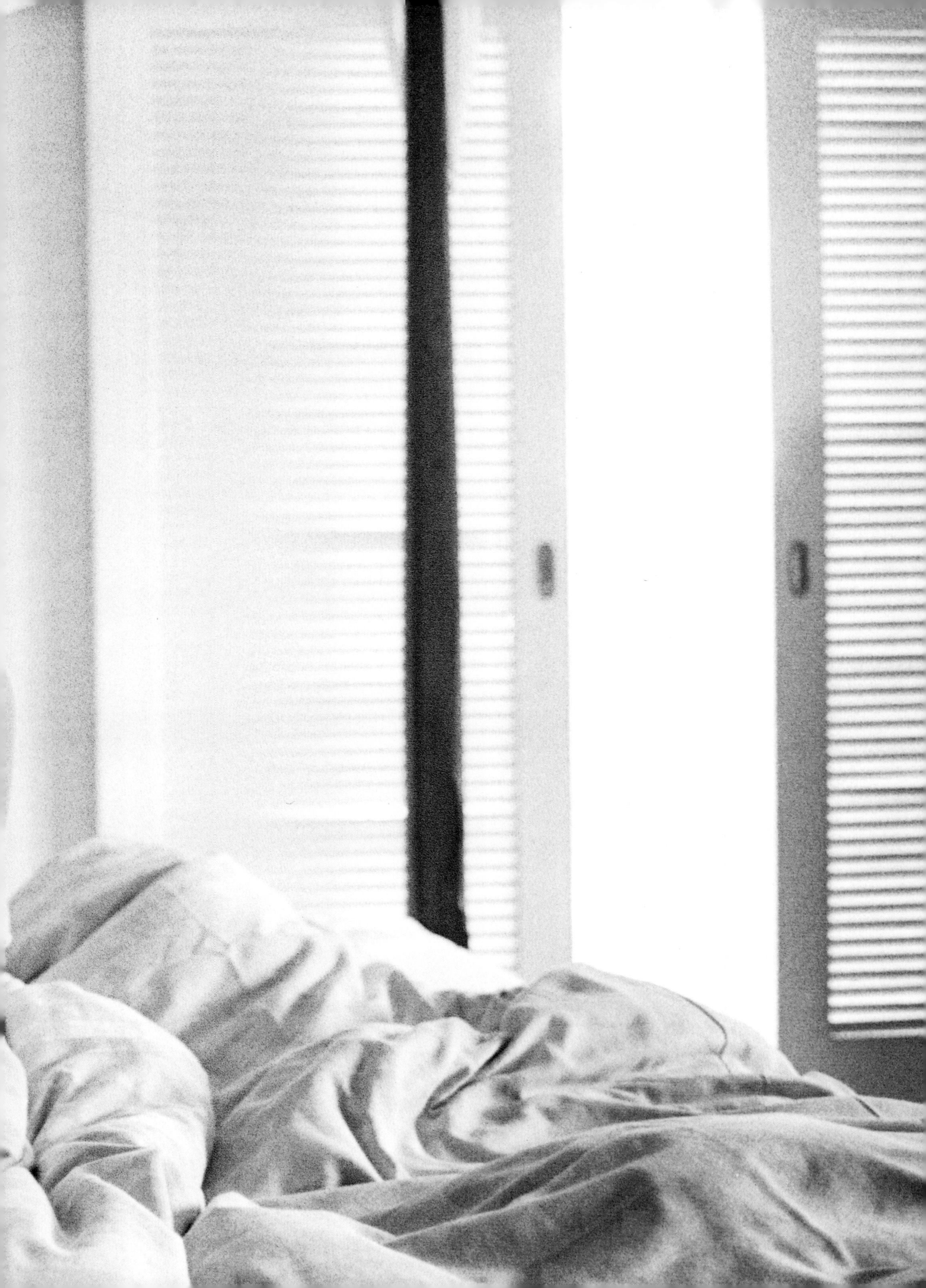

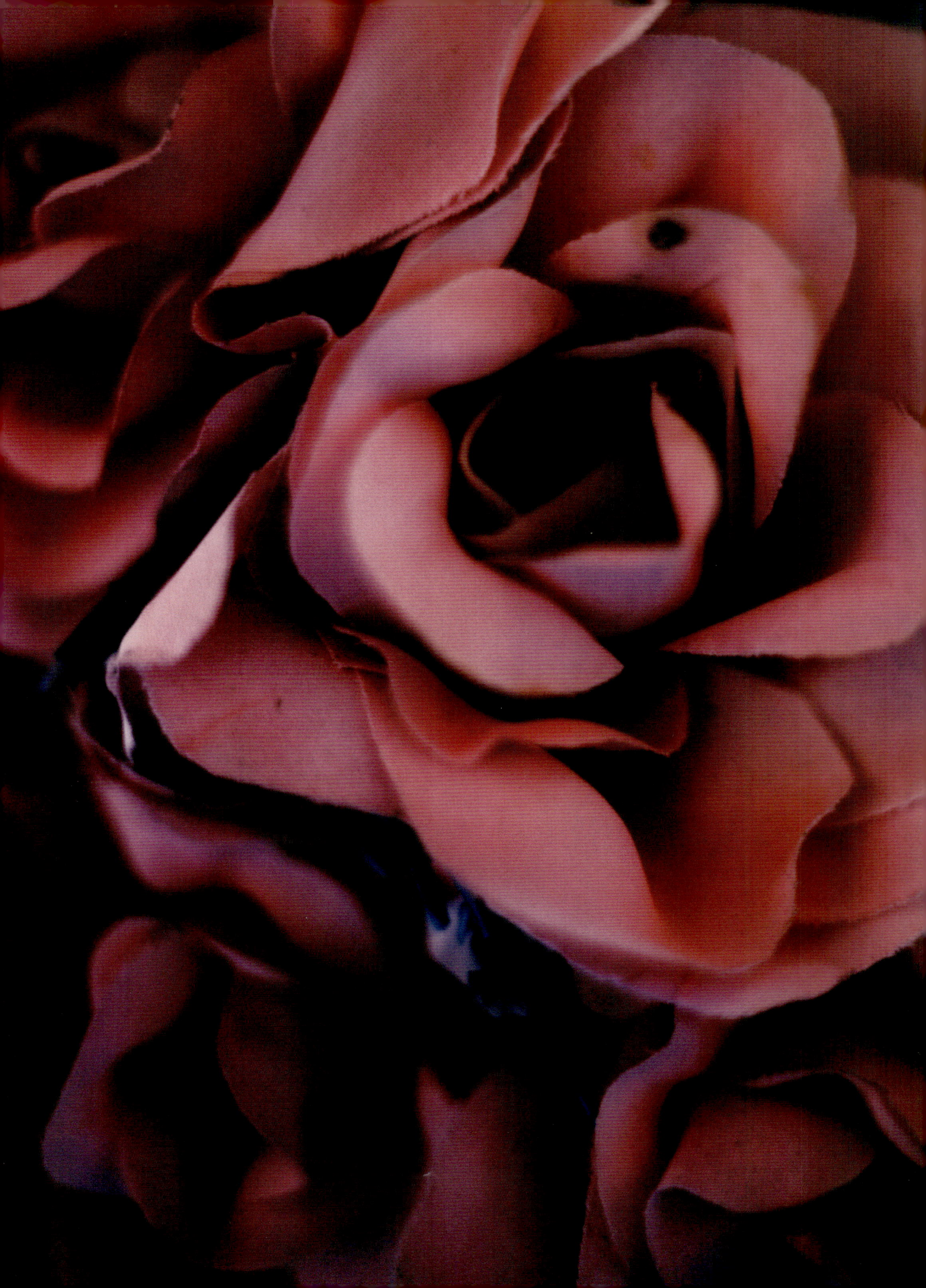

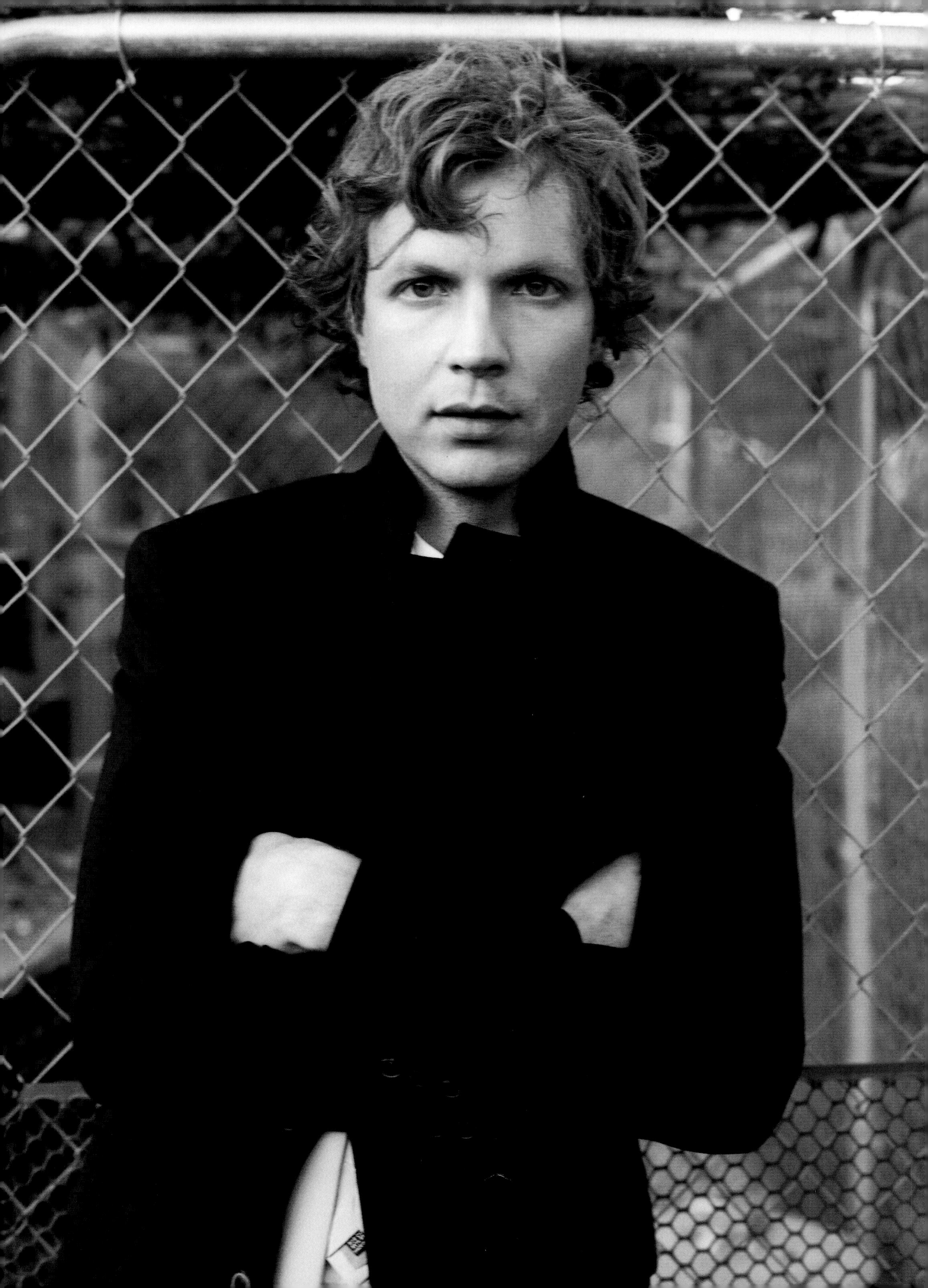

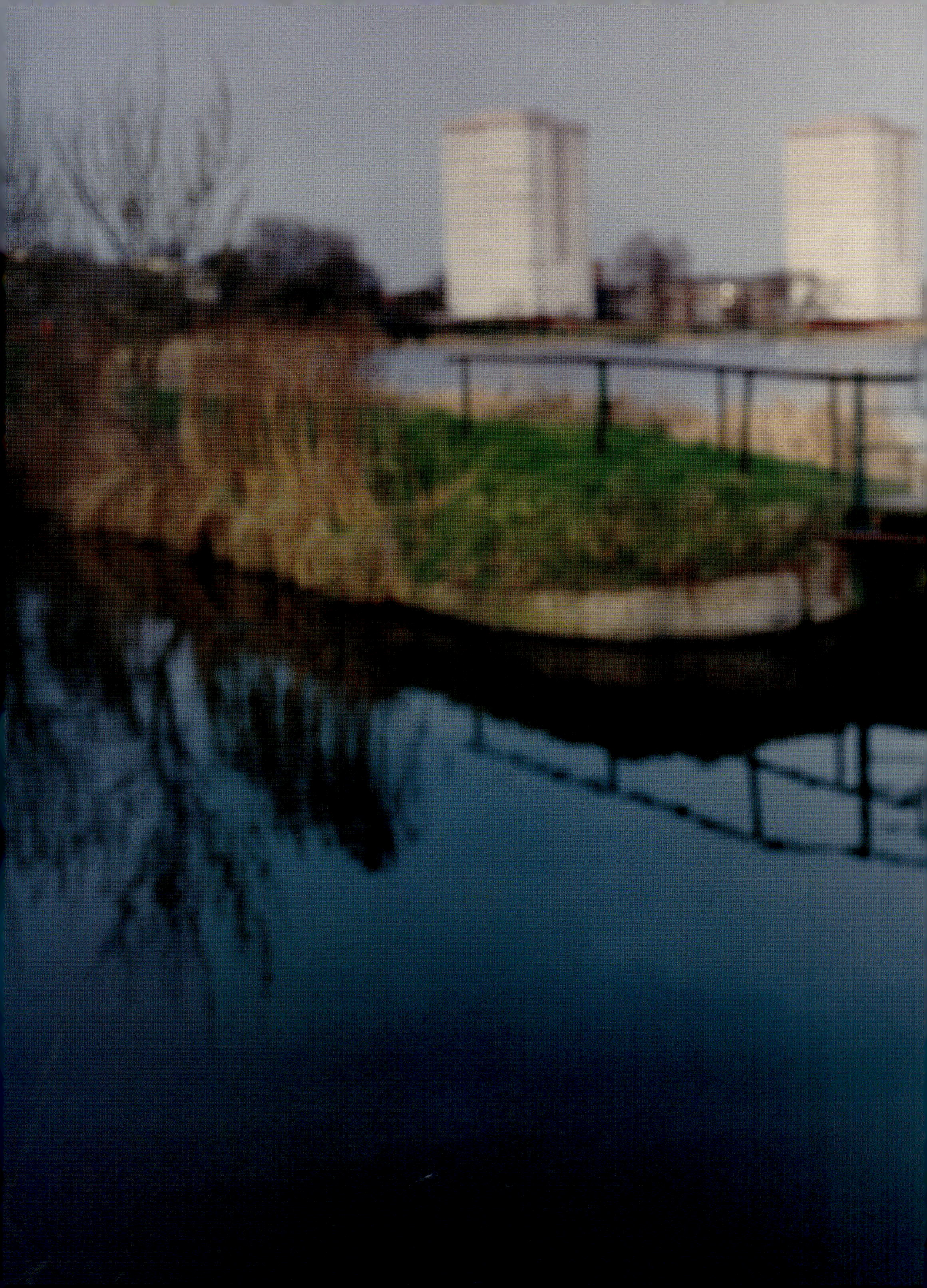

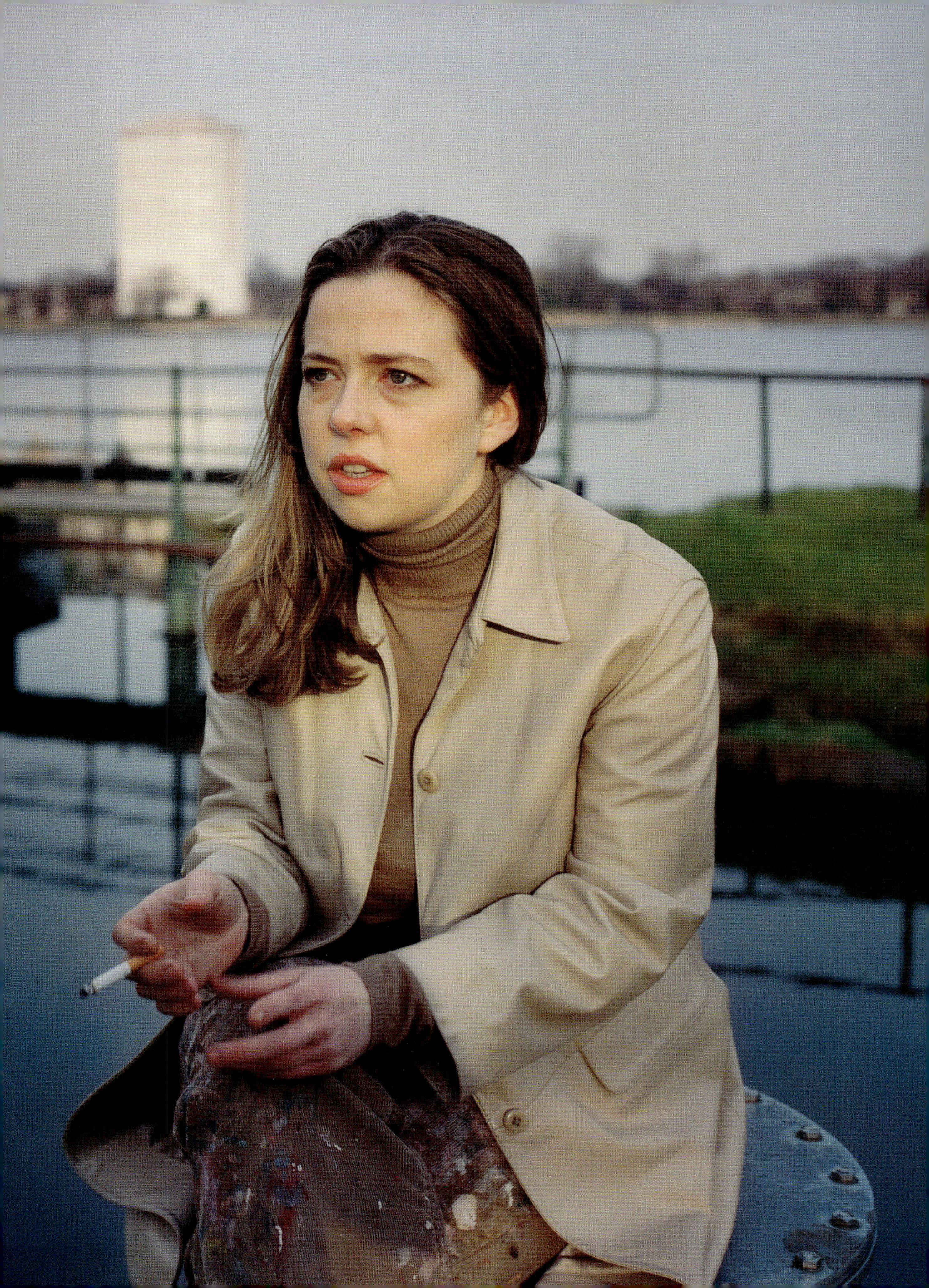

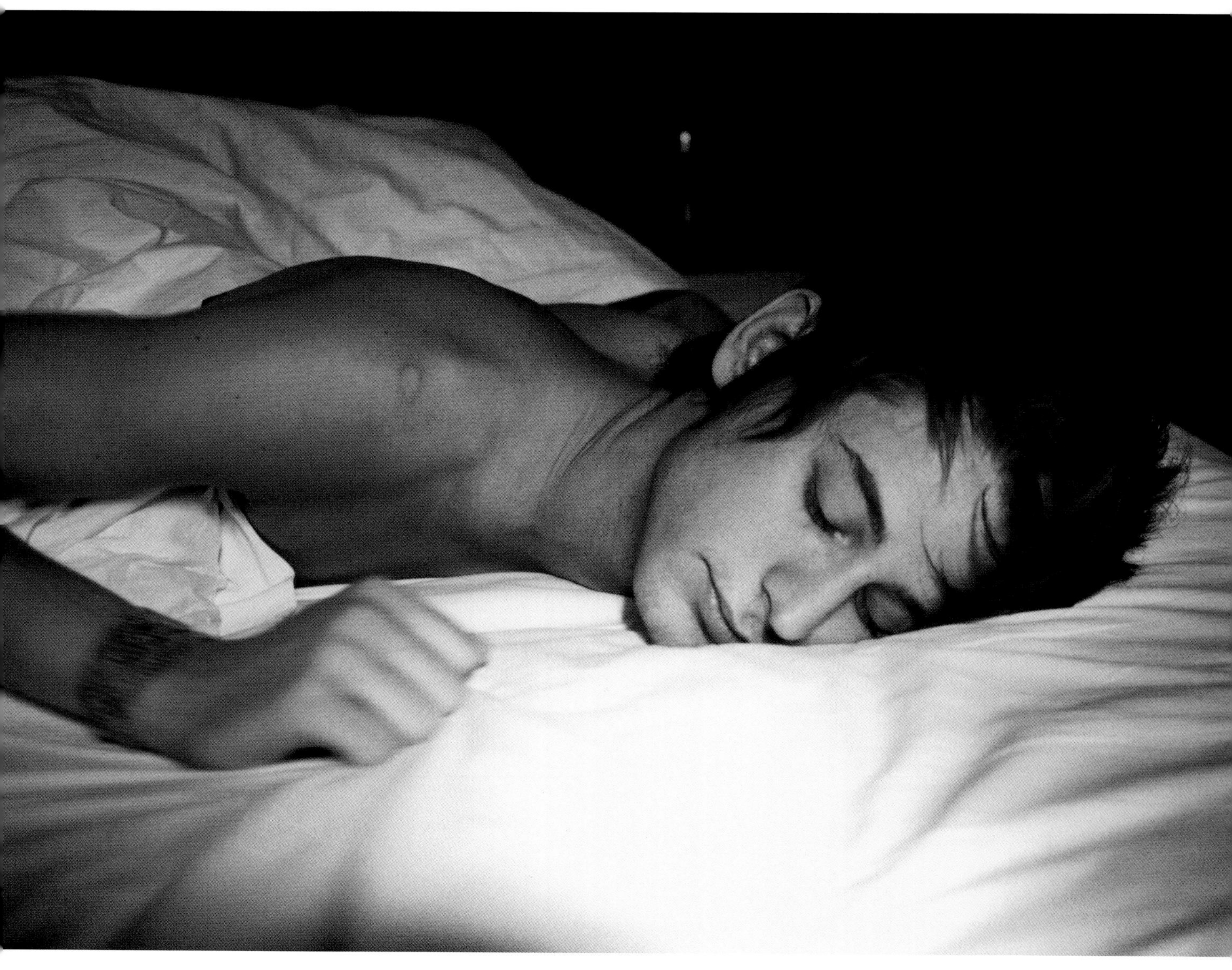

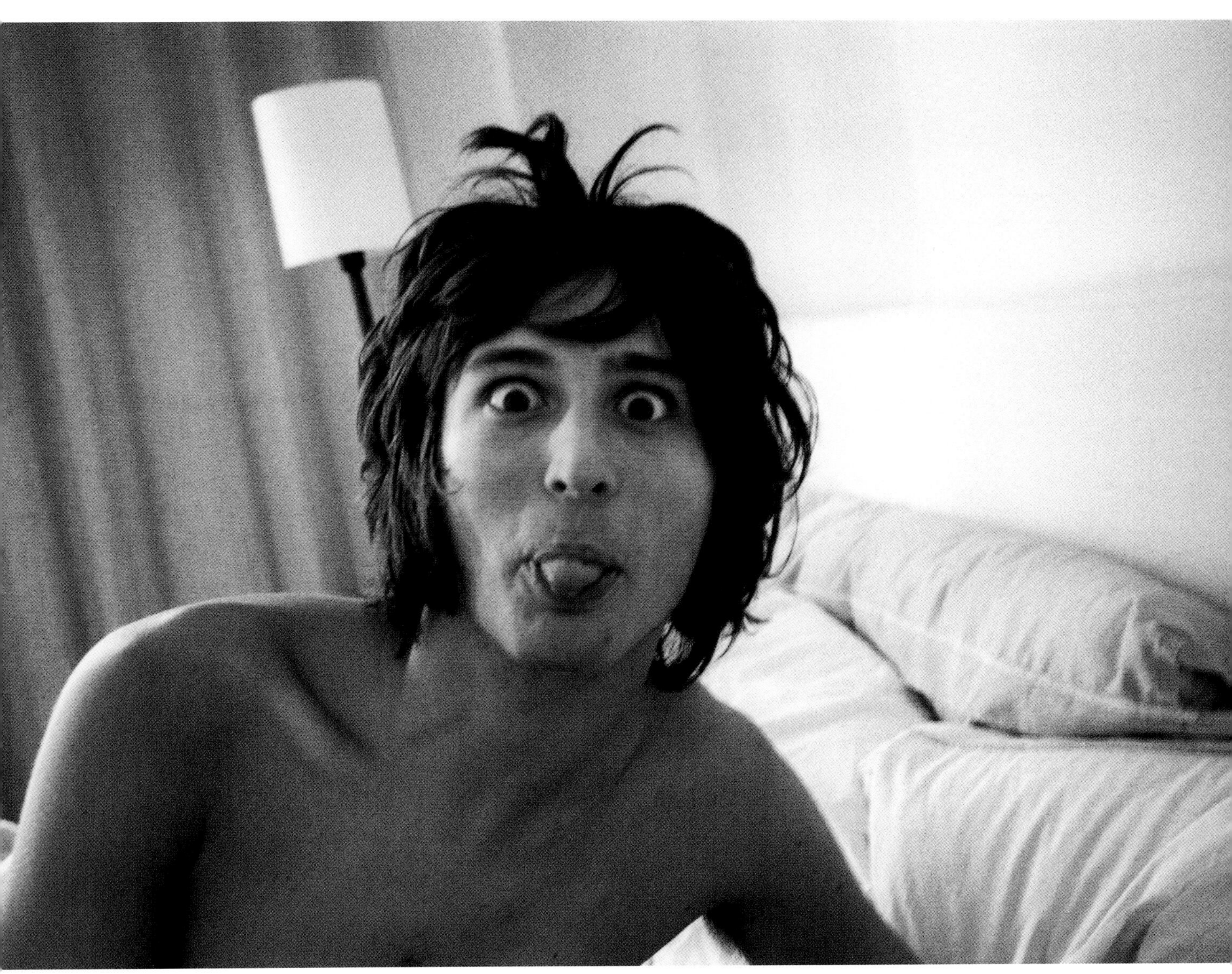

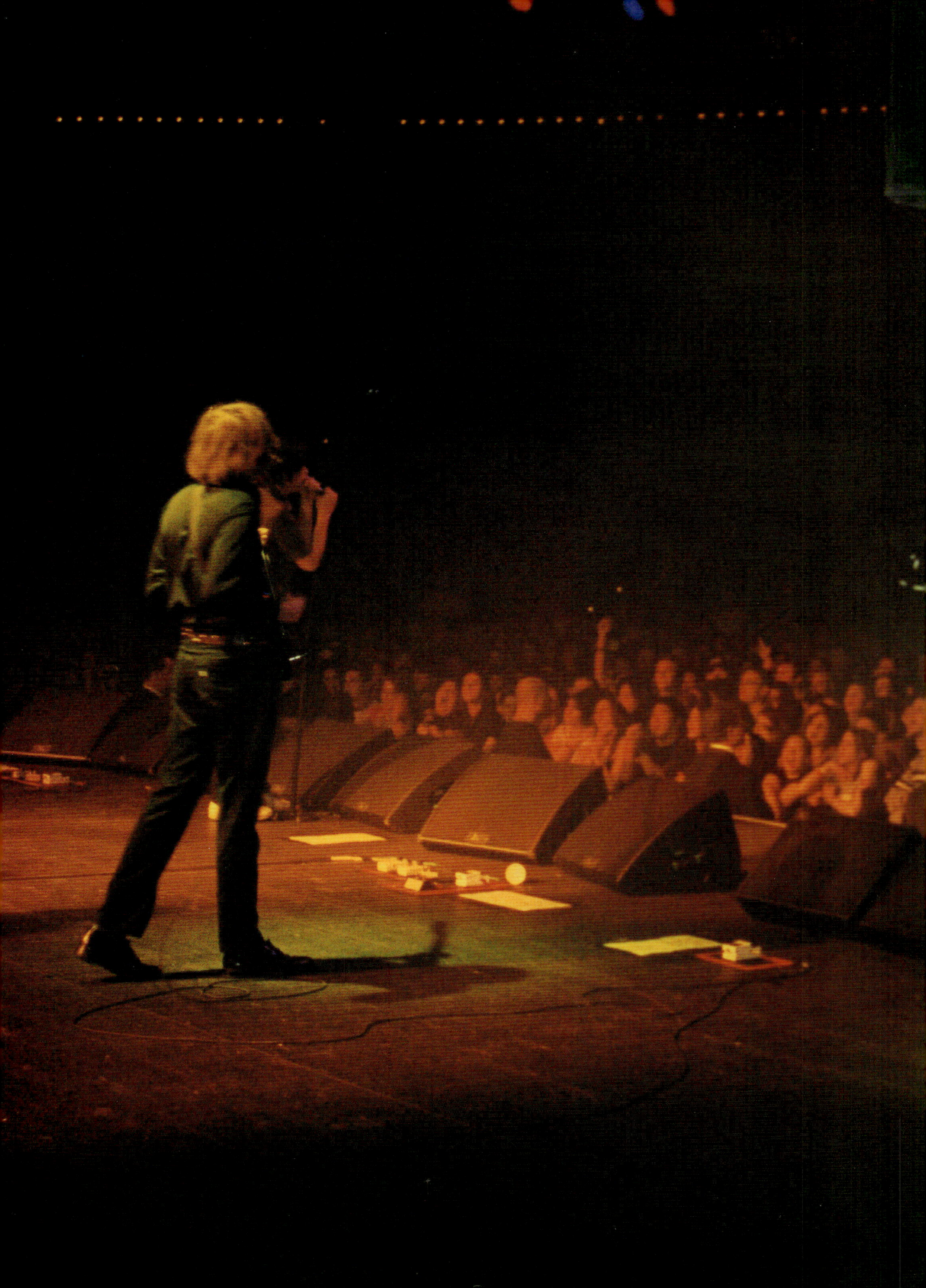

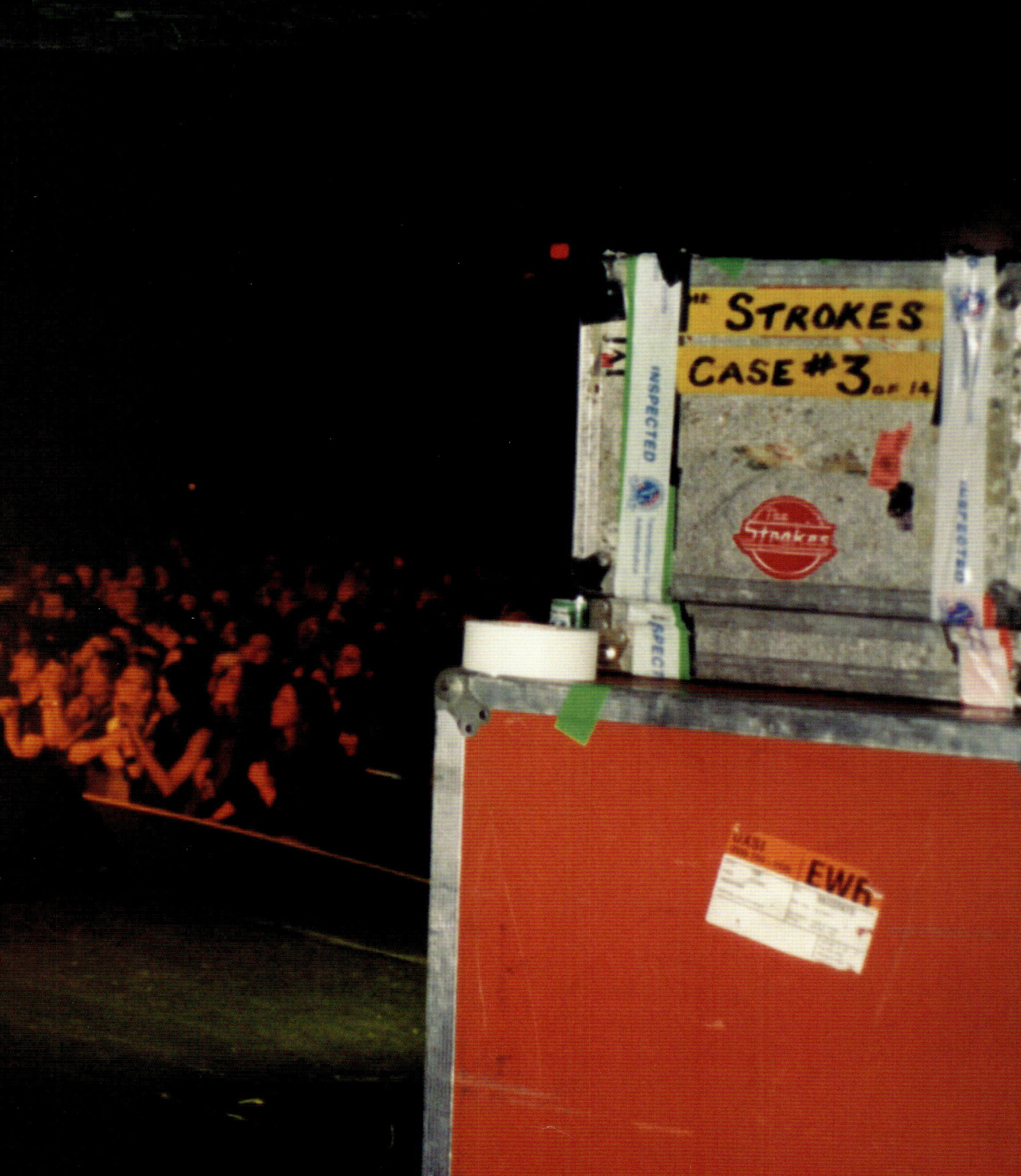
STROKES
CASE #3 OF 14
INSPECTED
The Strokes

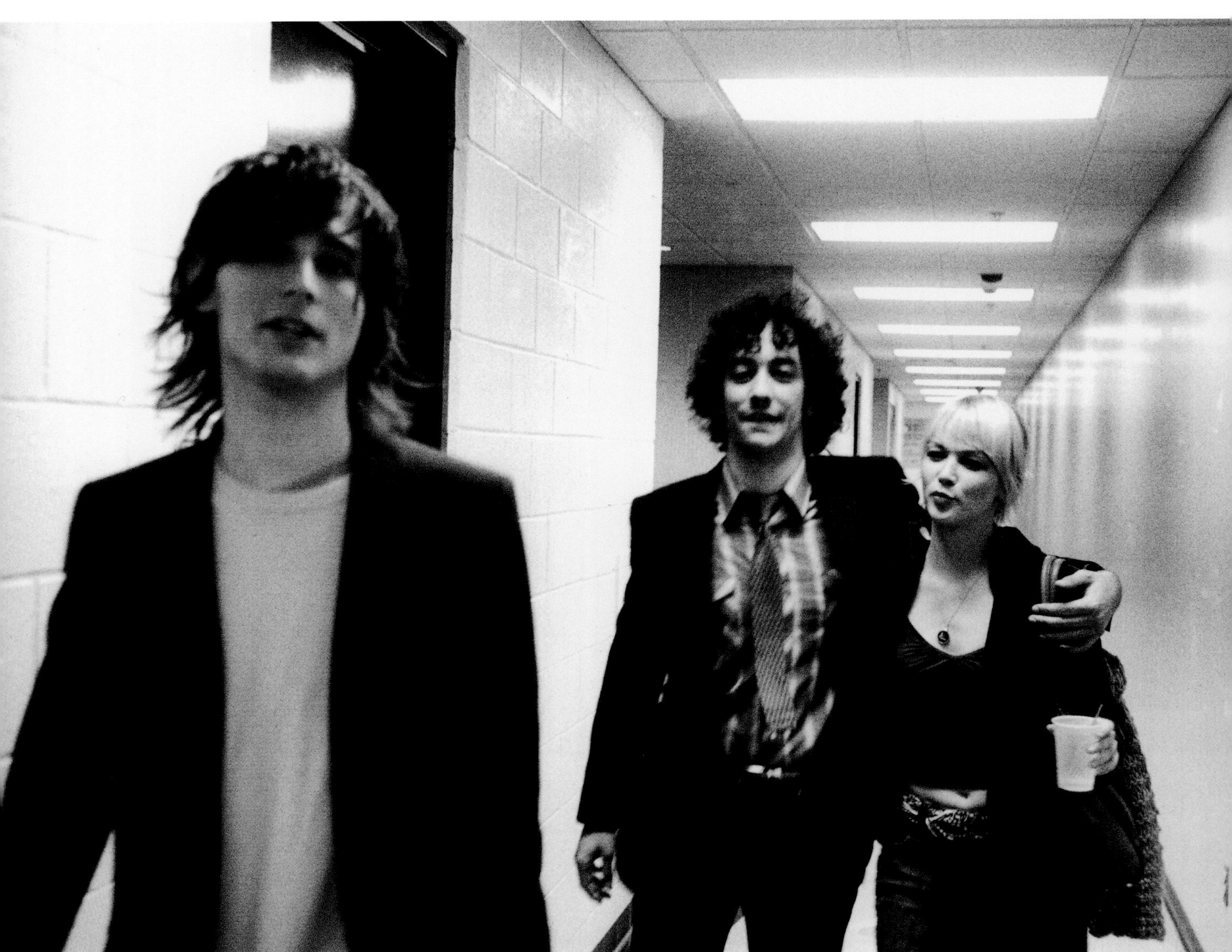

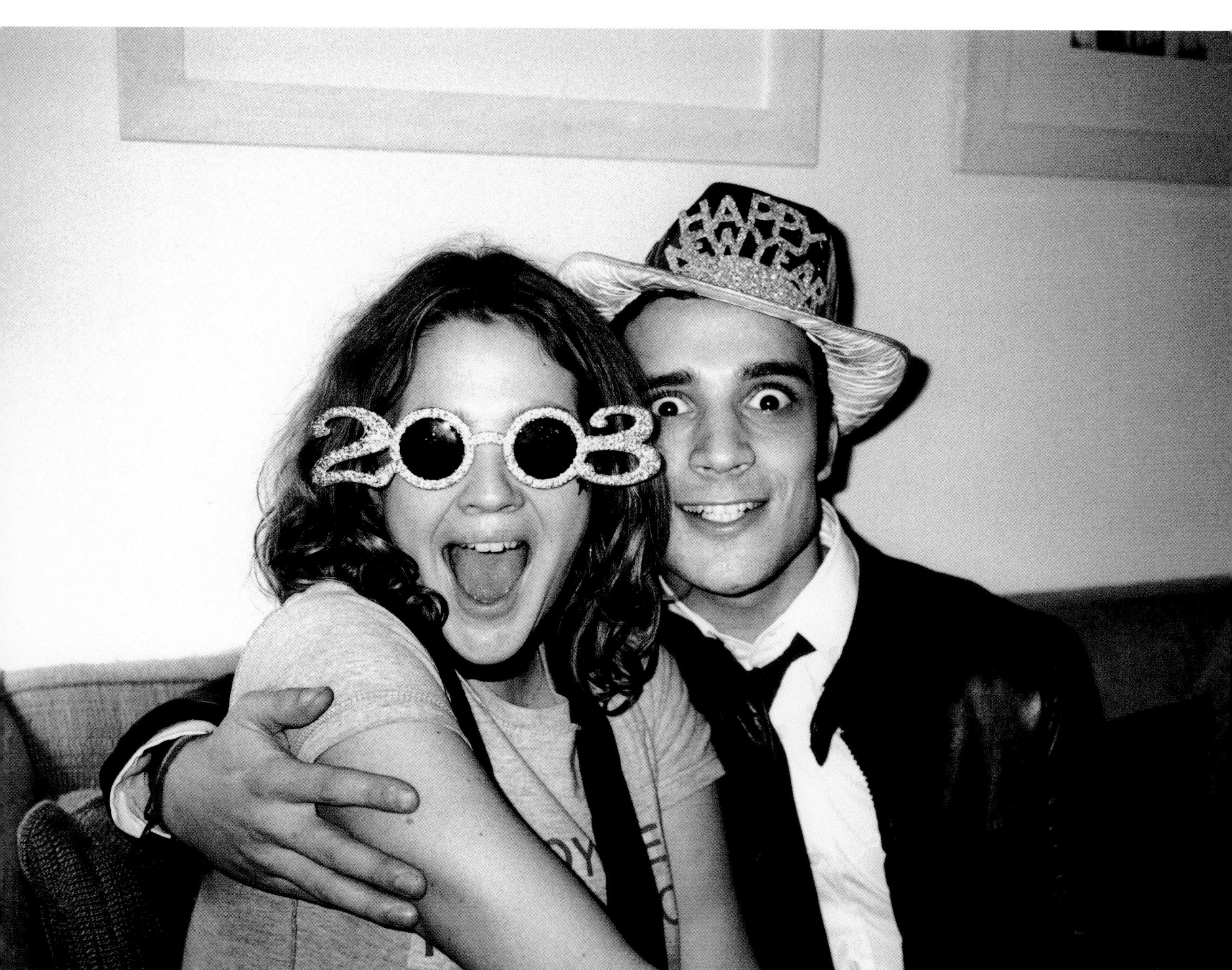
2003
HAPPY NEW YEAR

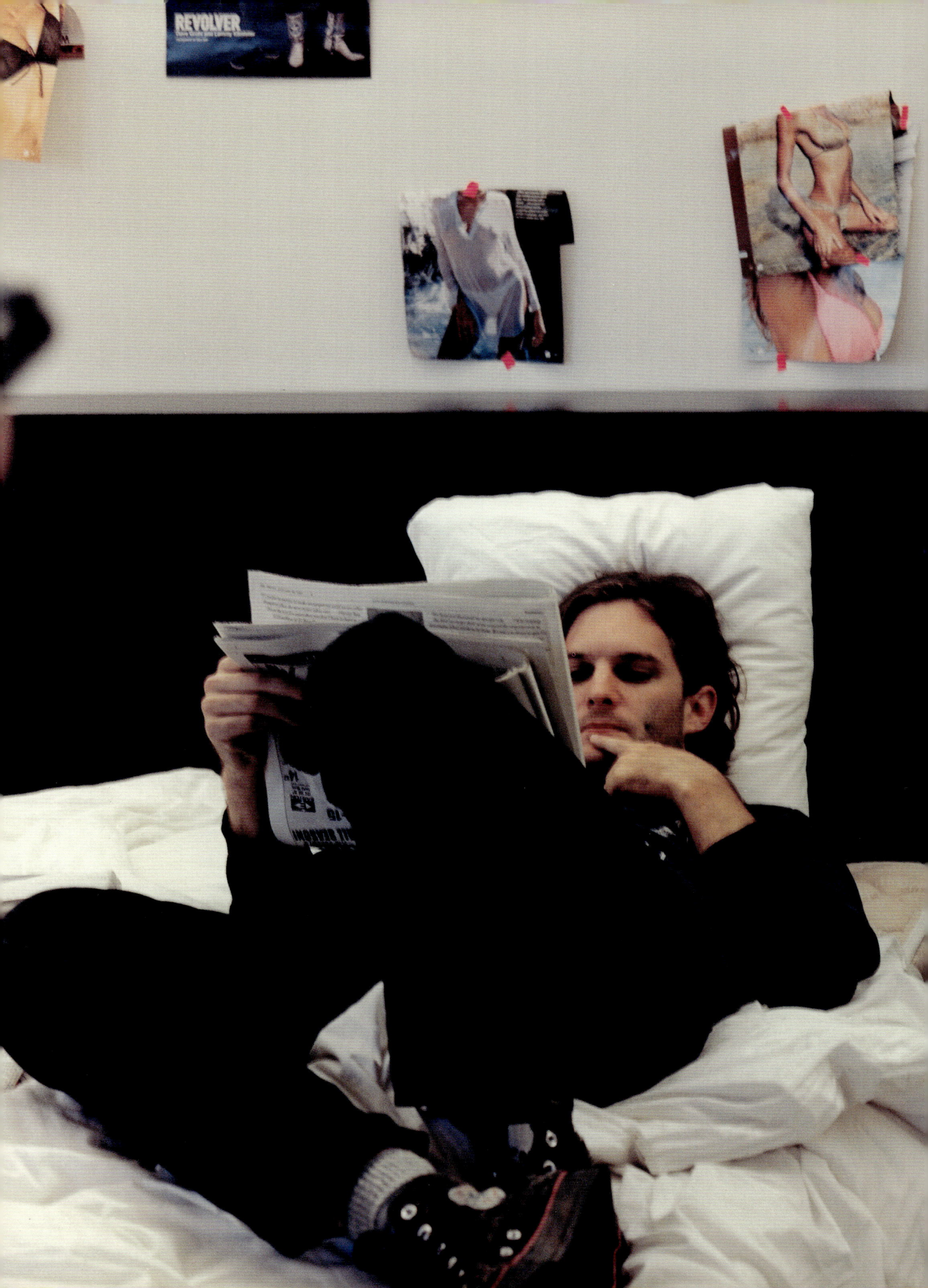
REVOLVER

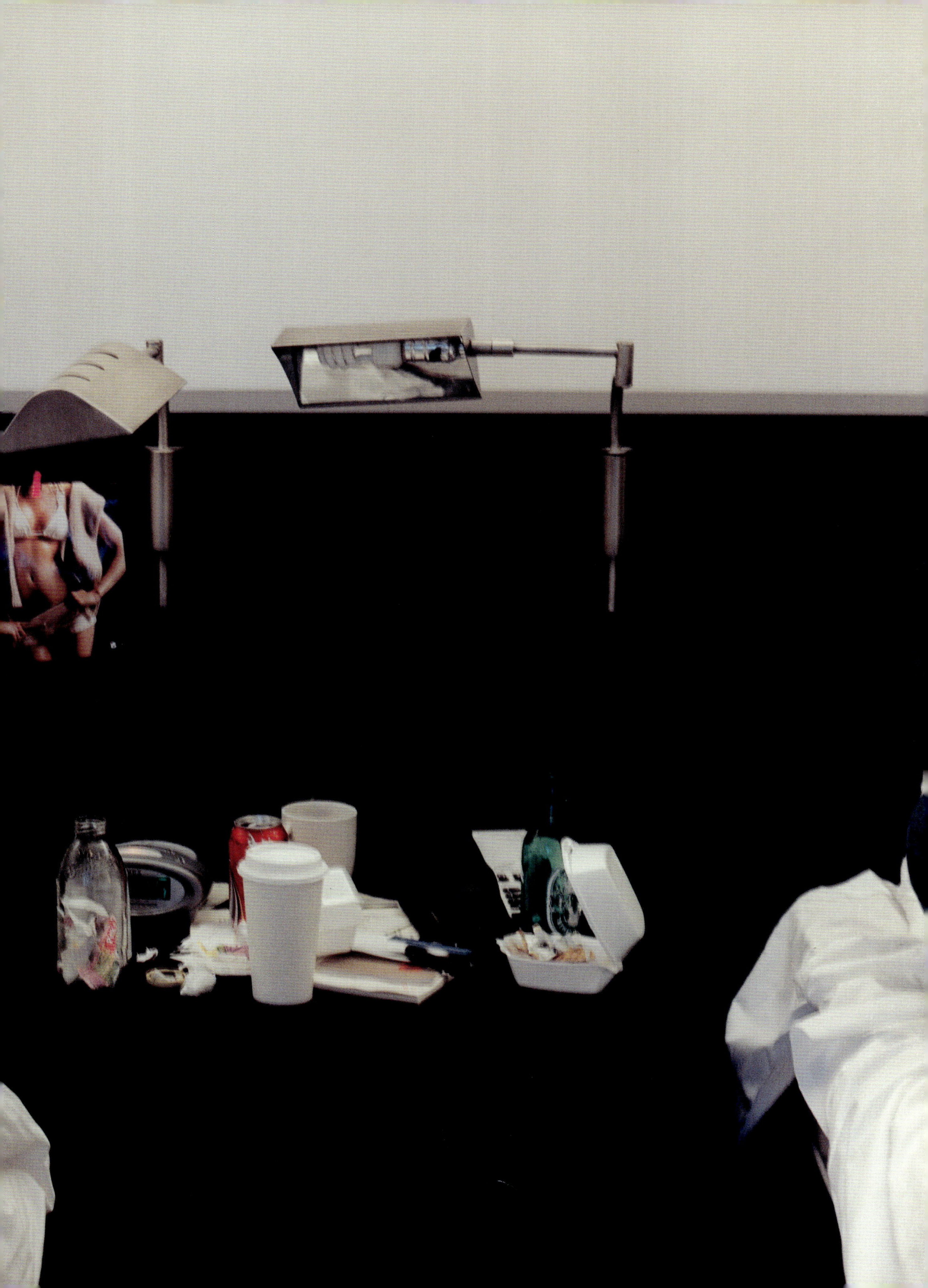

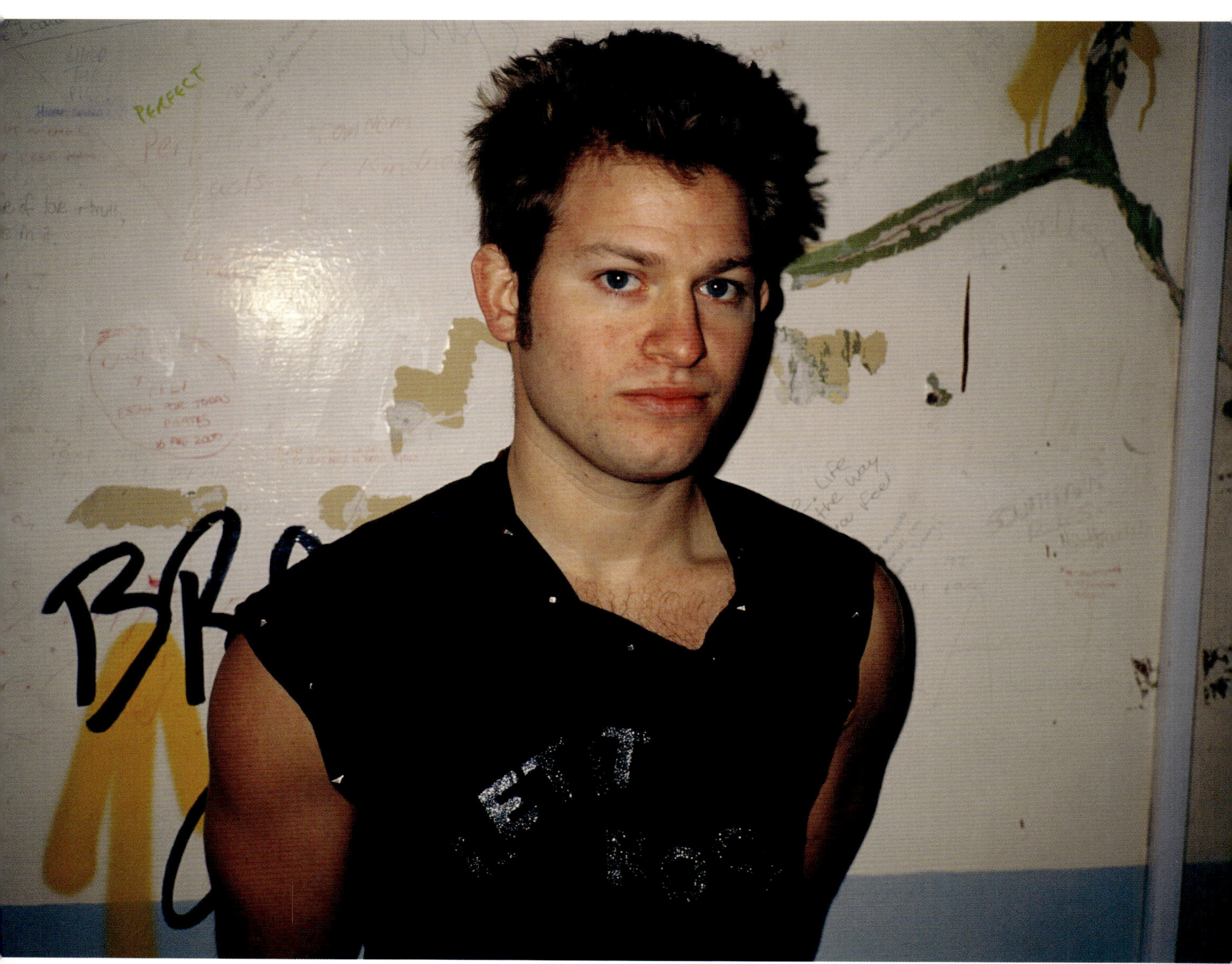

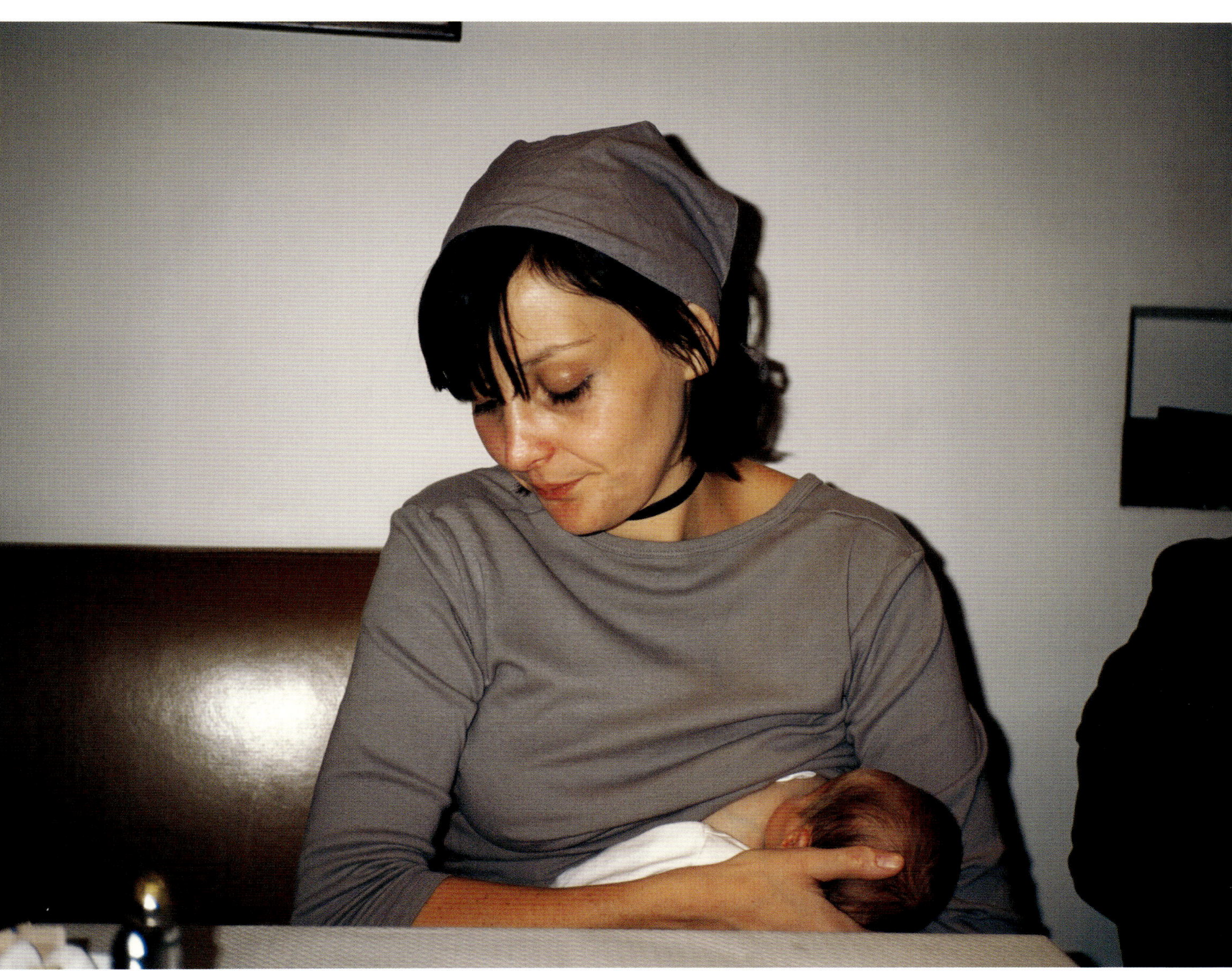

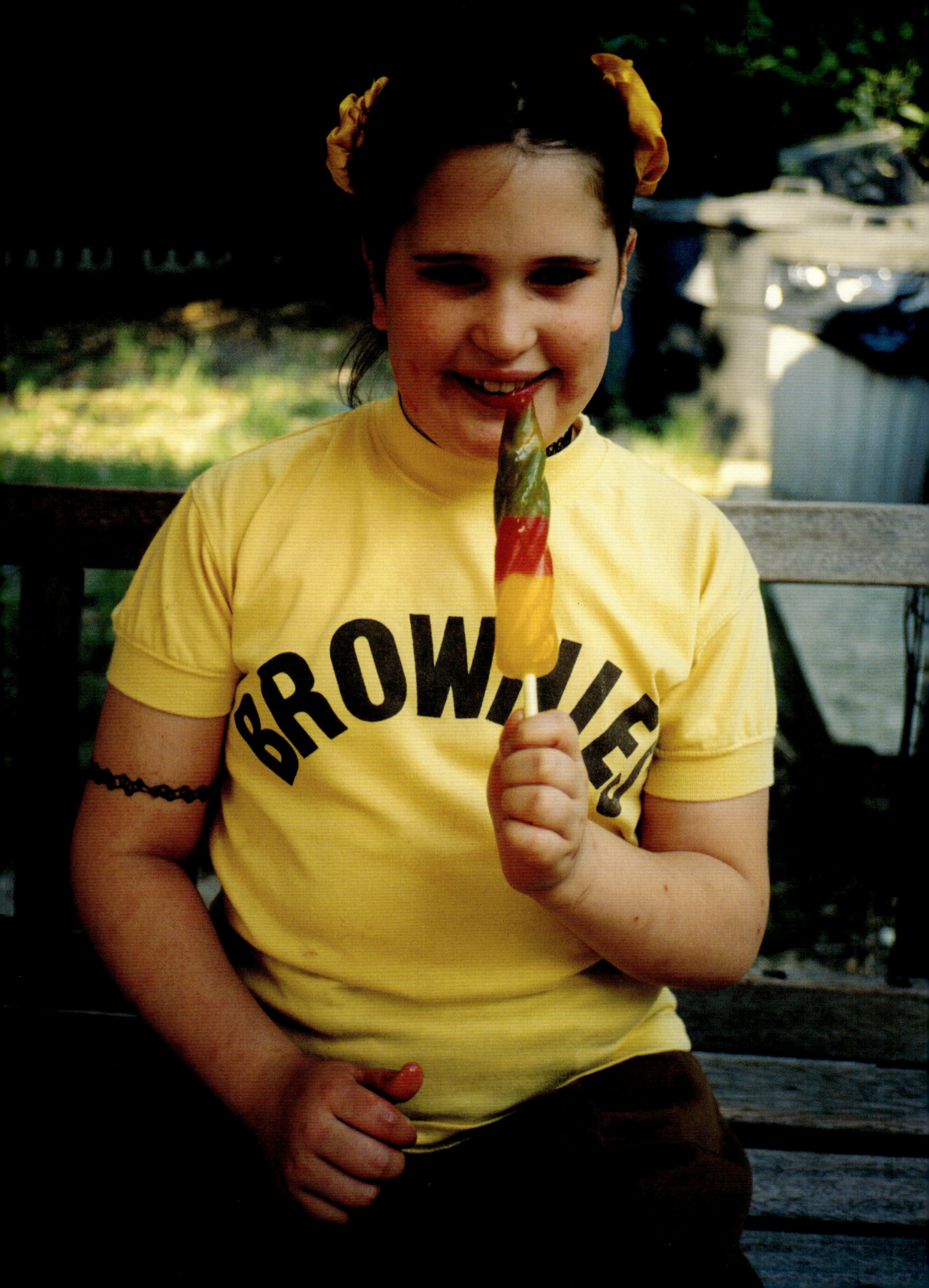

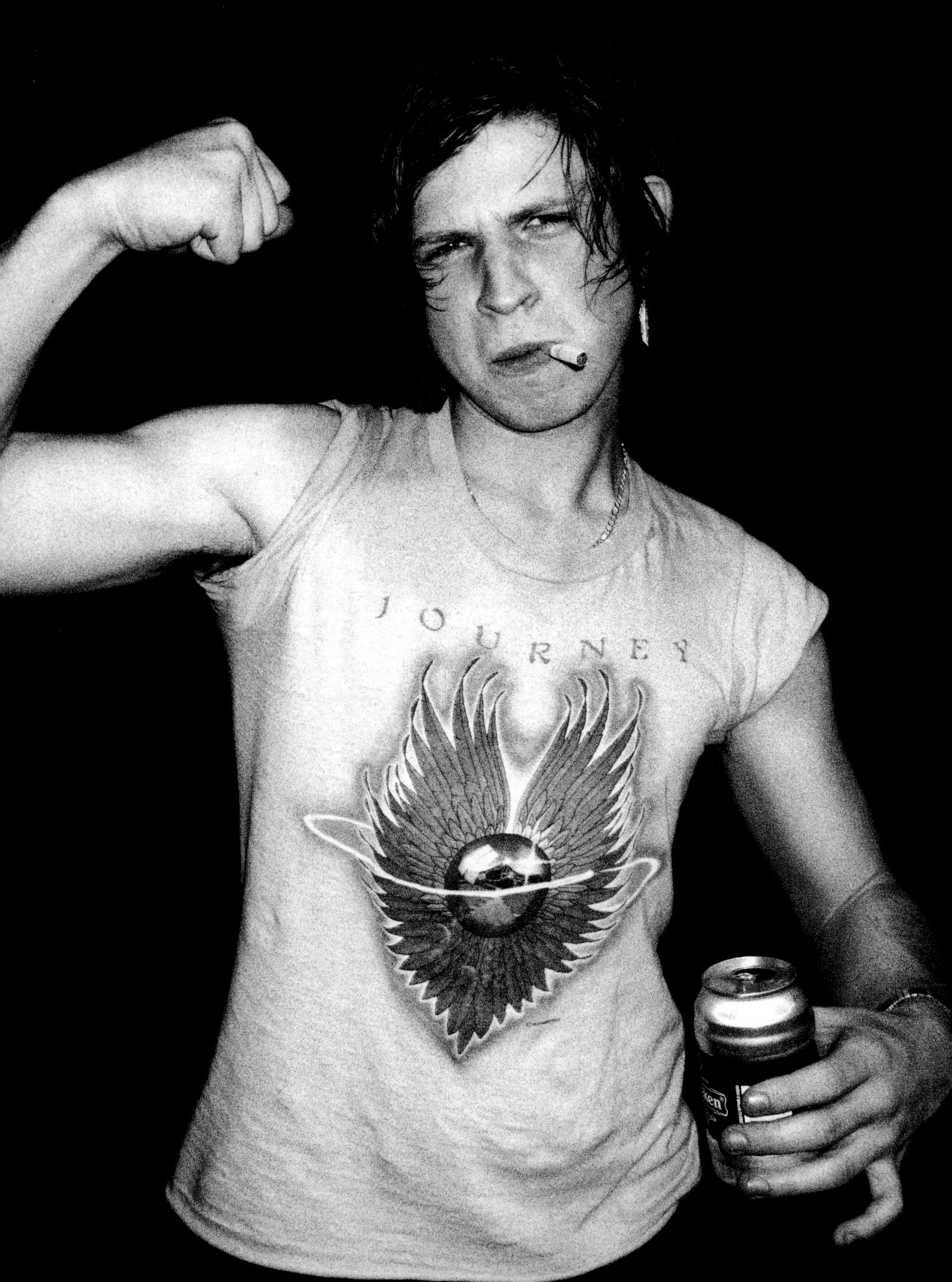
JOURNEY

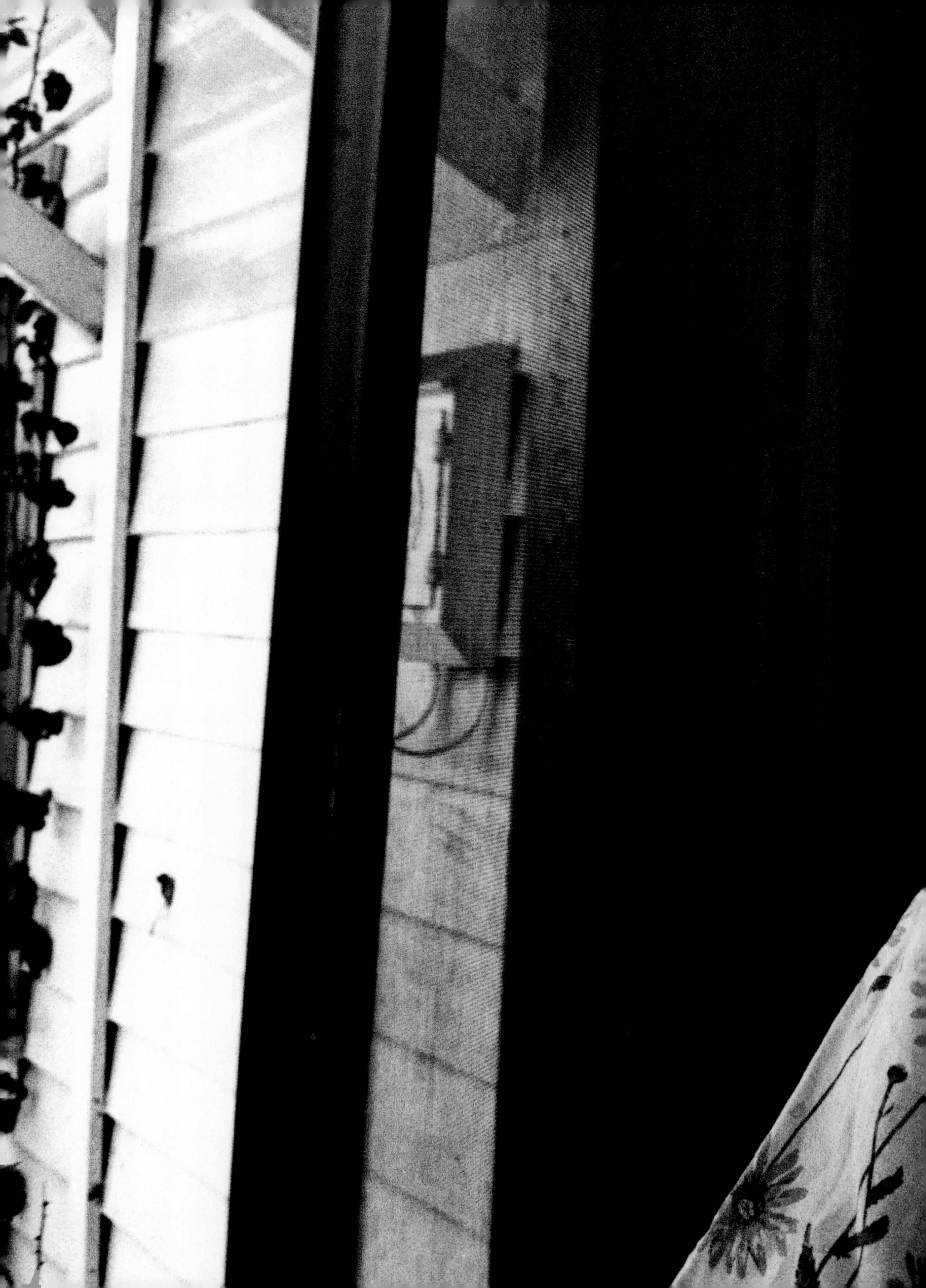

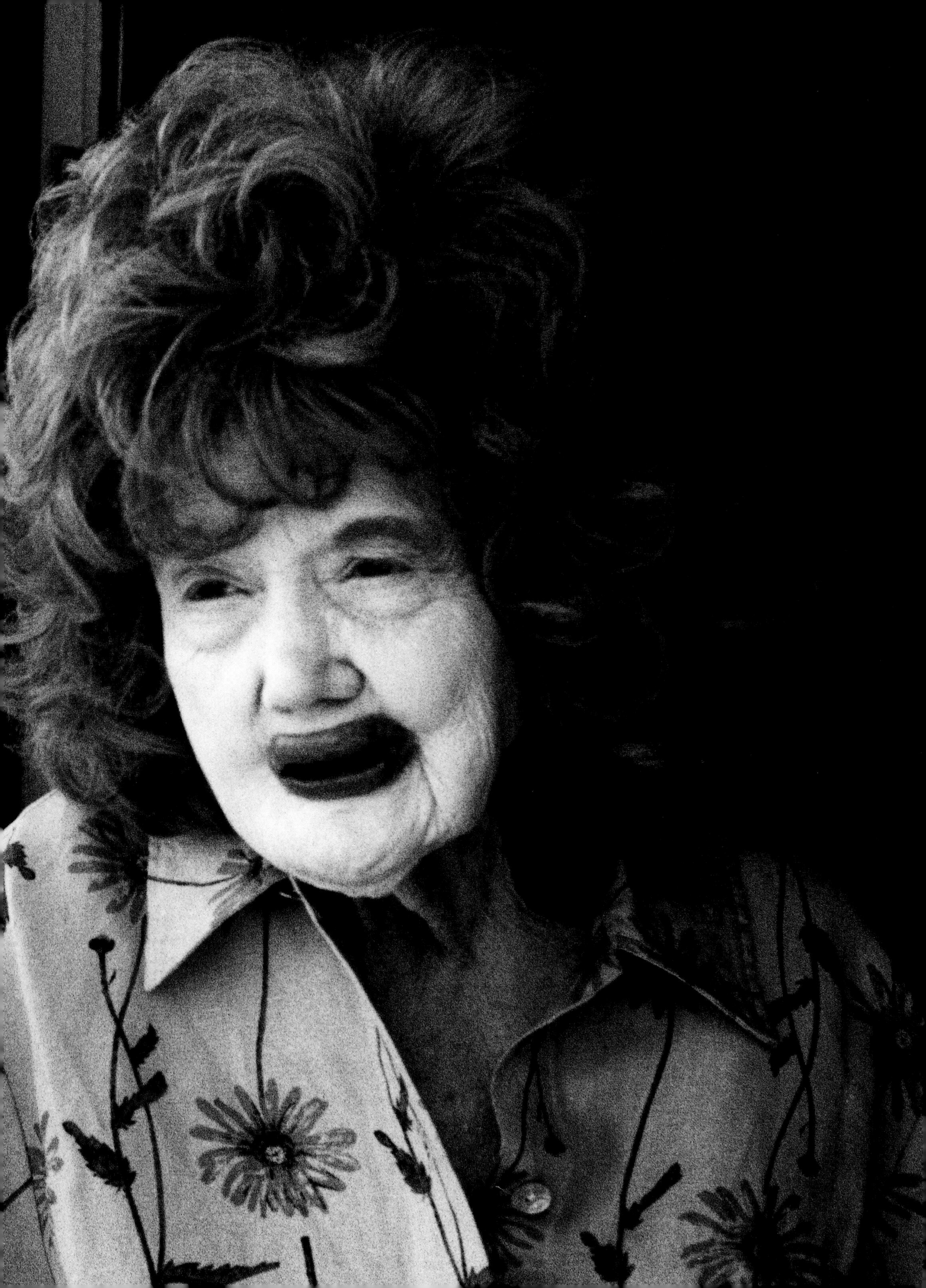

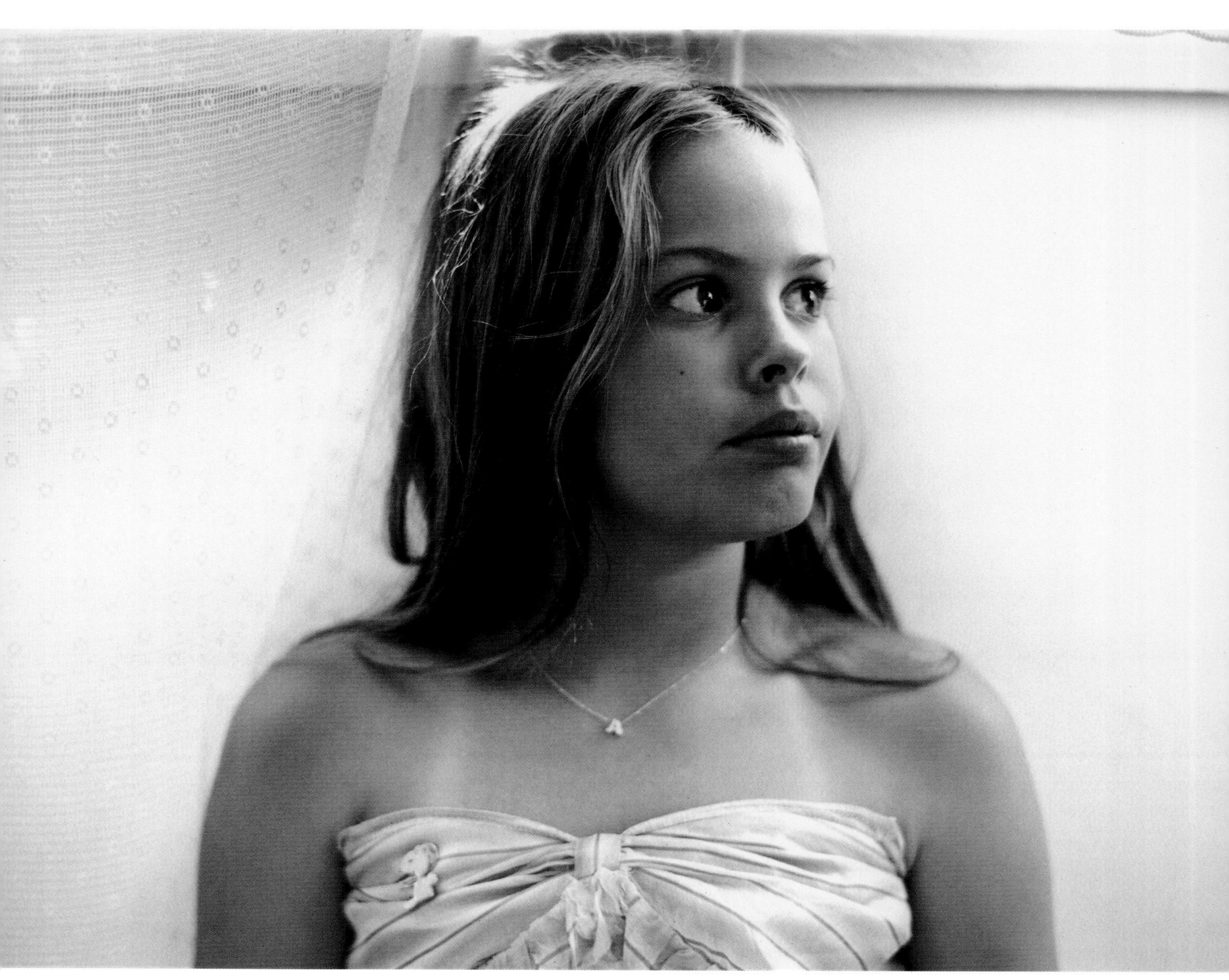

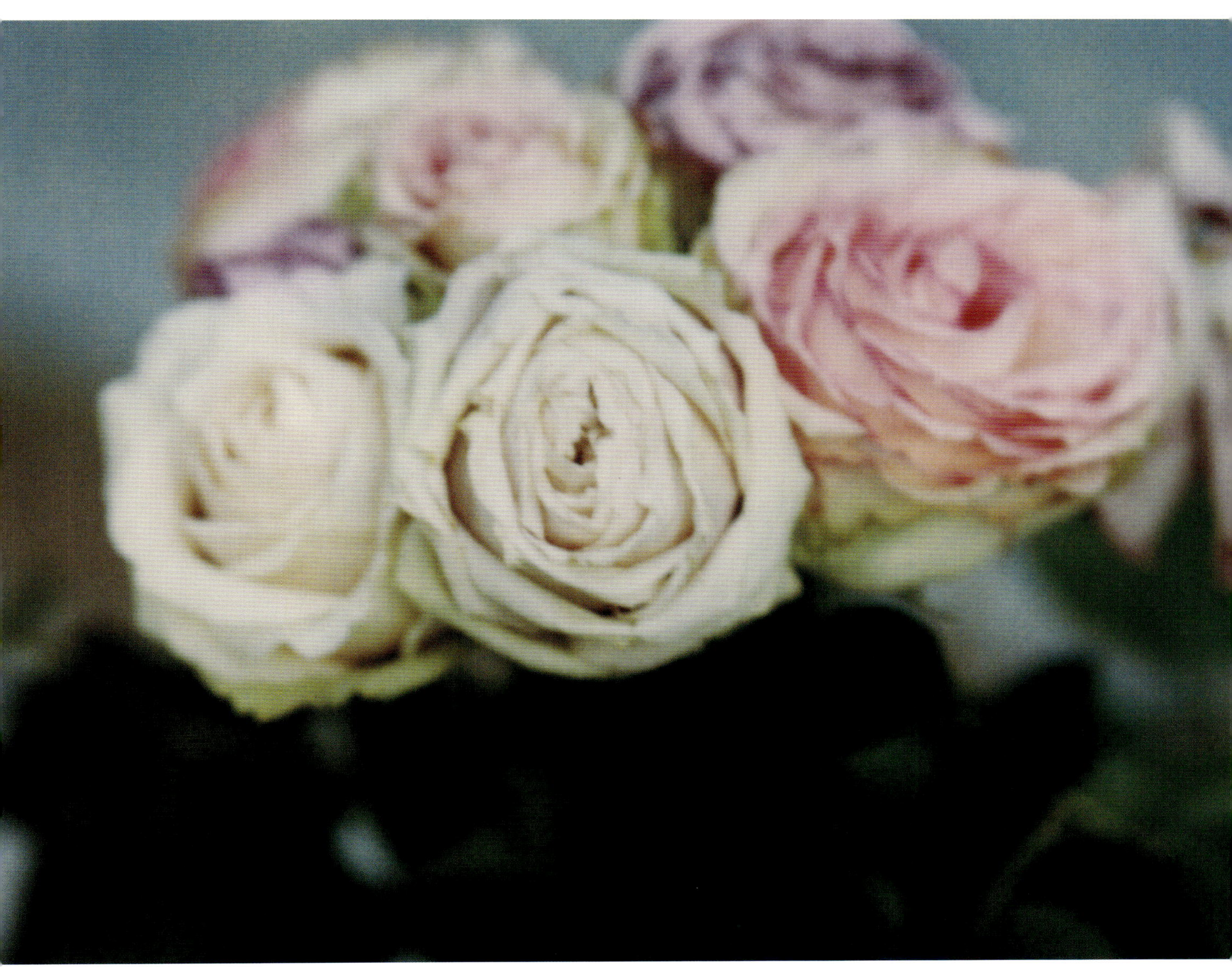

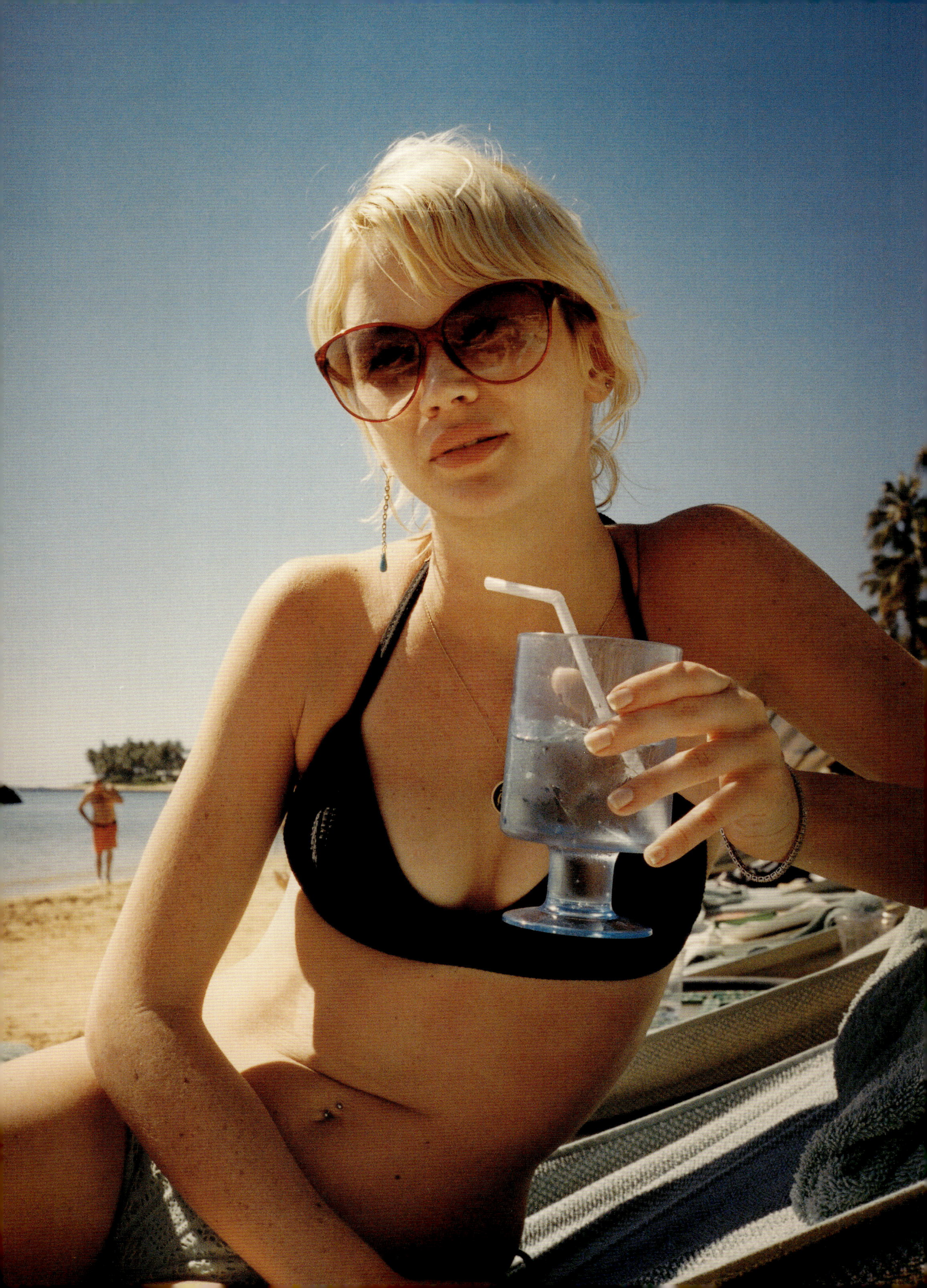

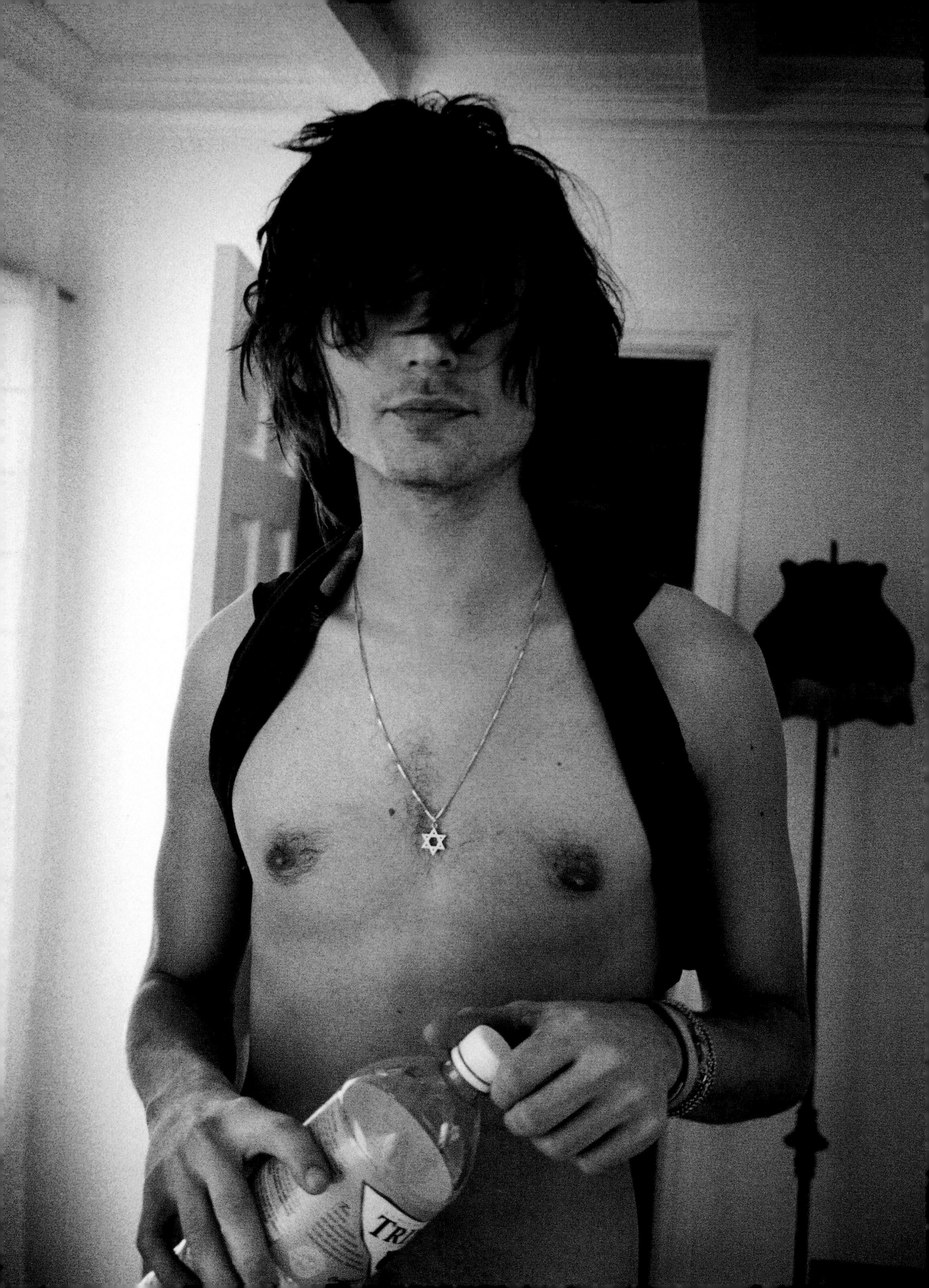

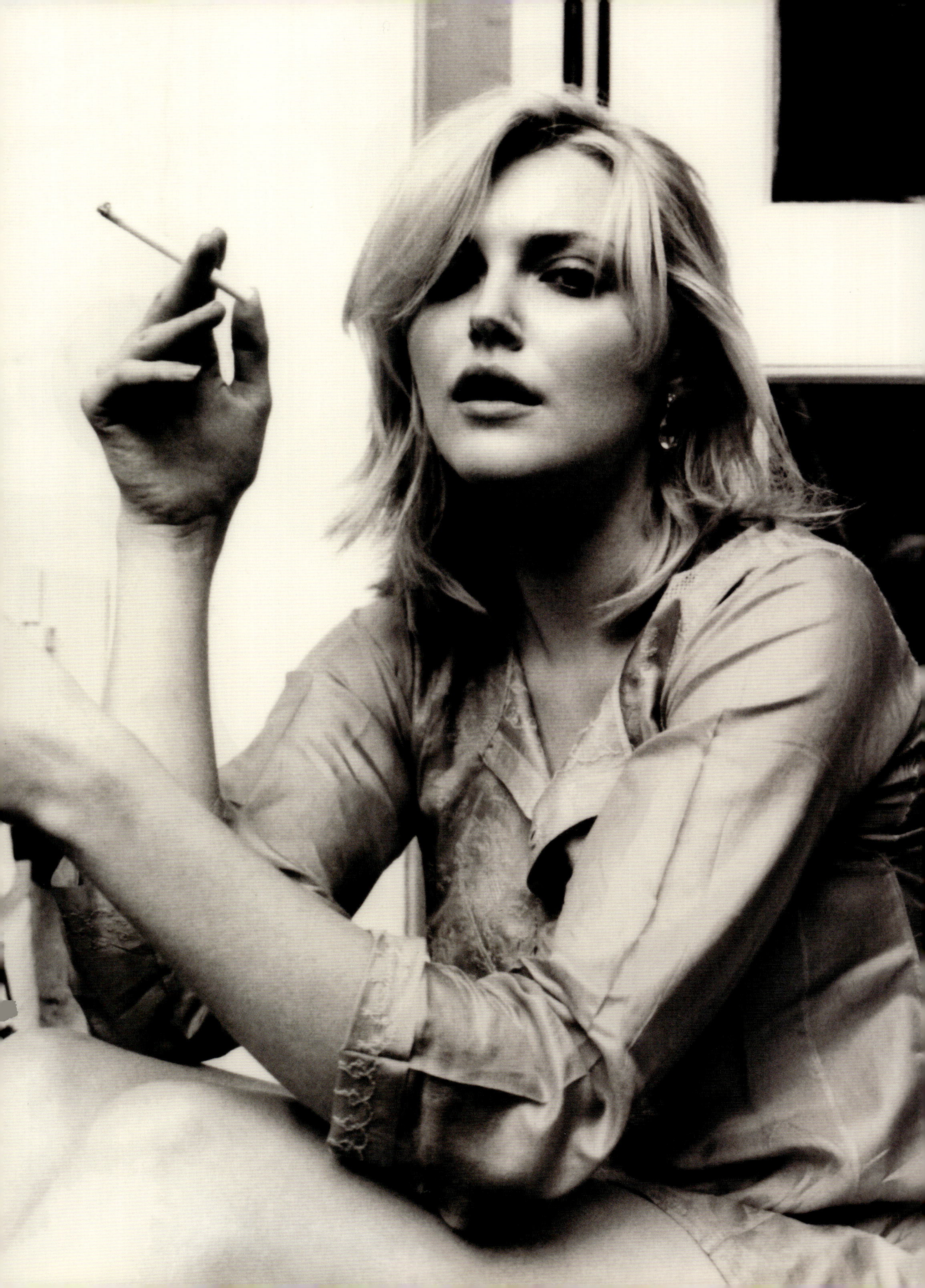

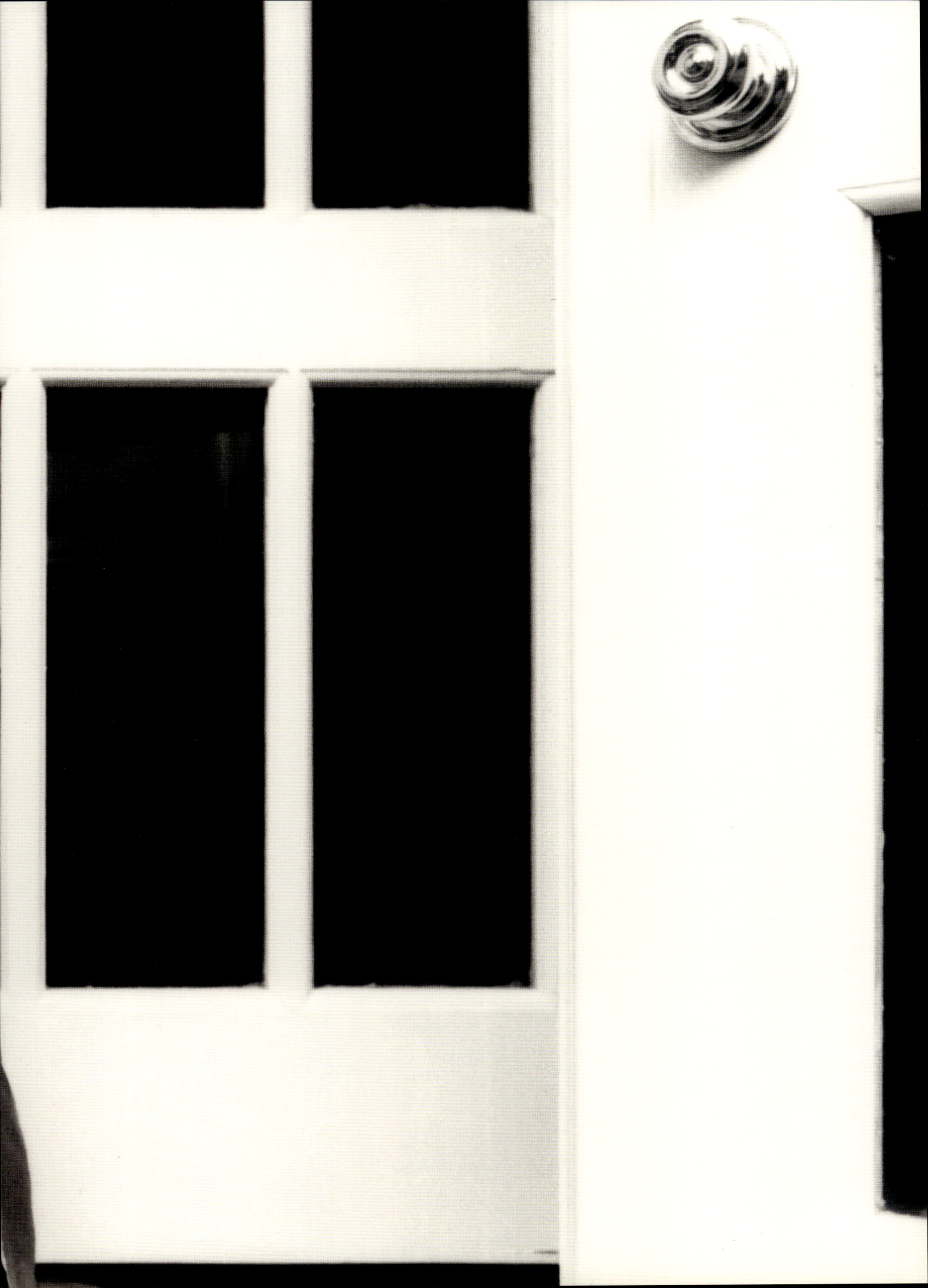

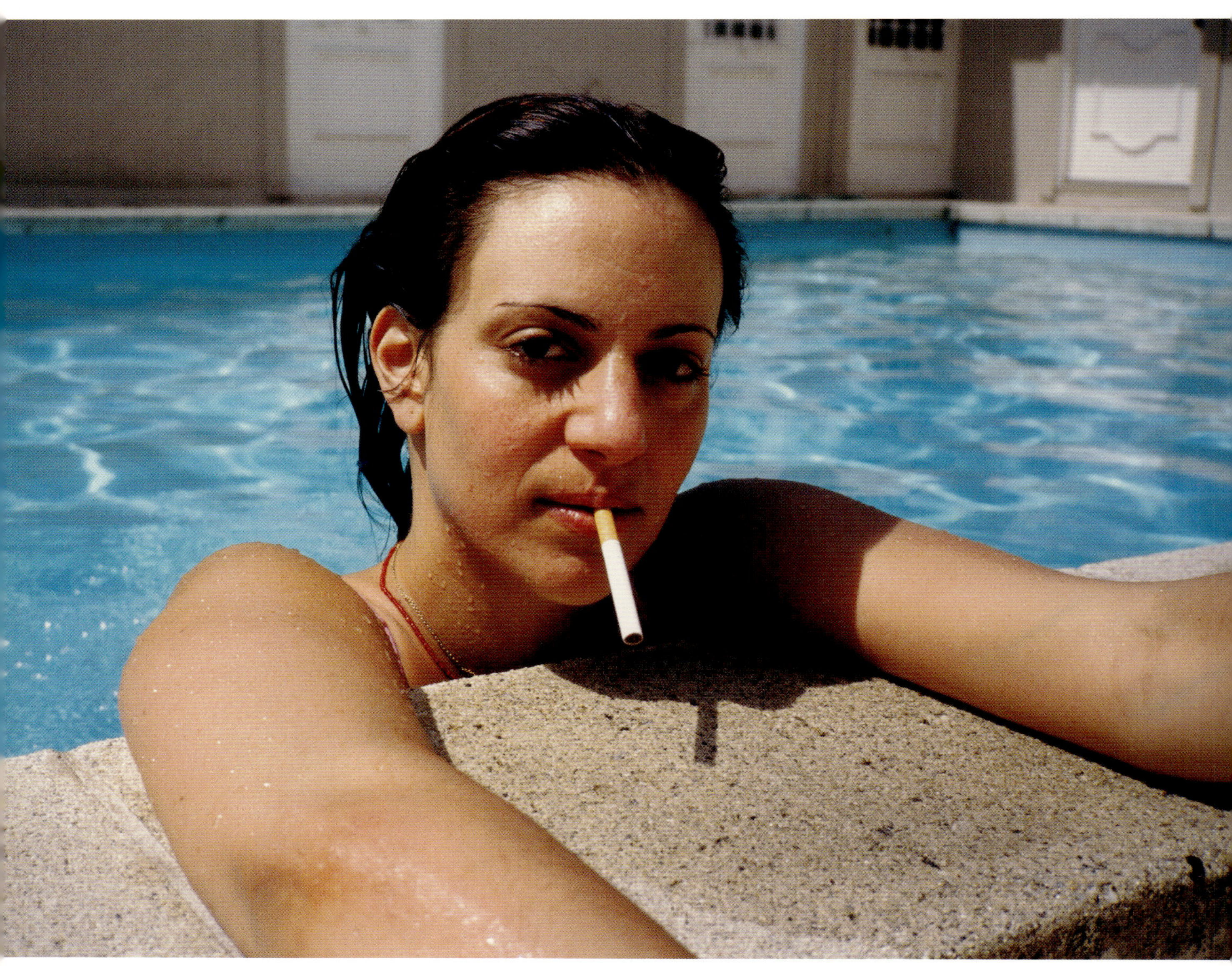

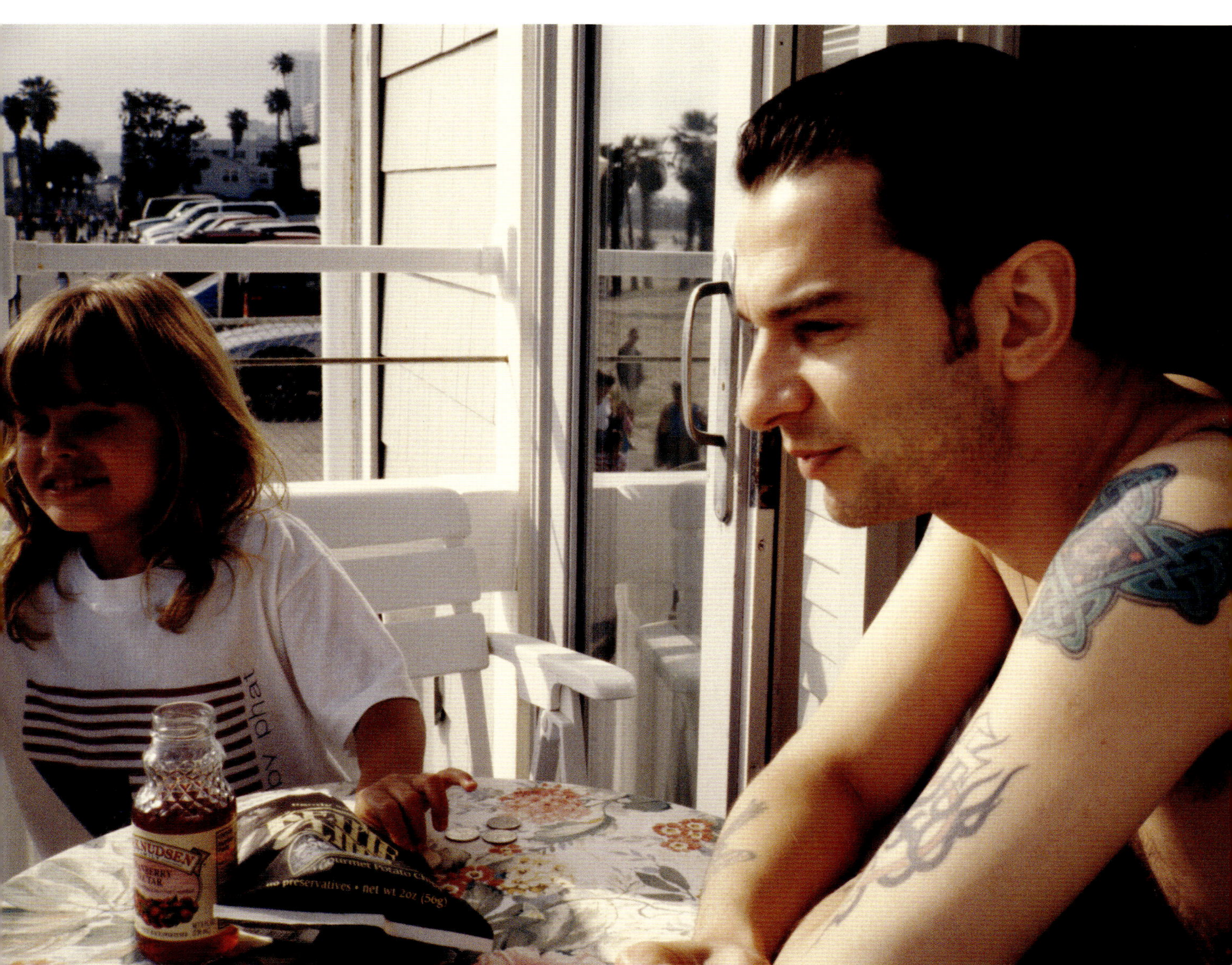
KNUDSEN
no preservatives • net wt 2oz (56g)

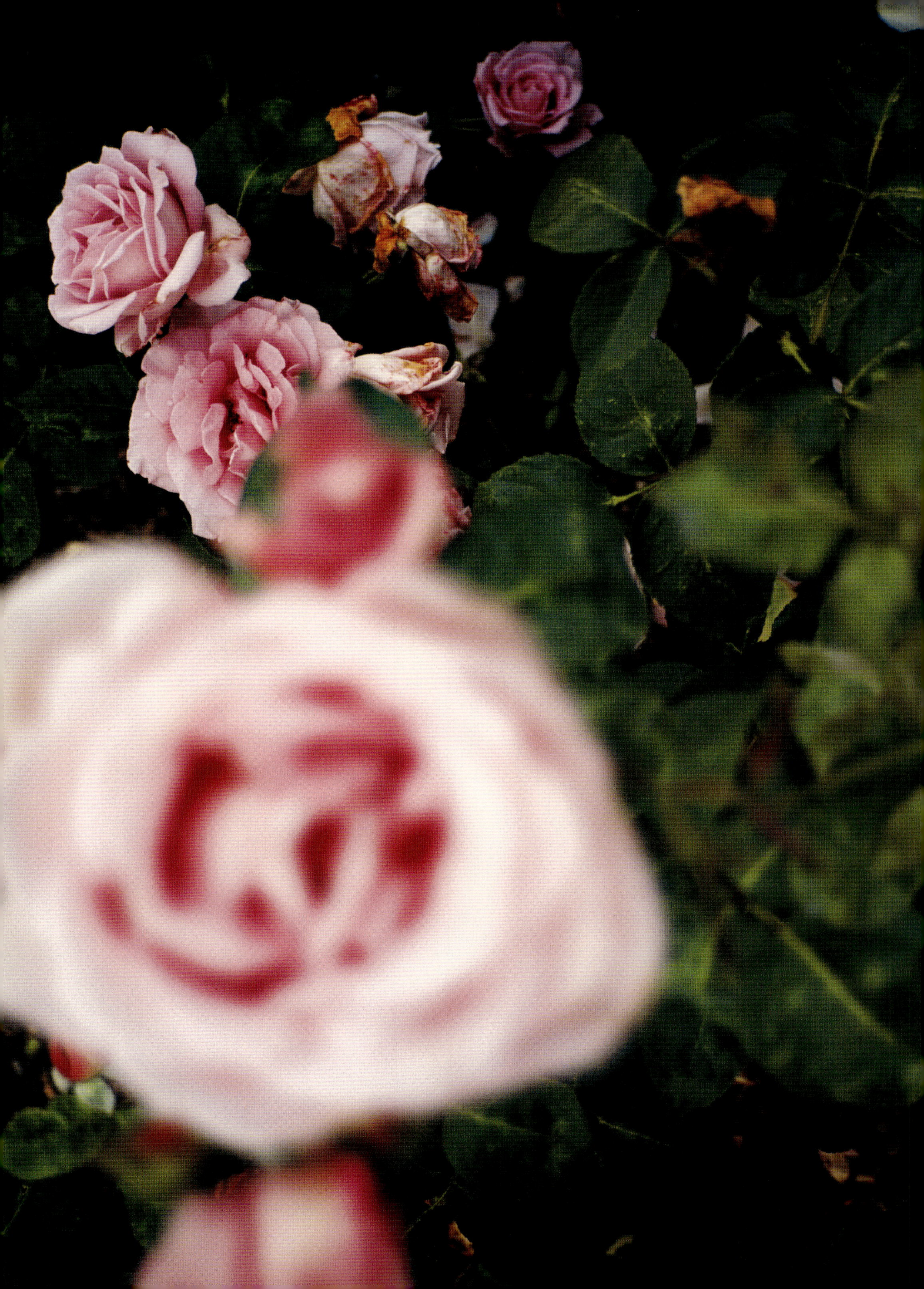

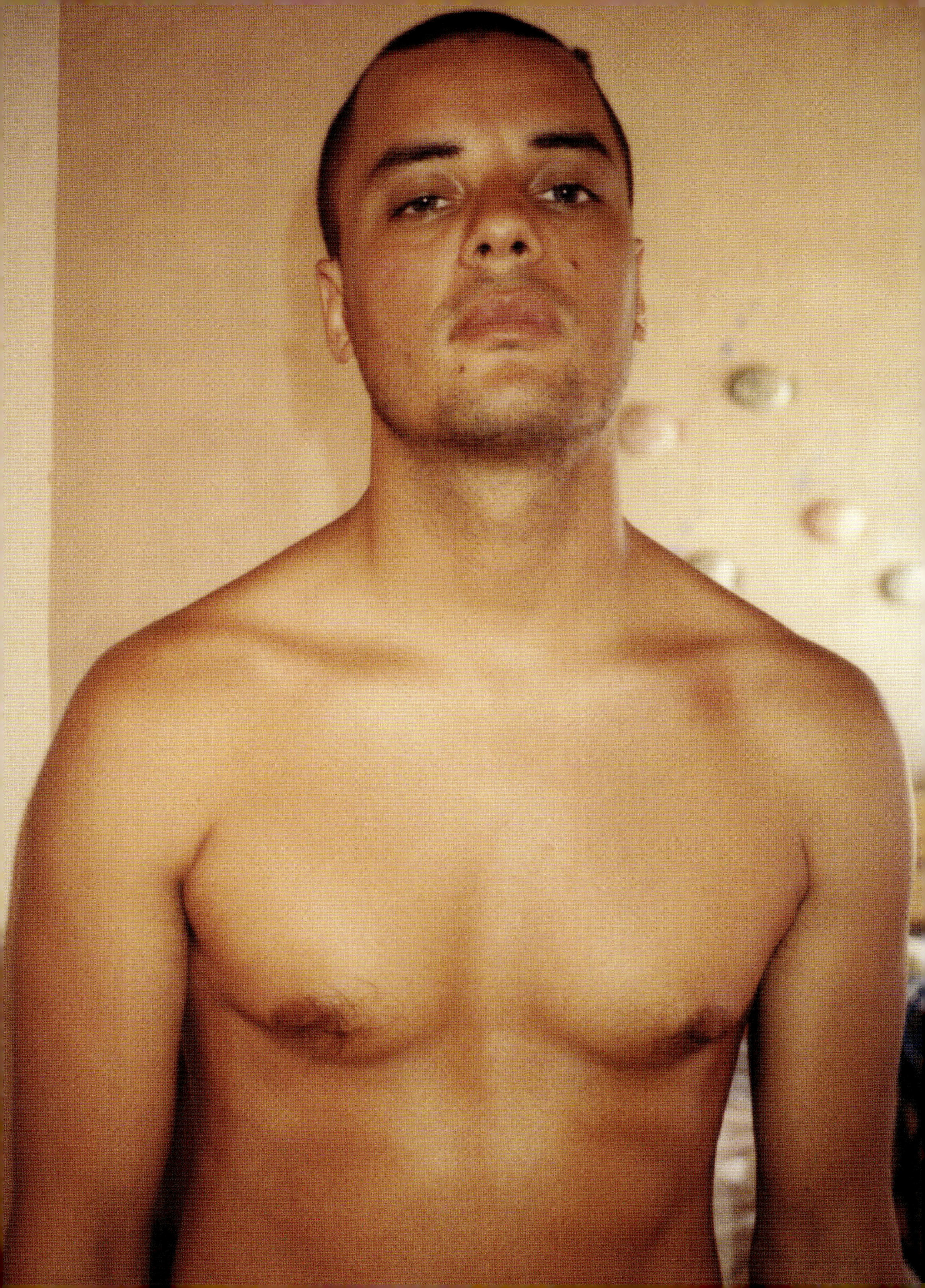

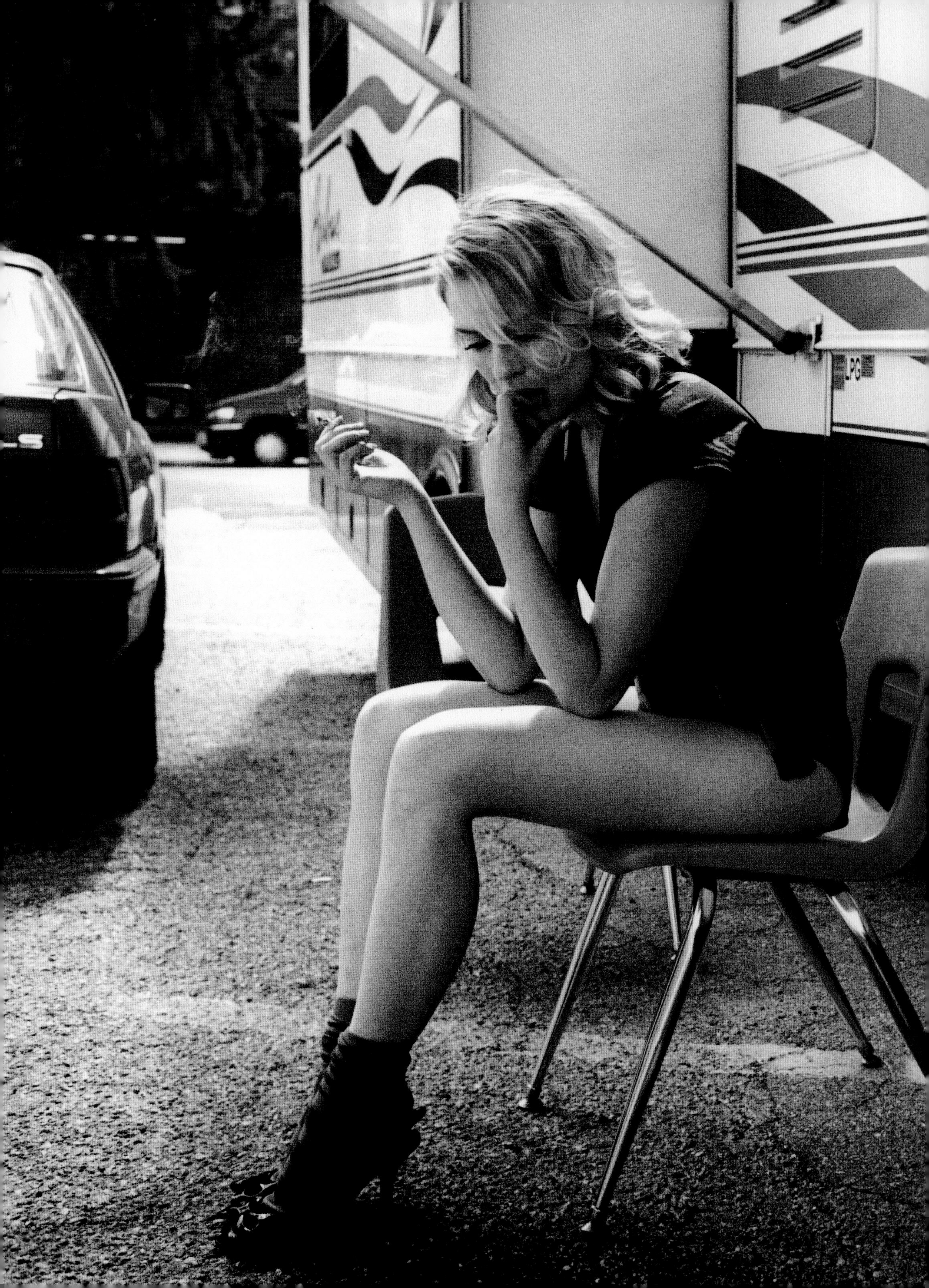
LPG

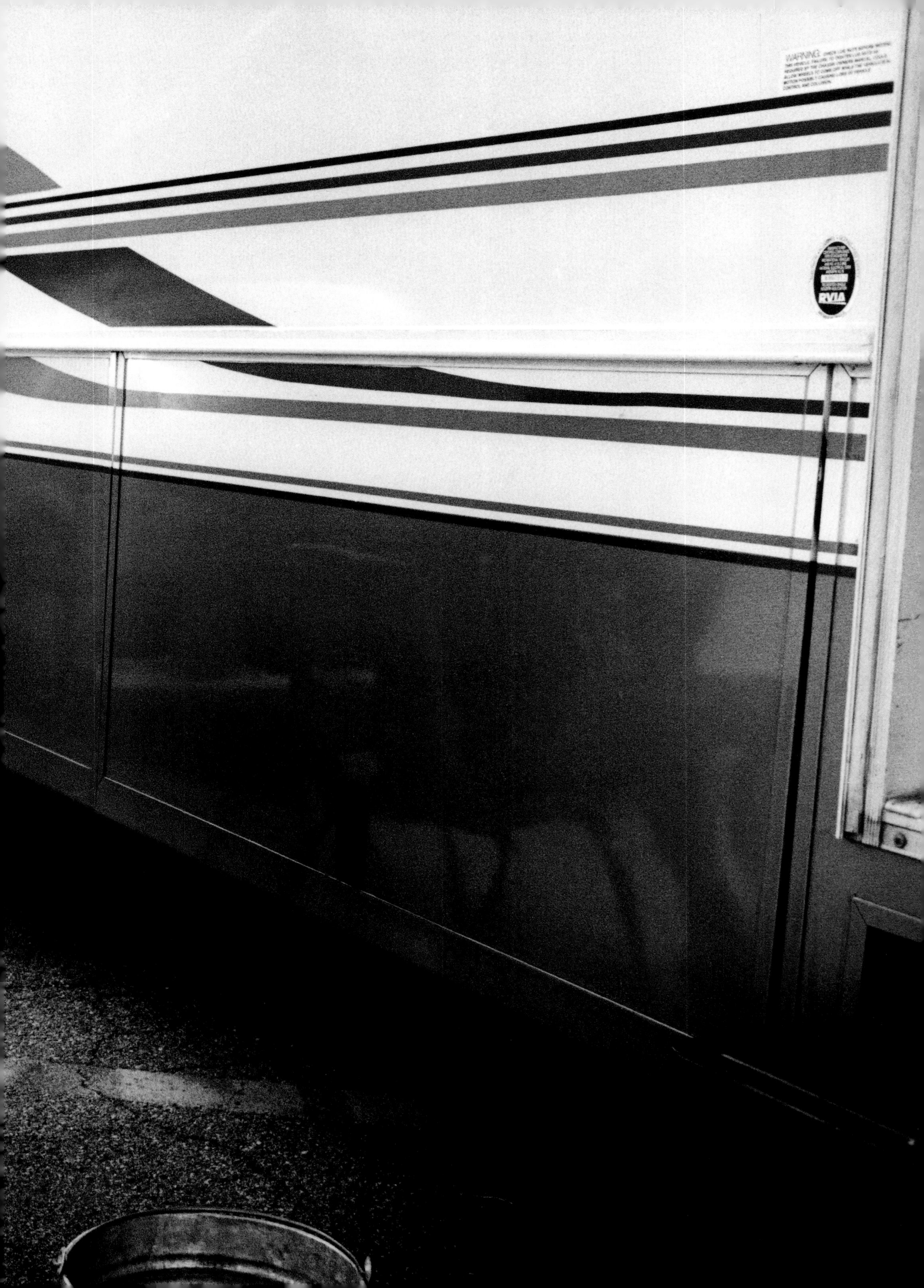
WARNING
RVIA

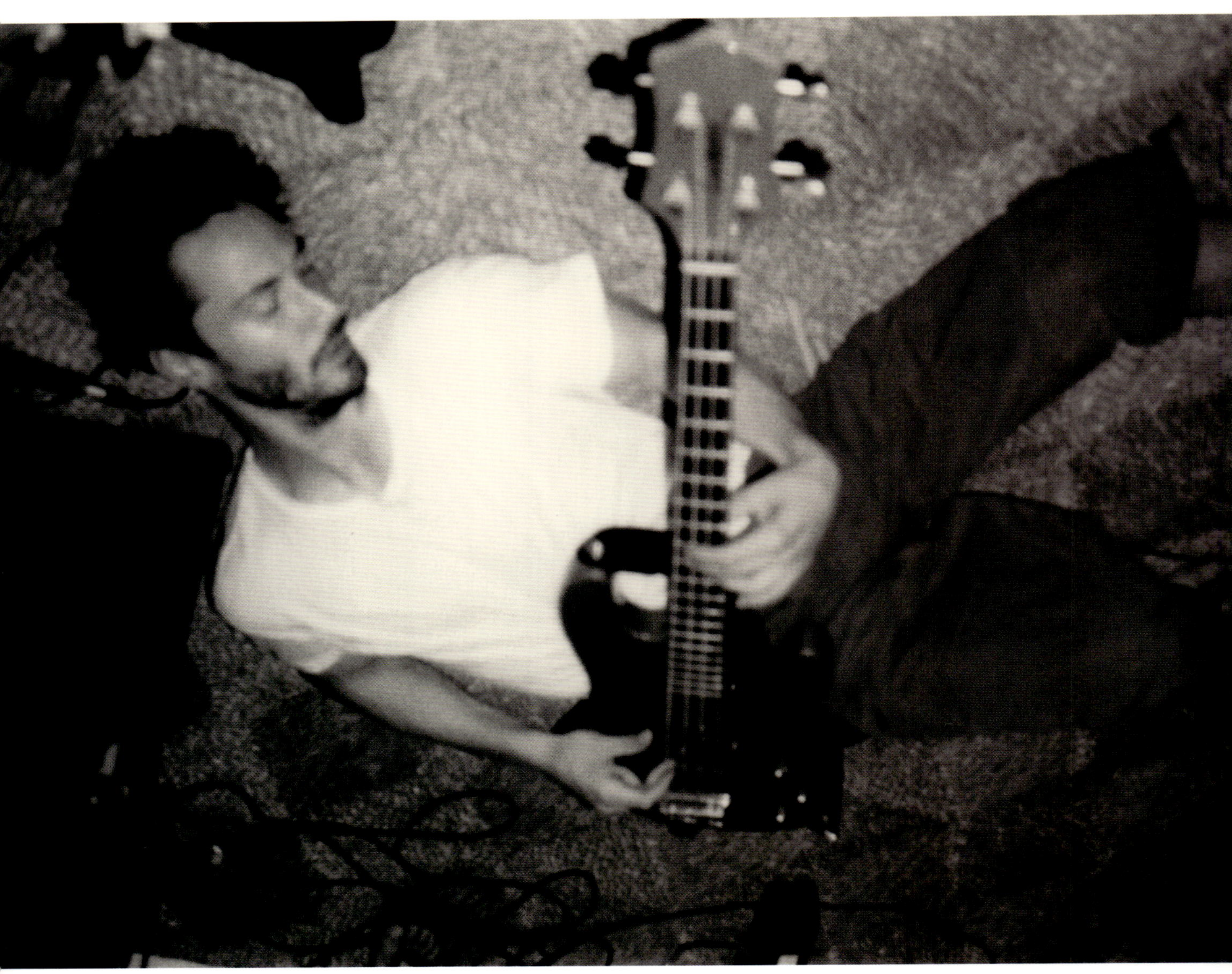

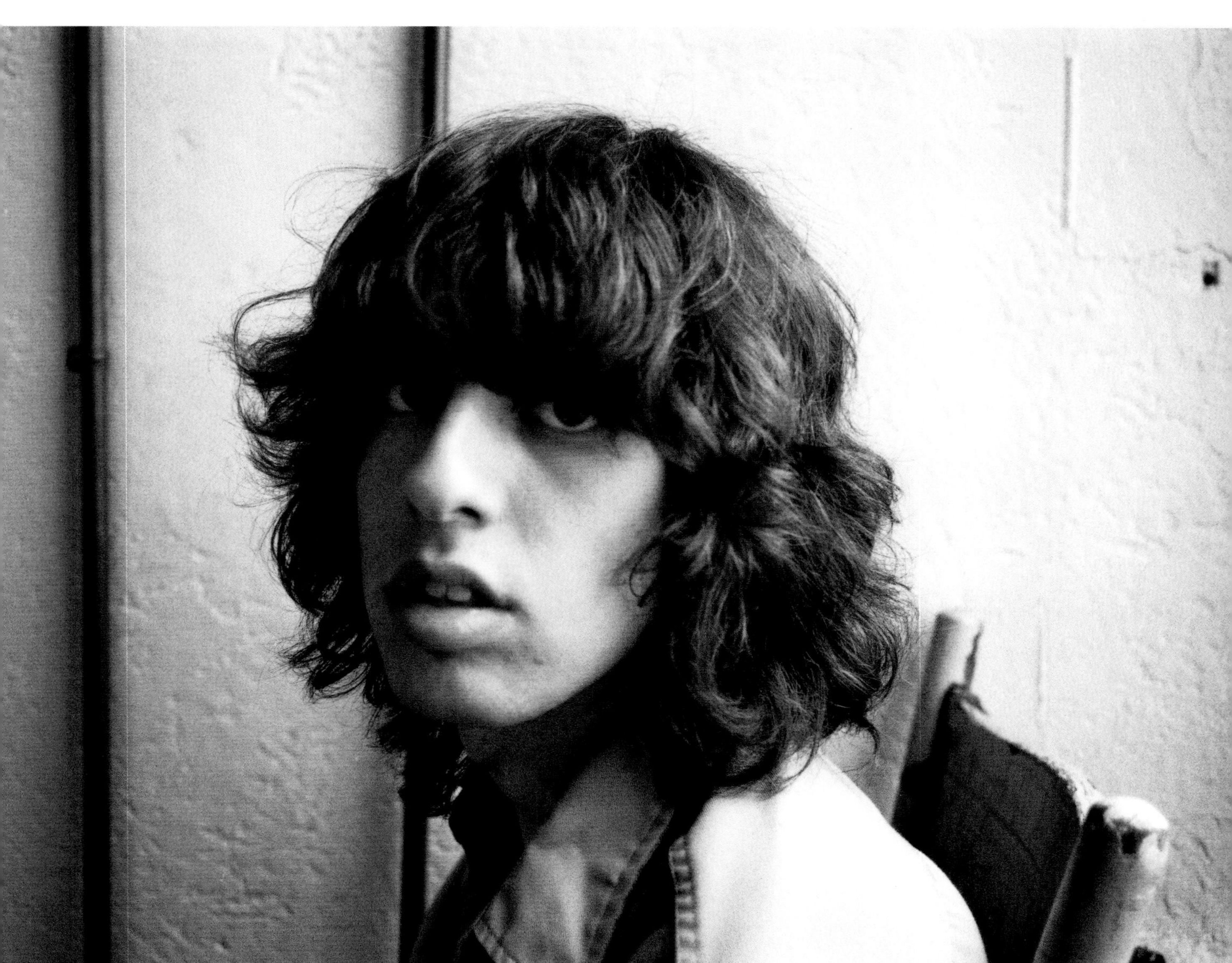

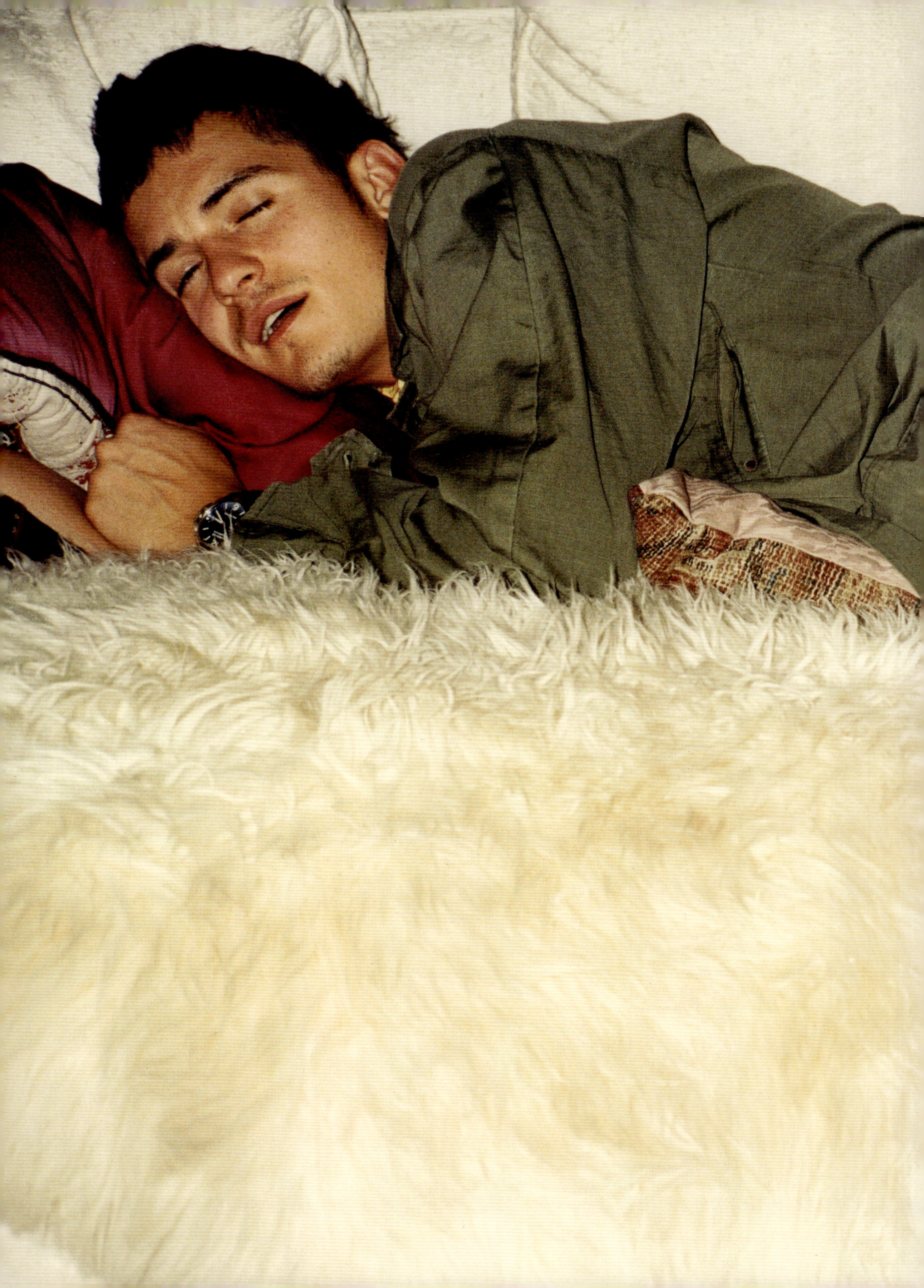

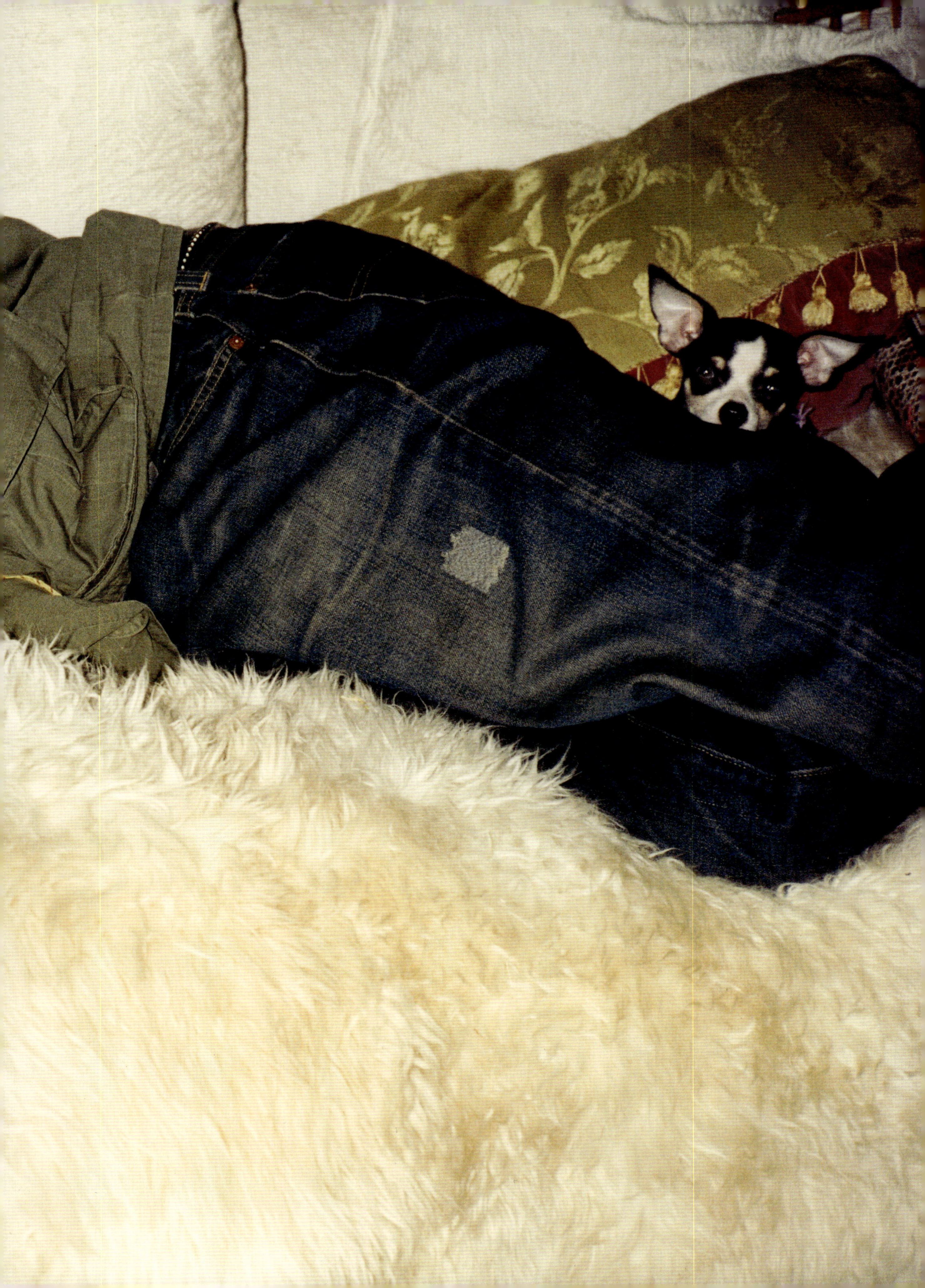

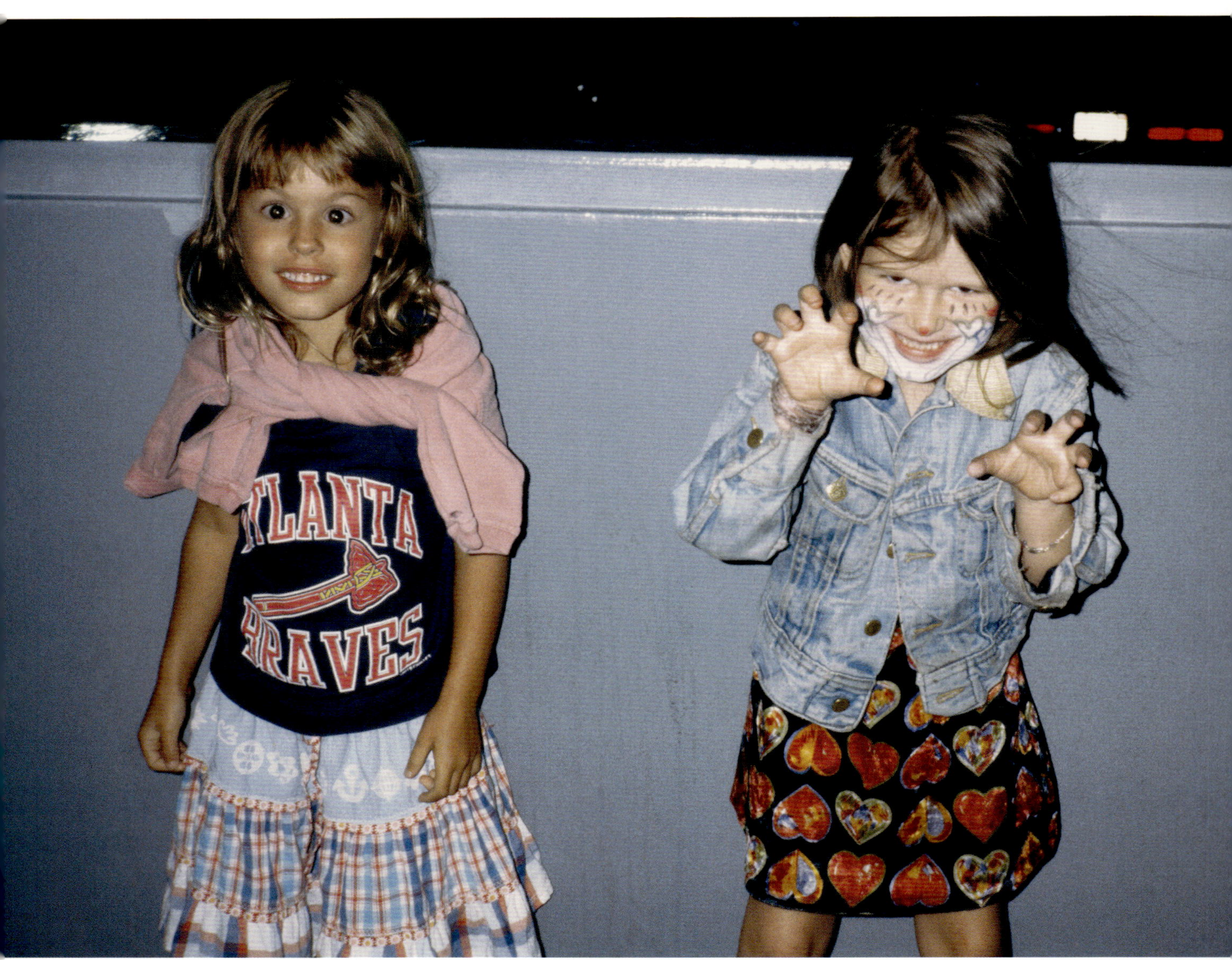
ATLANTA
BRAVES

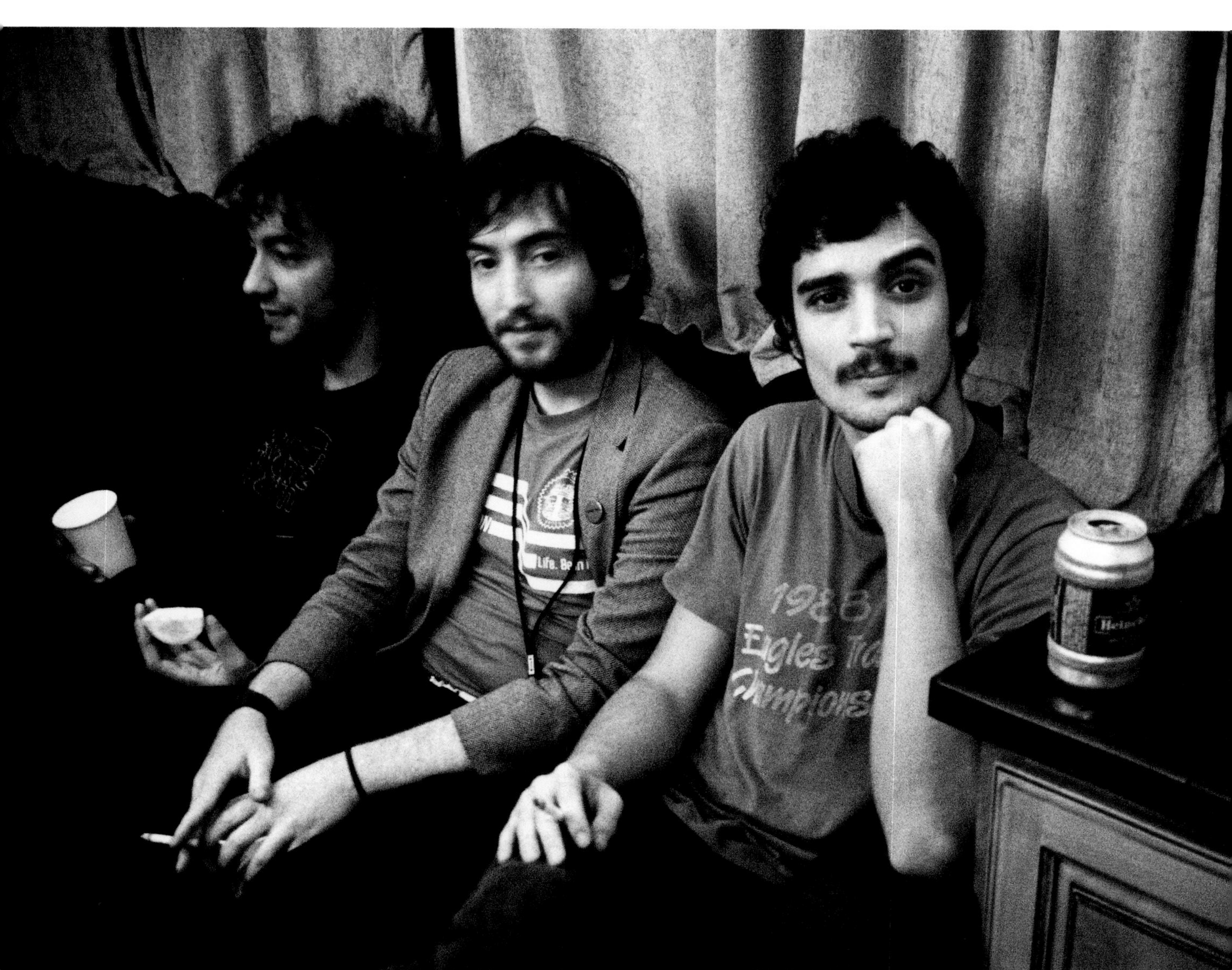

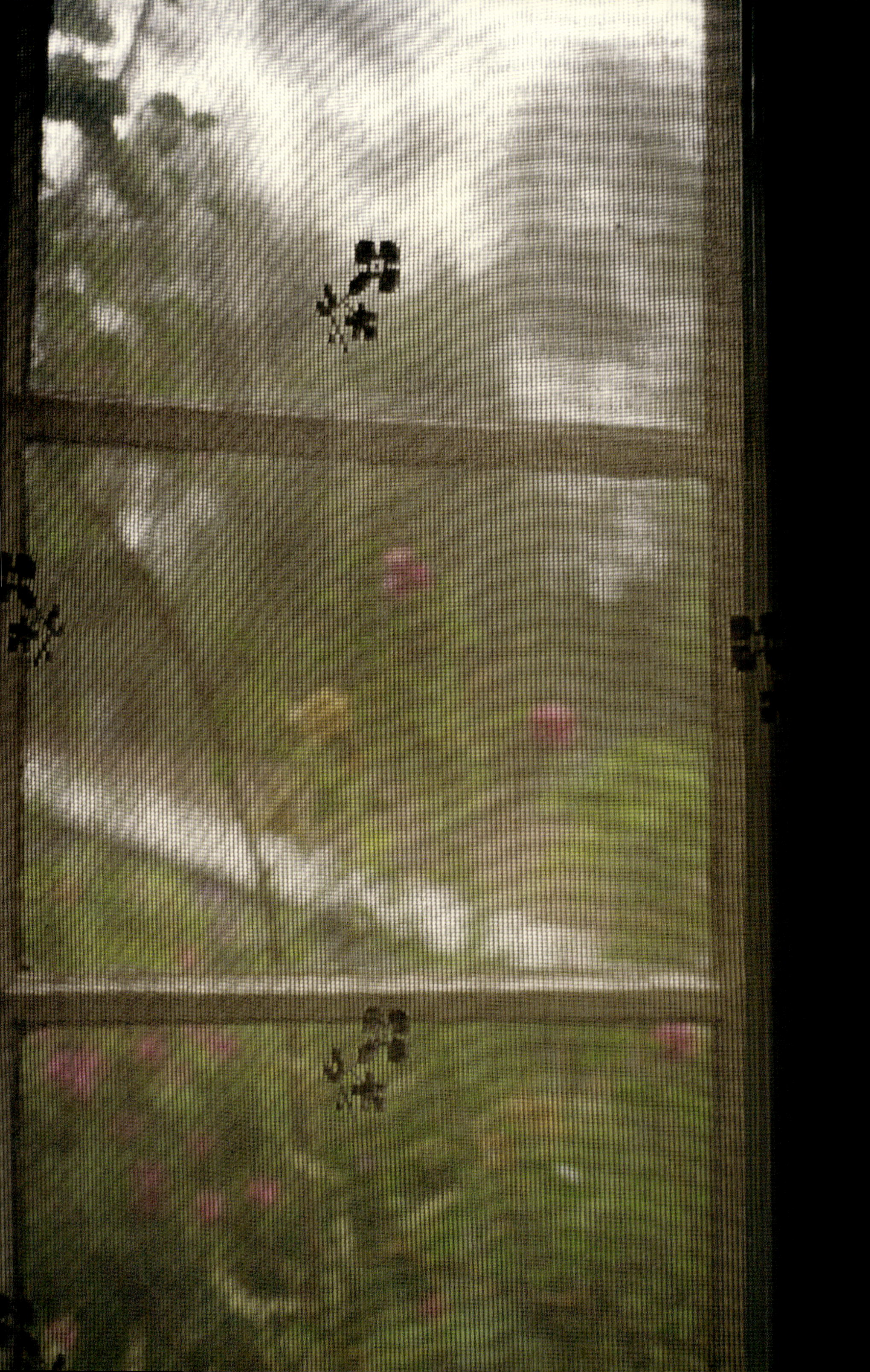

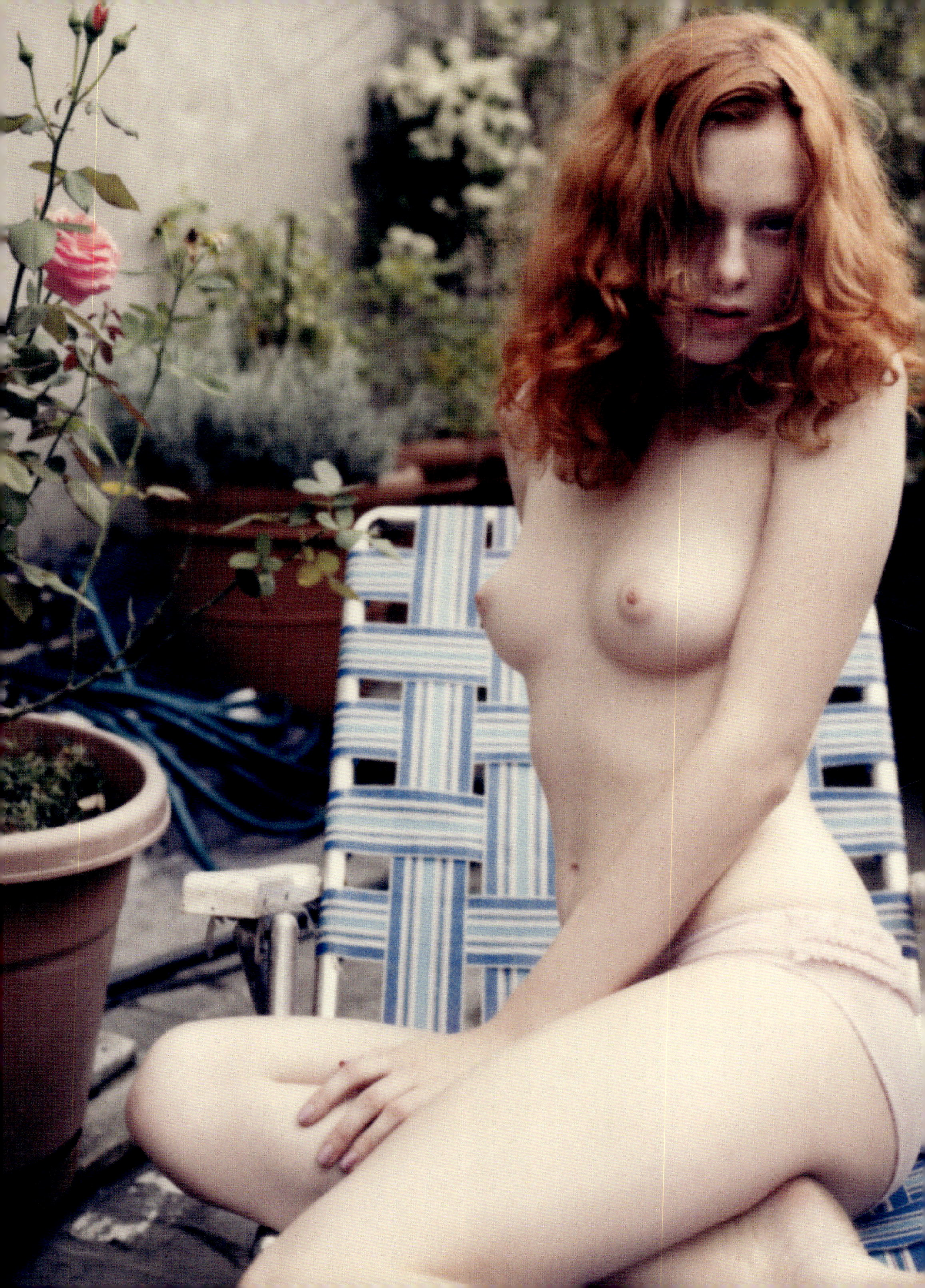

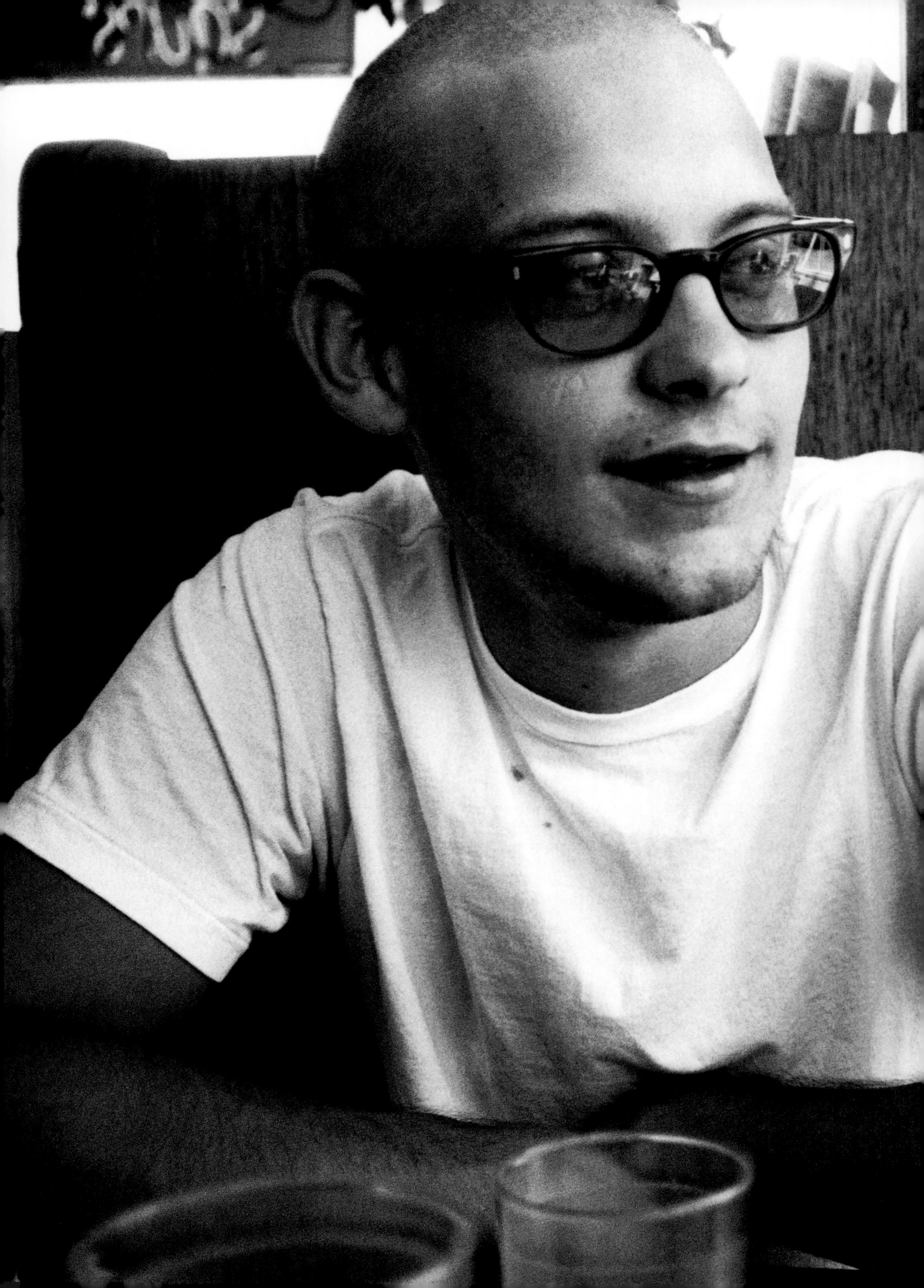

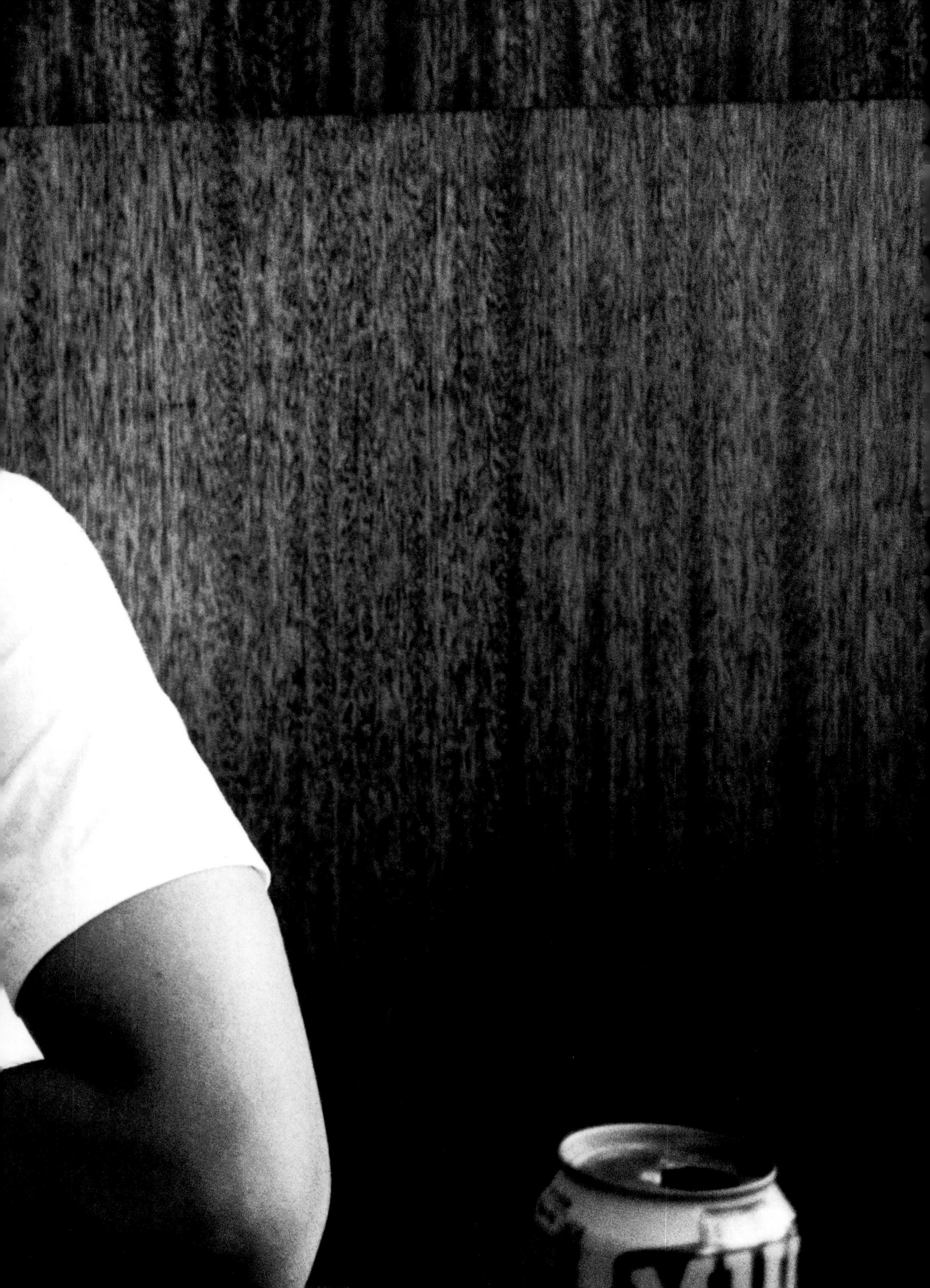

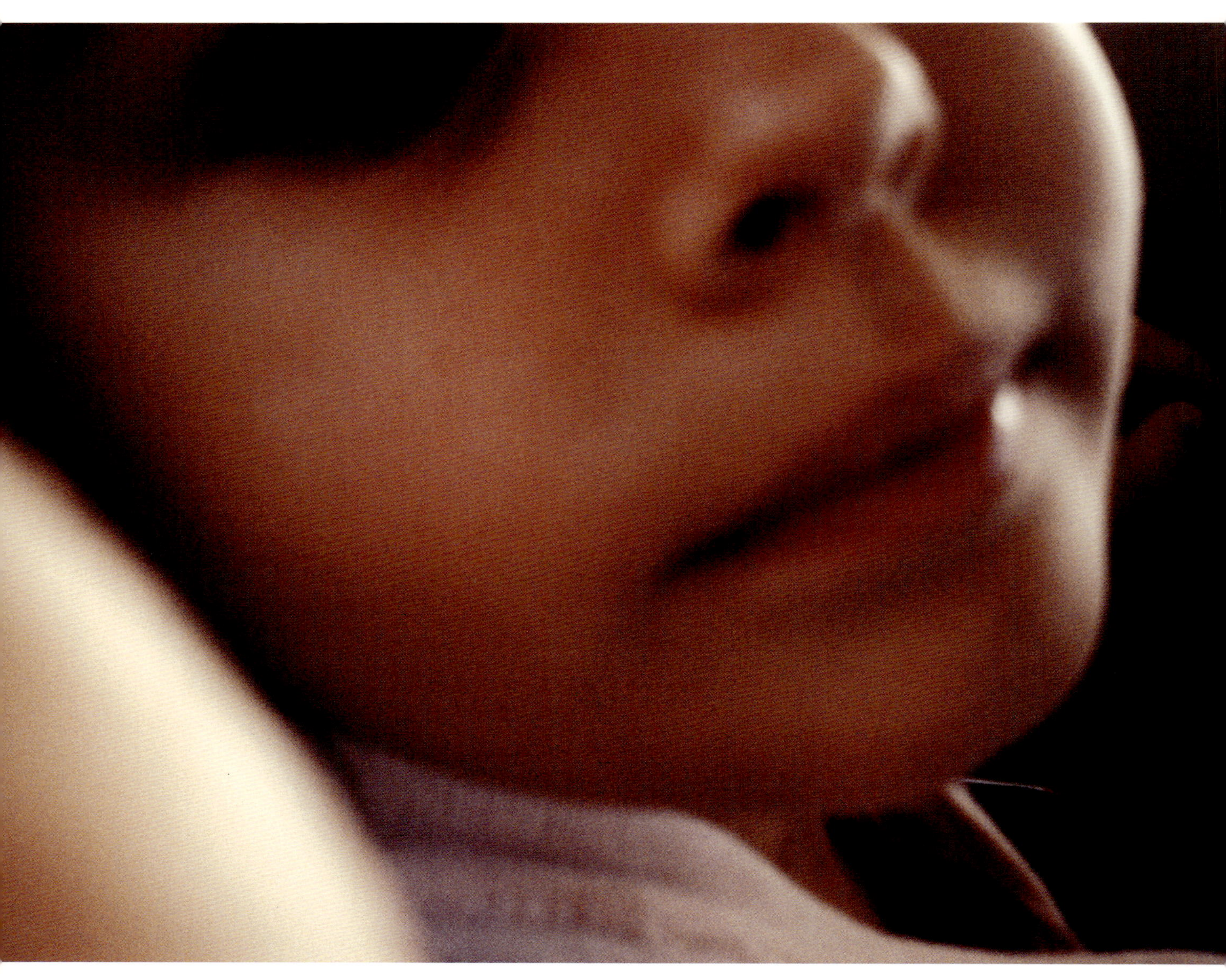

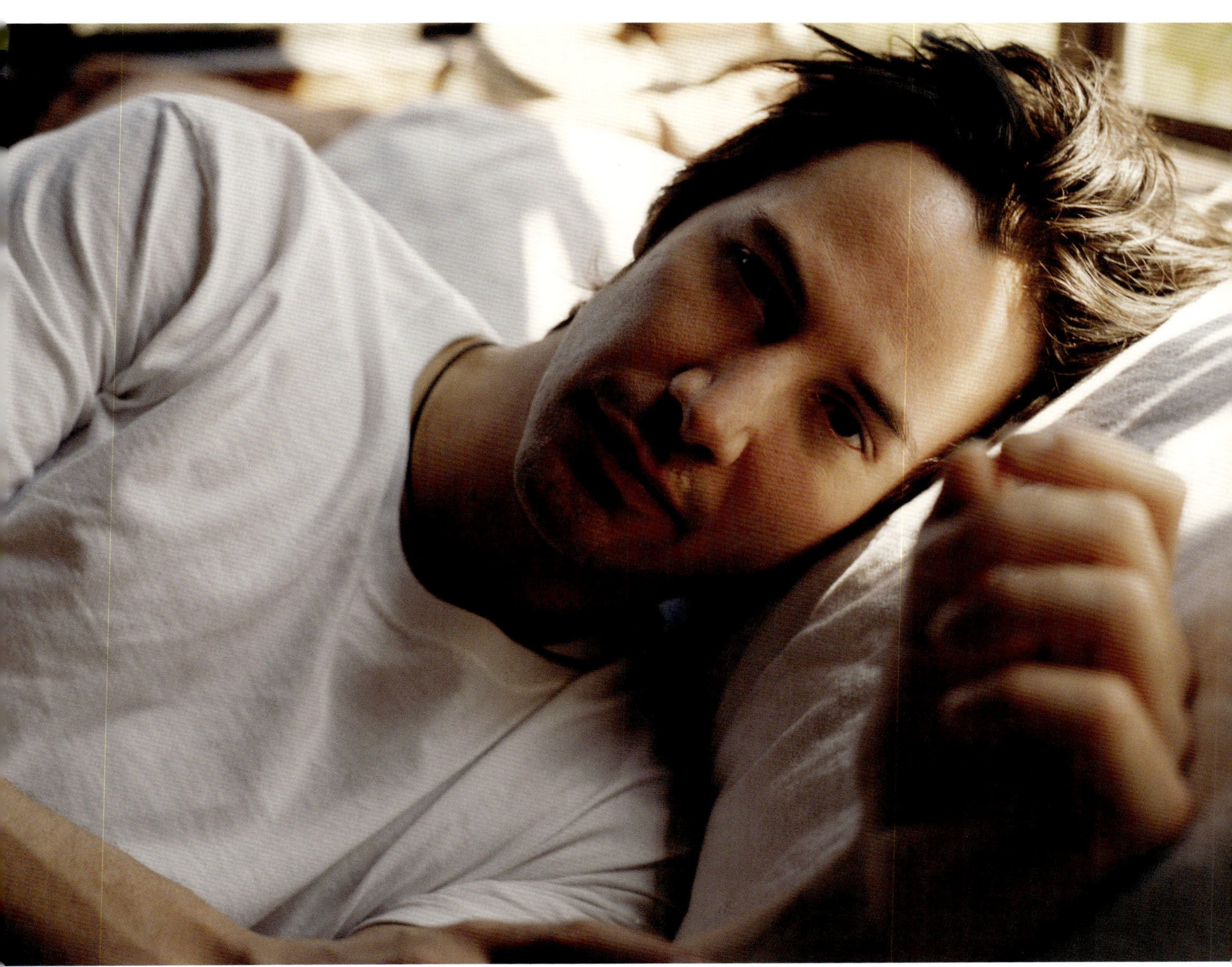

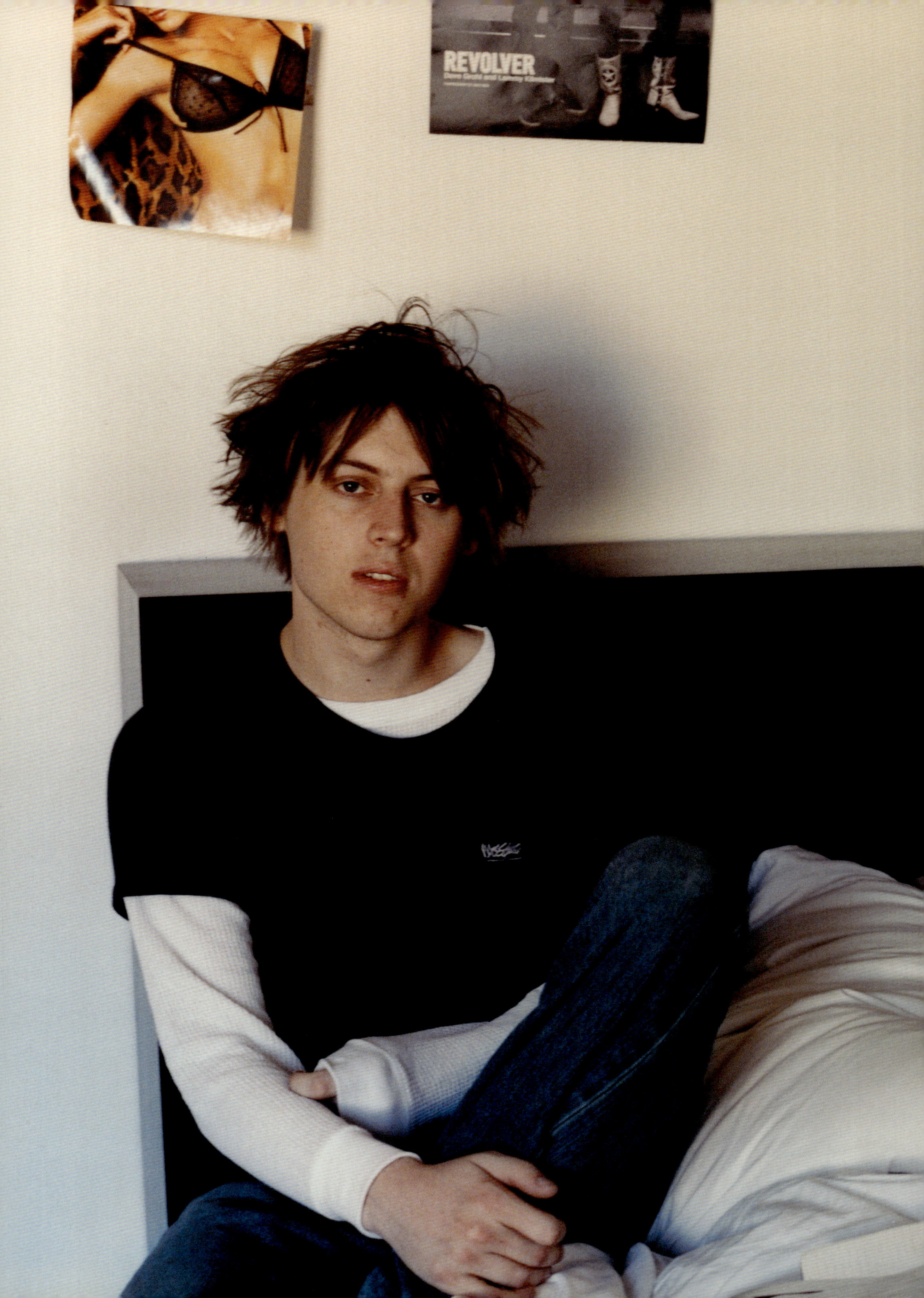
REVOLVER

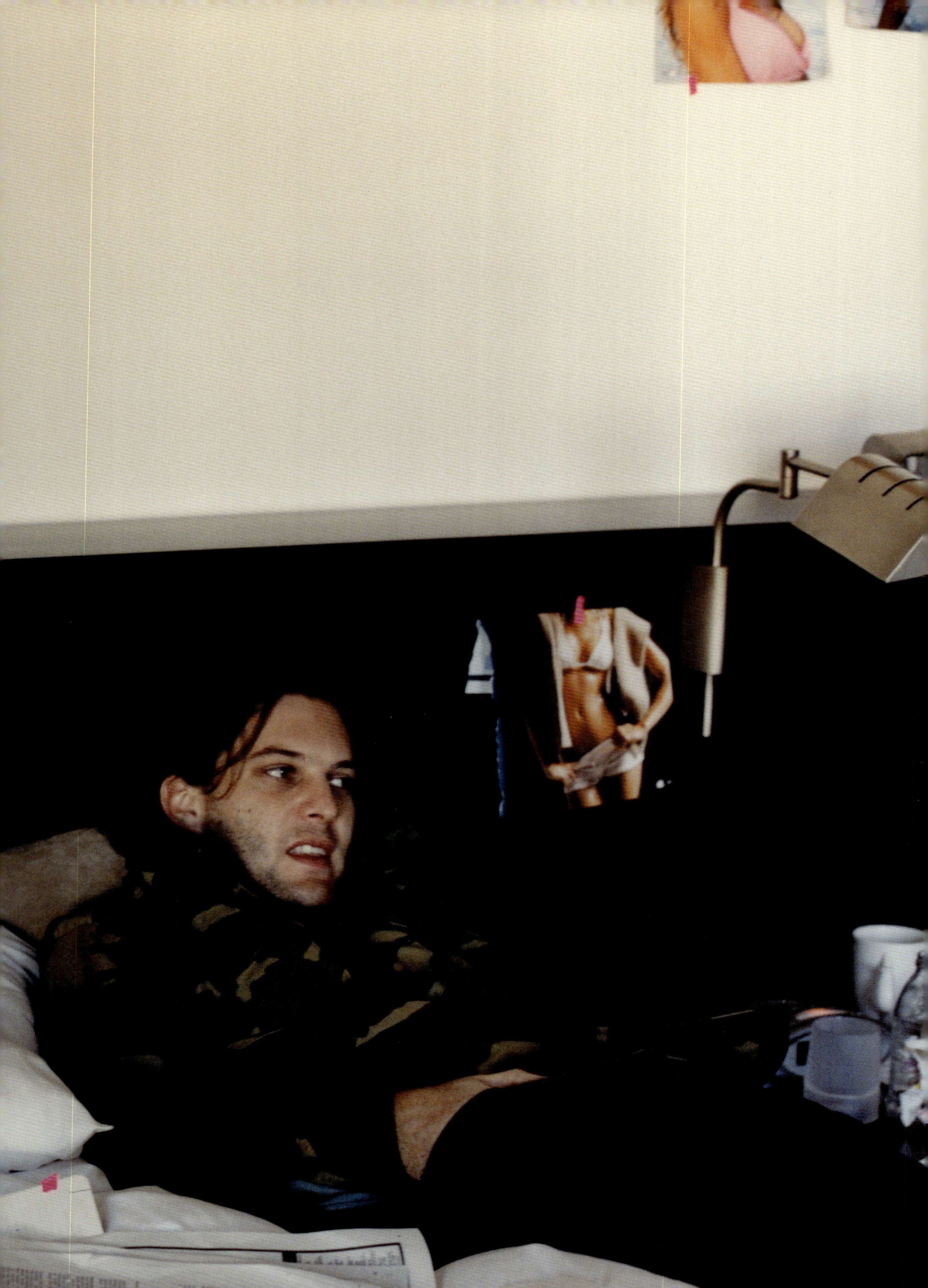

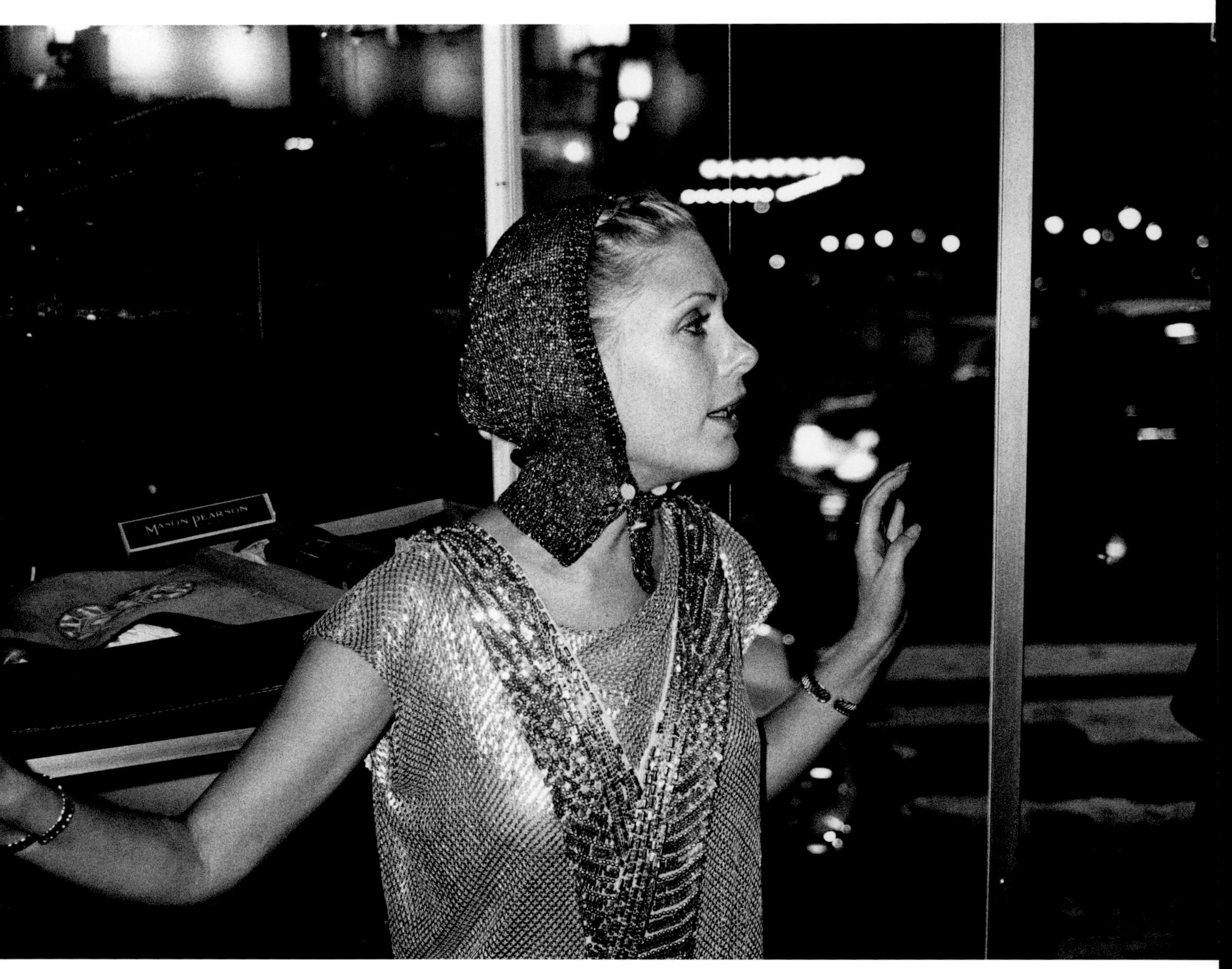
MASON PEARSON

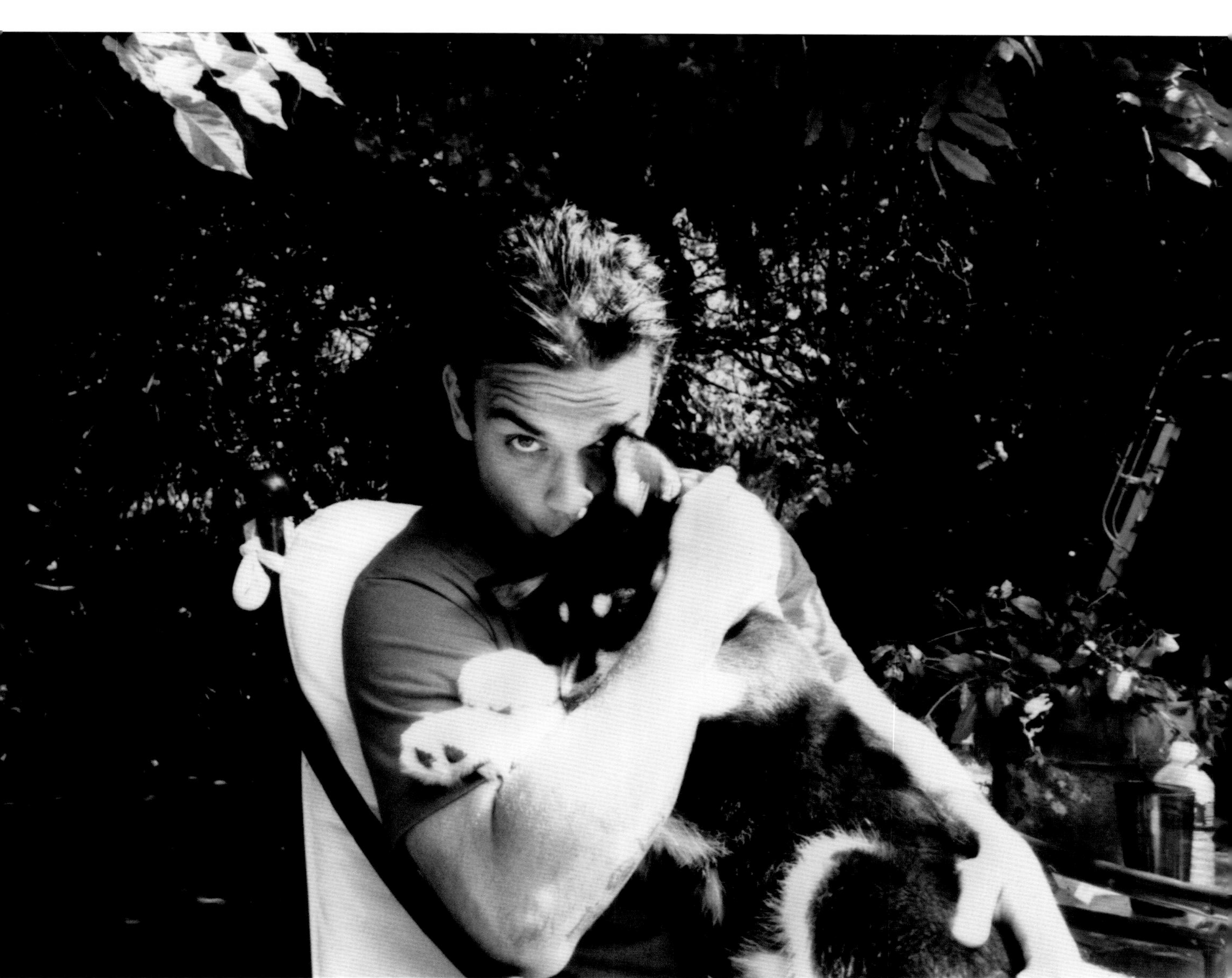

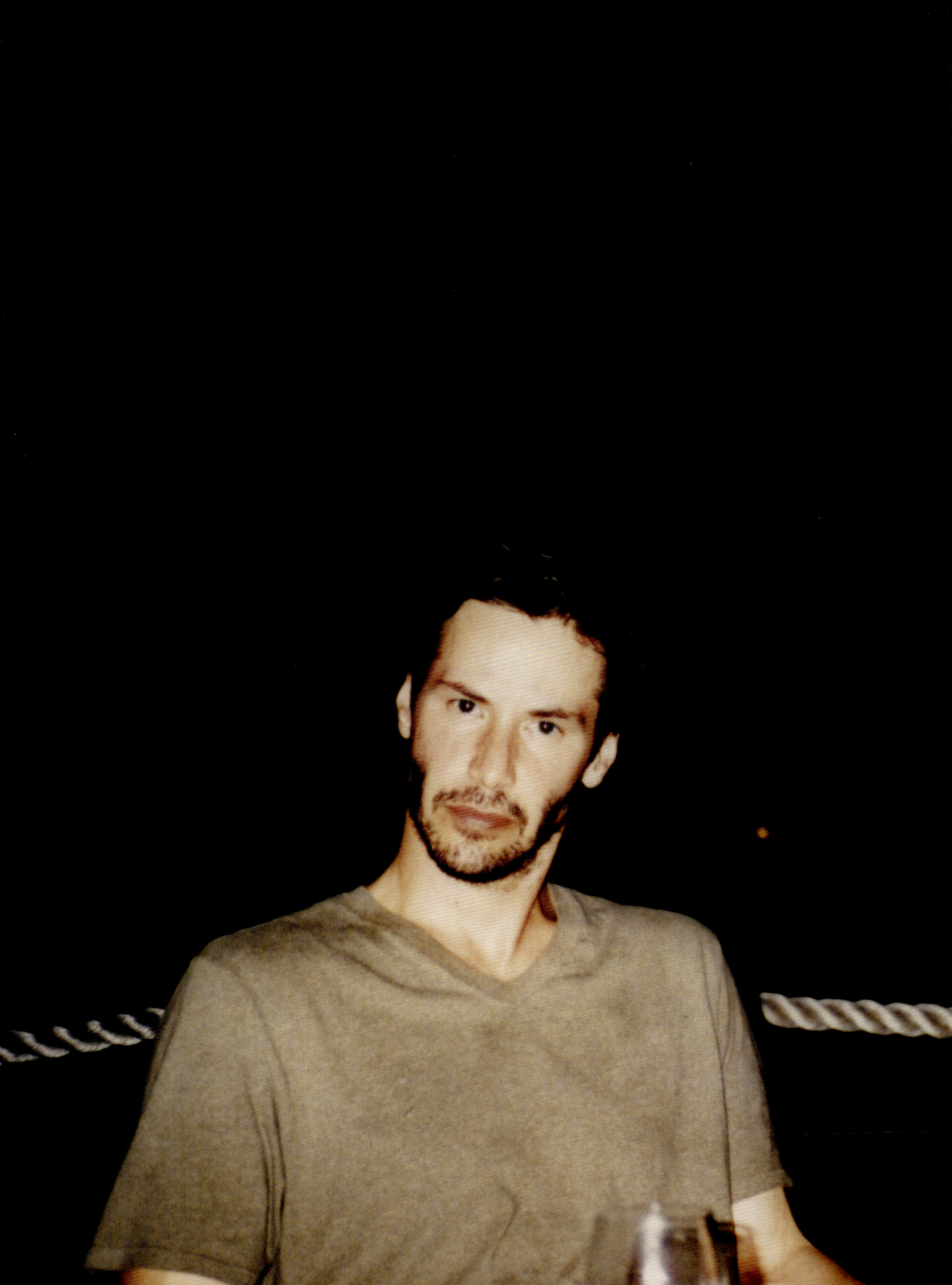

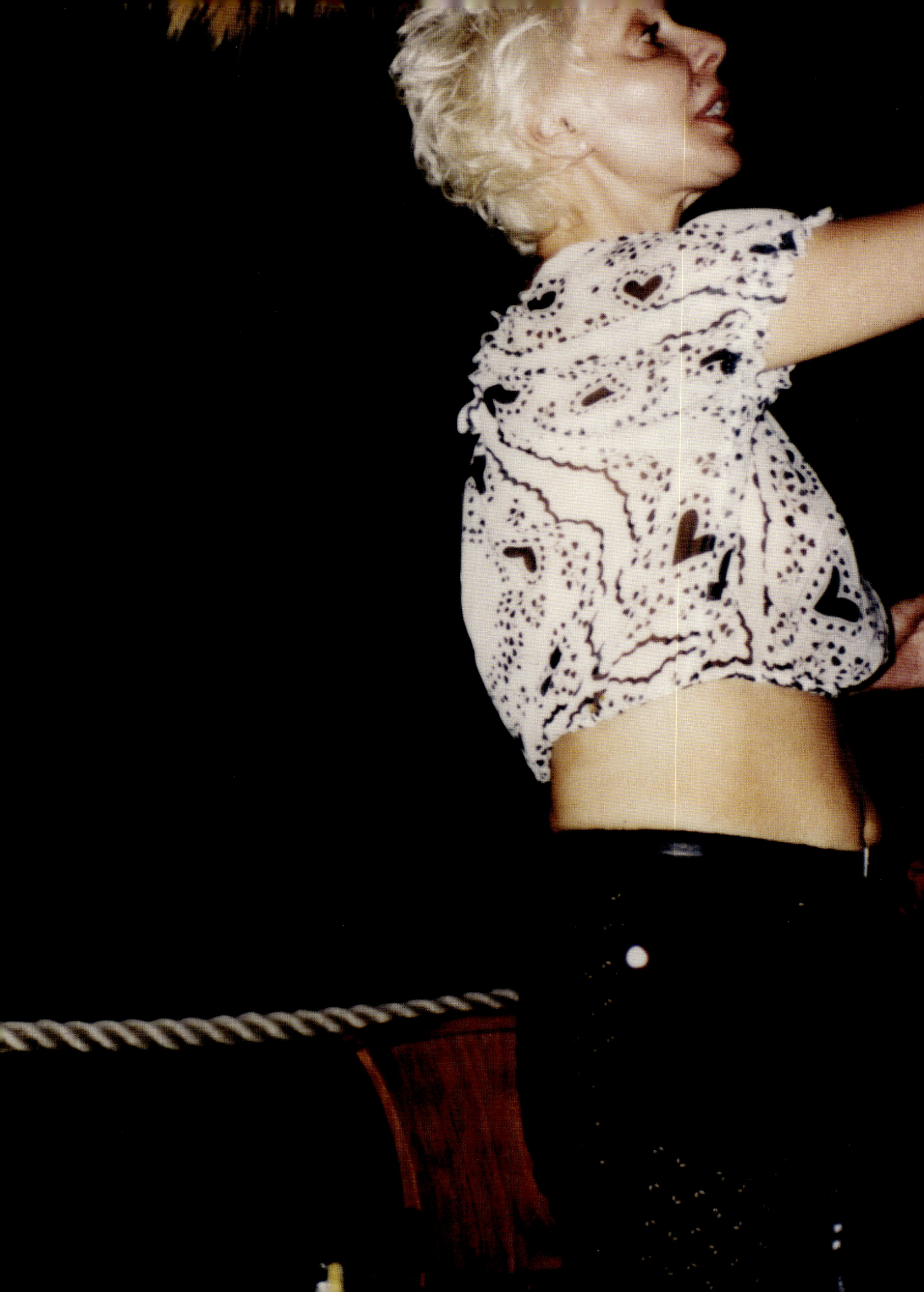

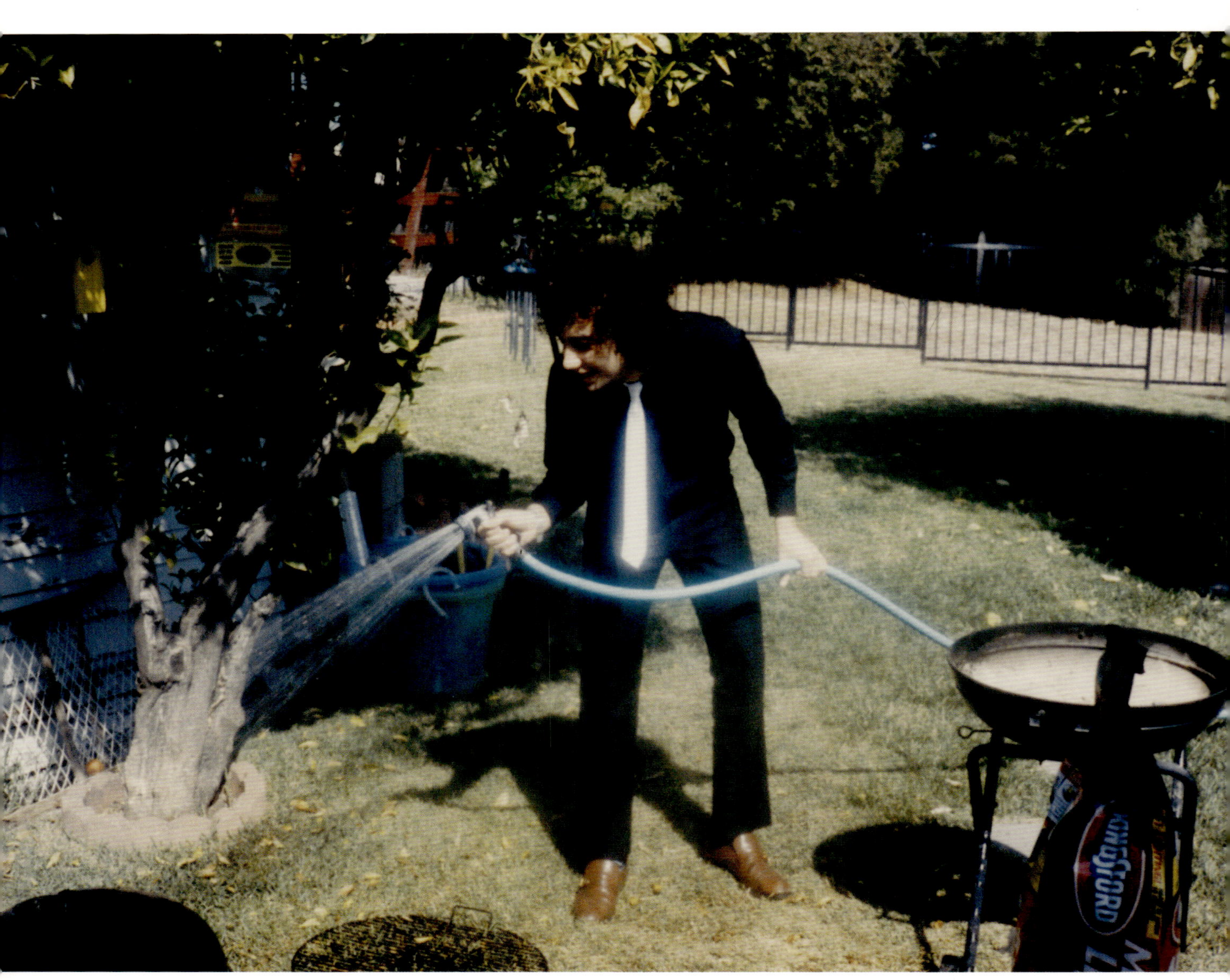

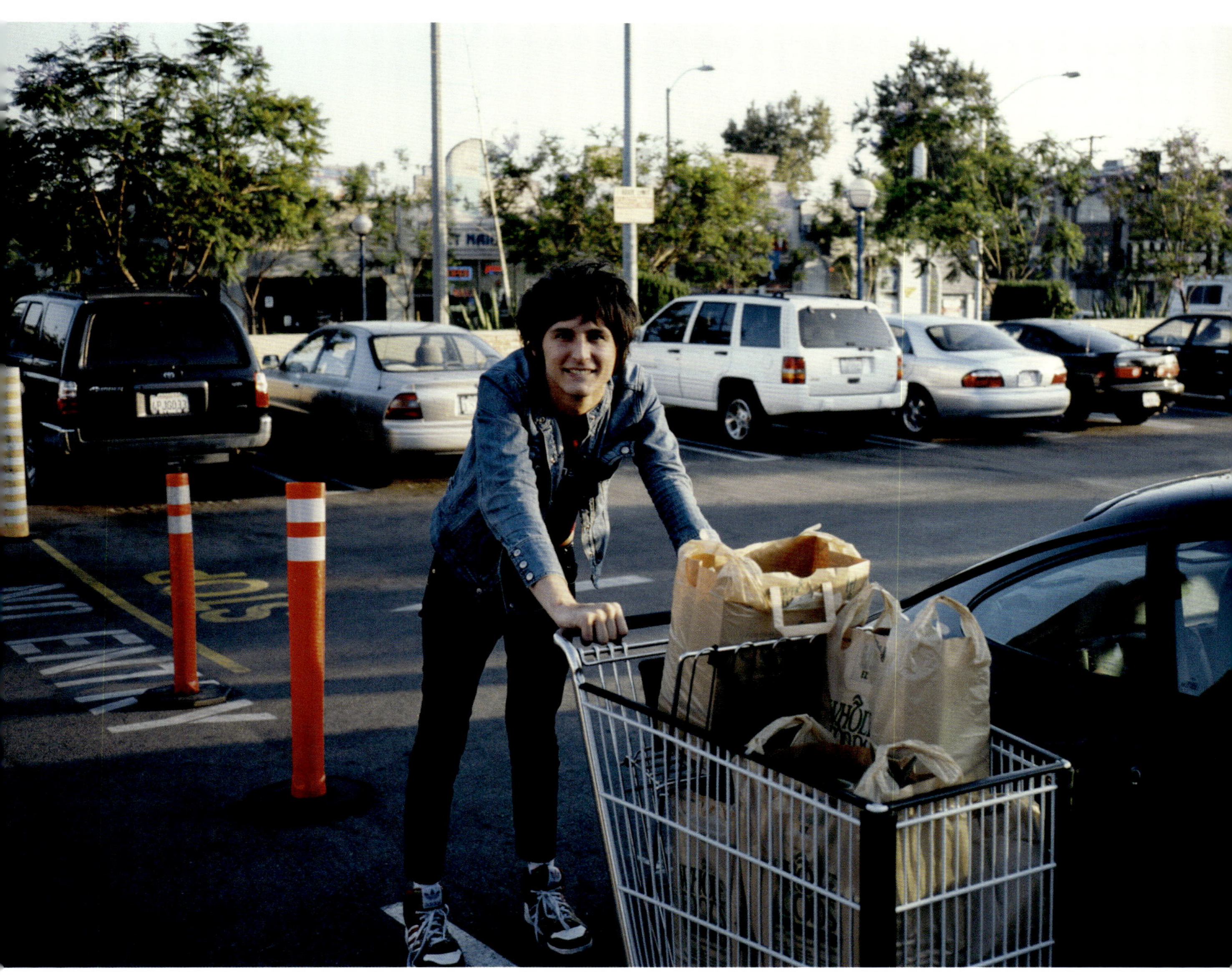

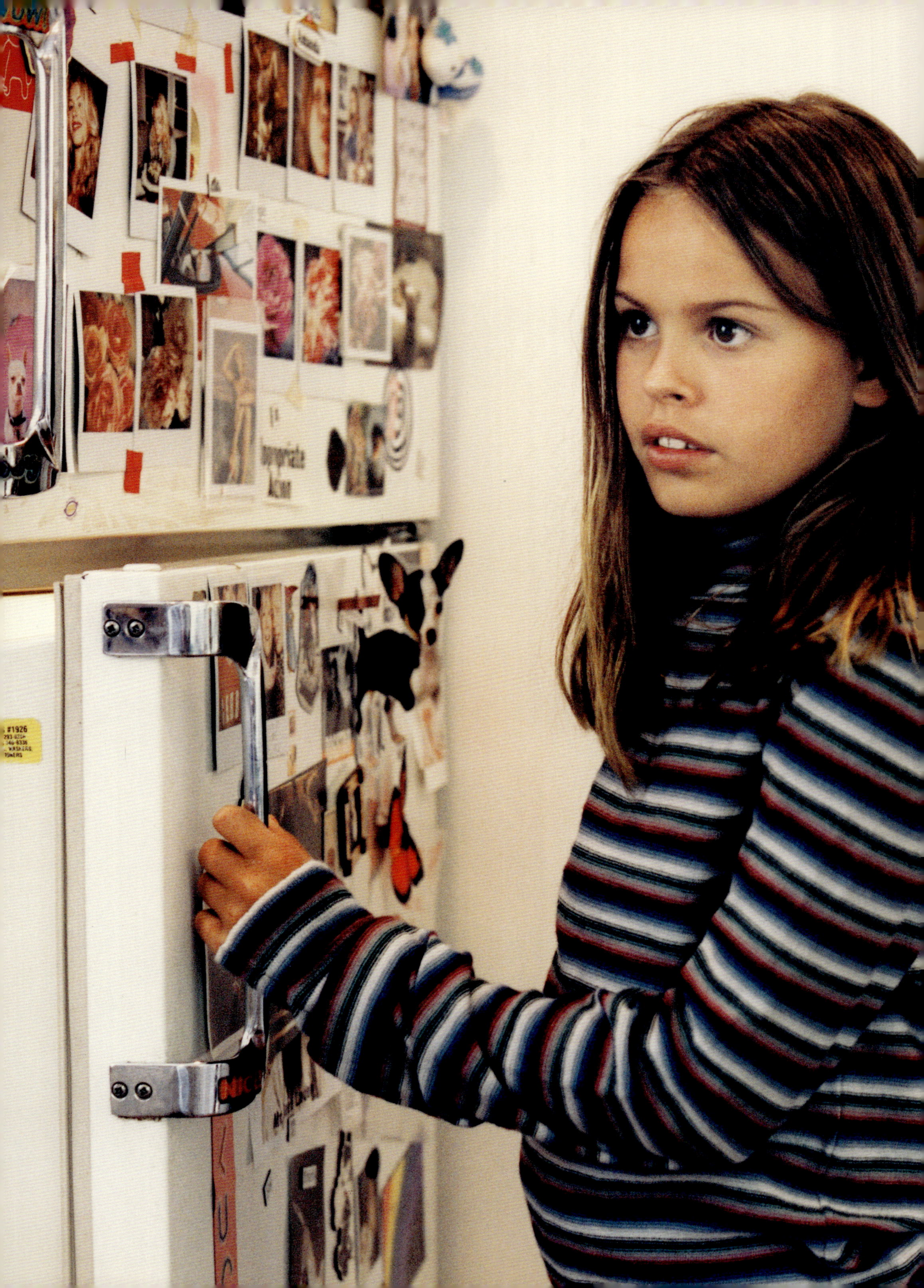

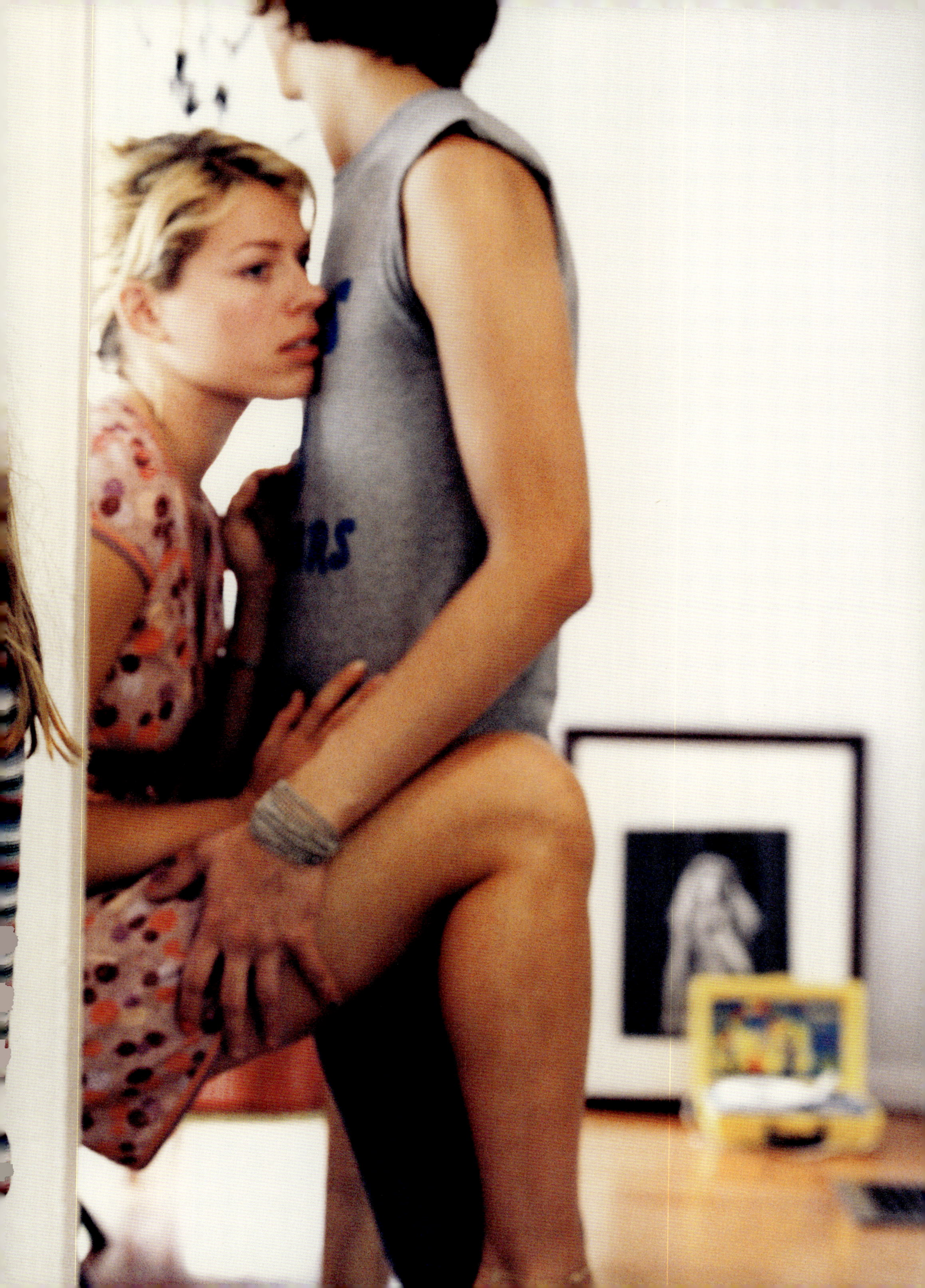

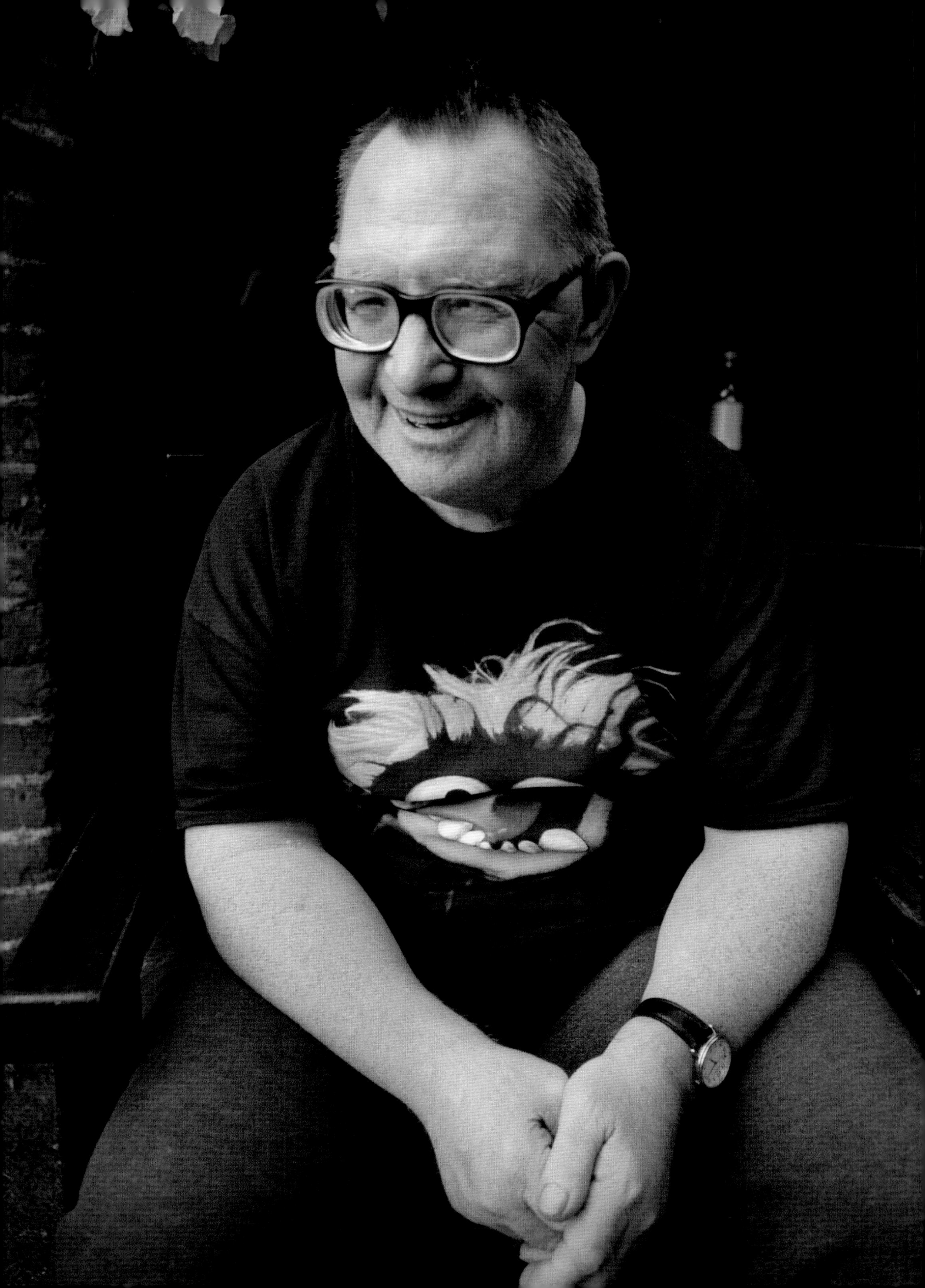

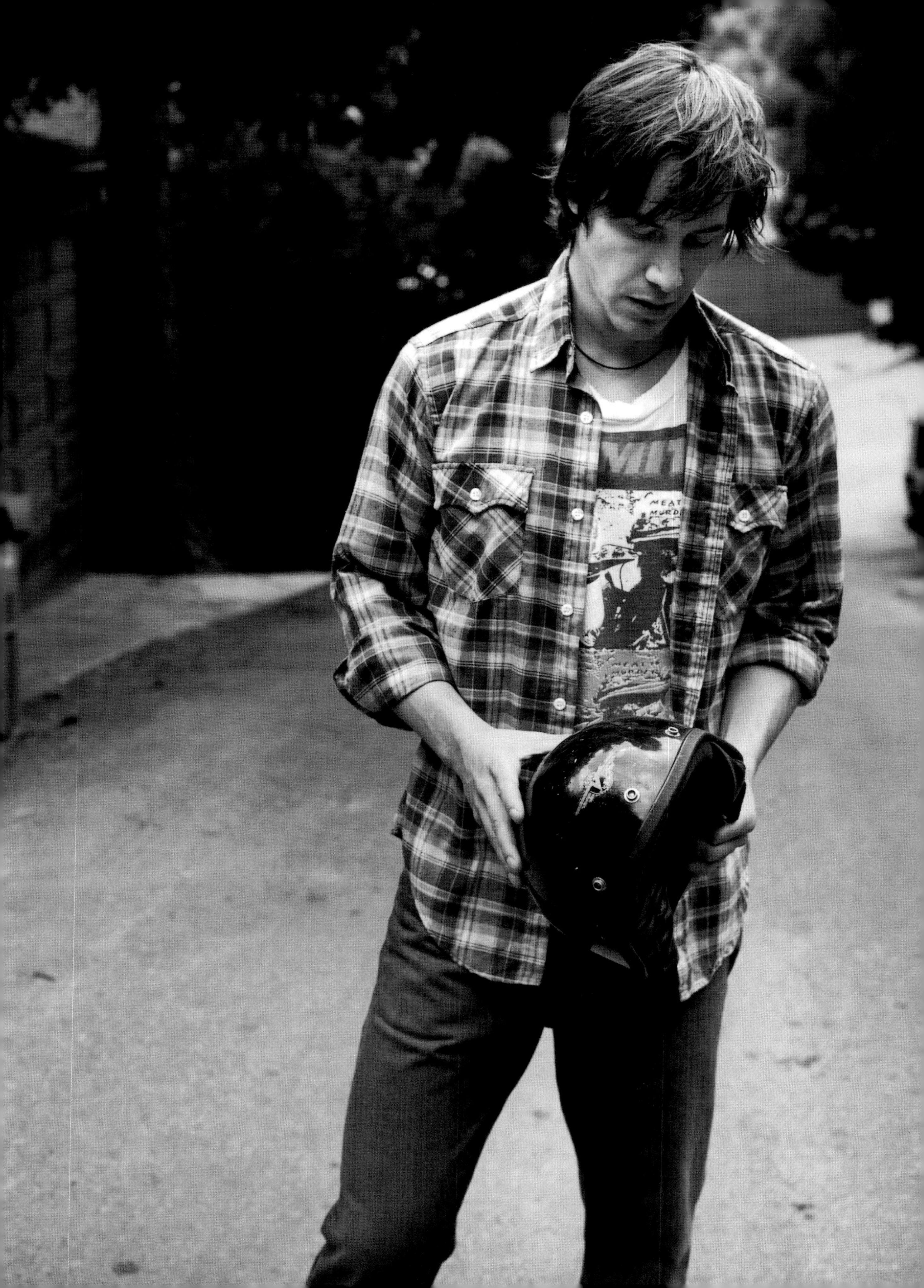
MEAT

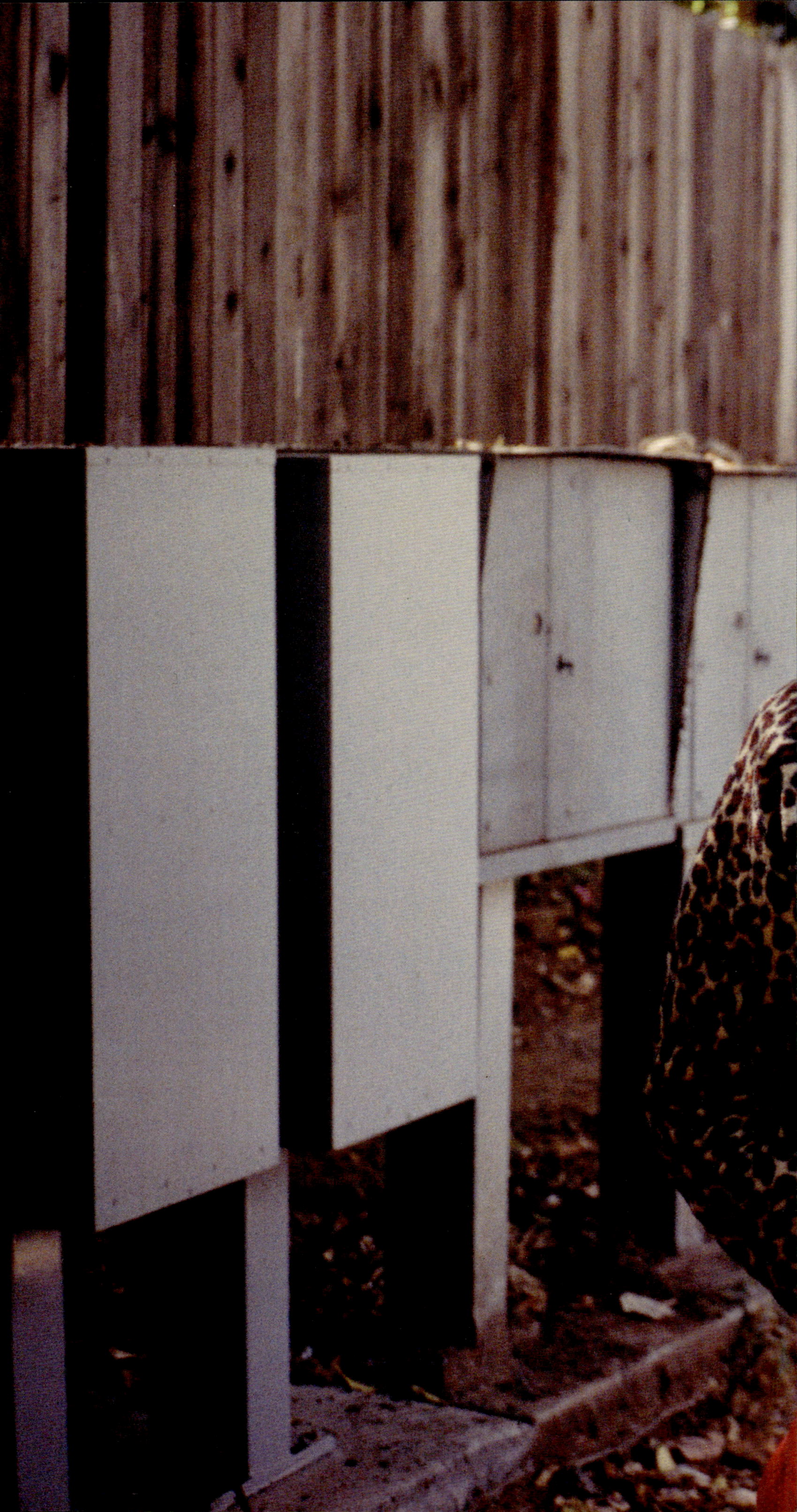

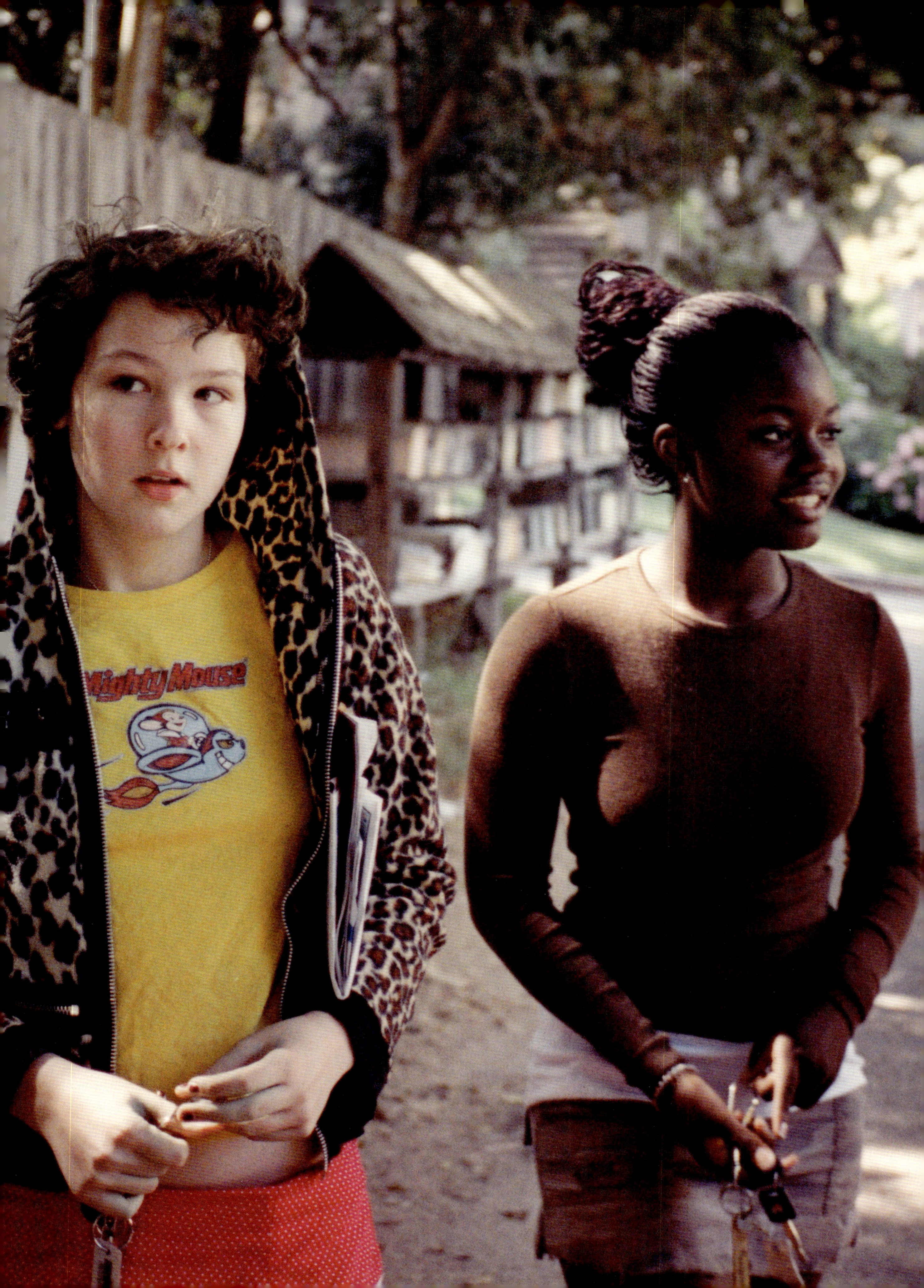
Mighty Mouse

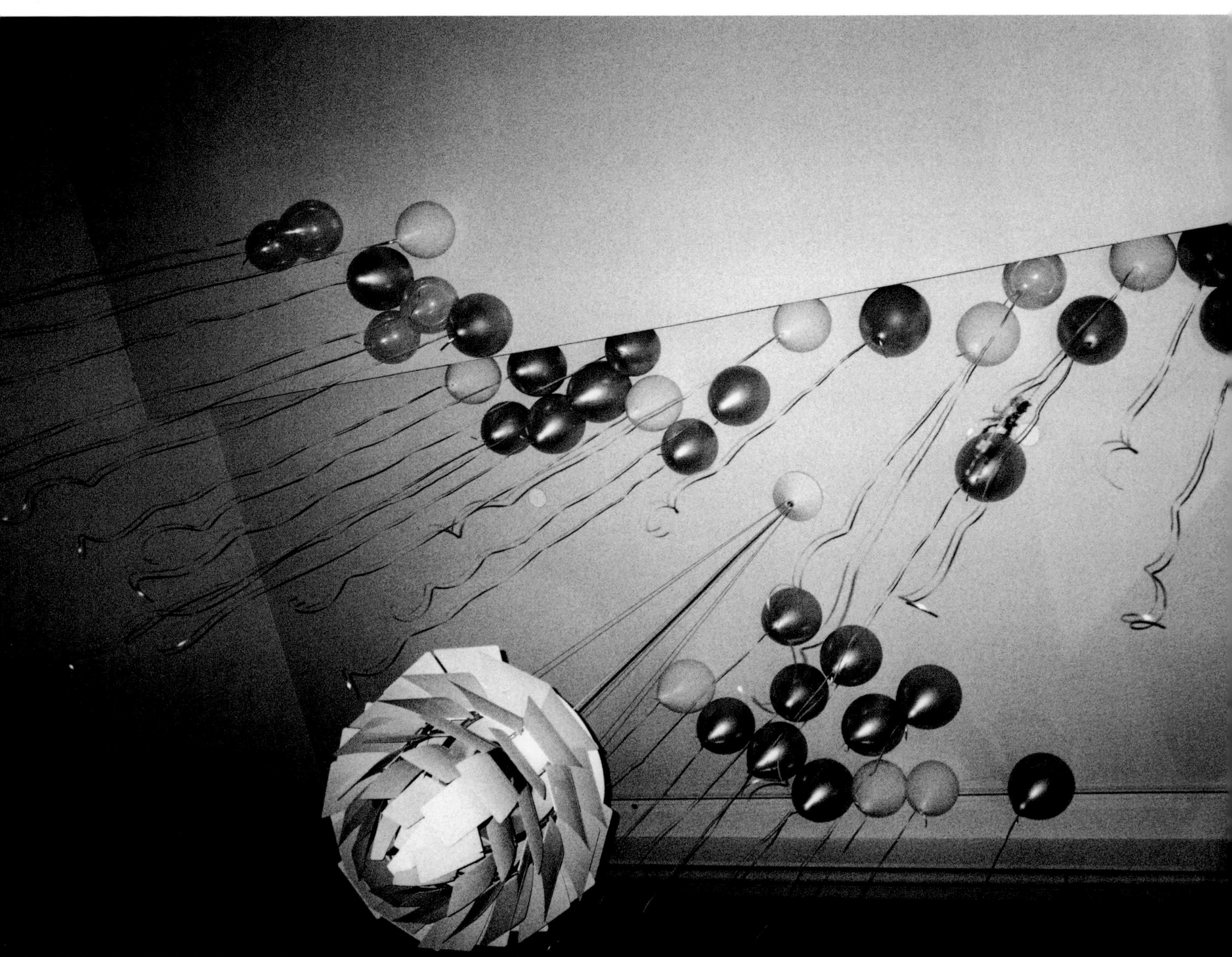

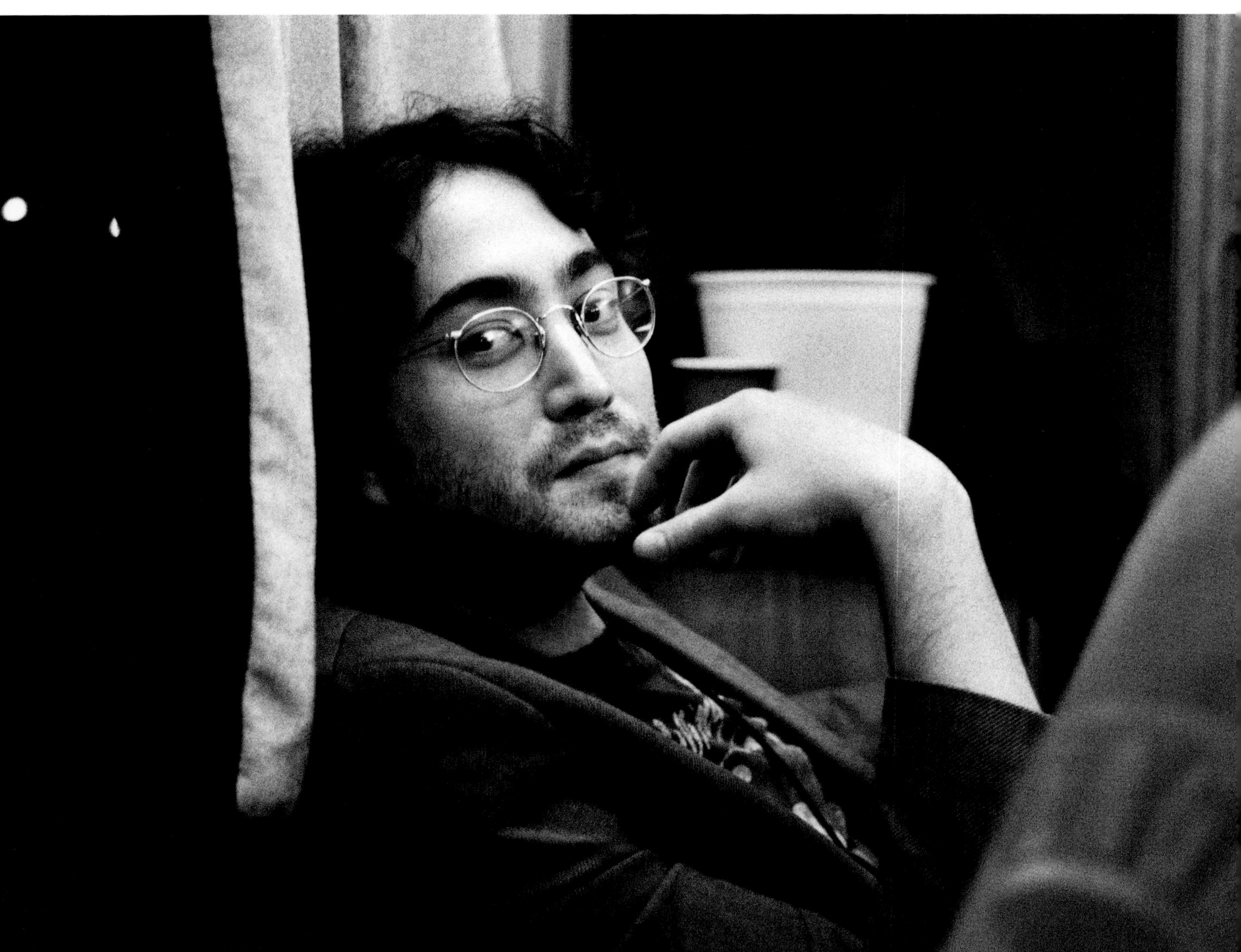

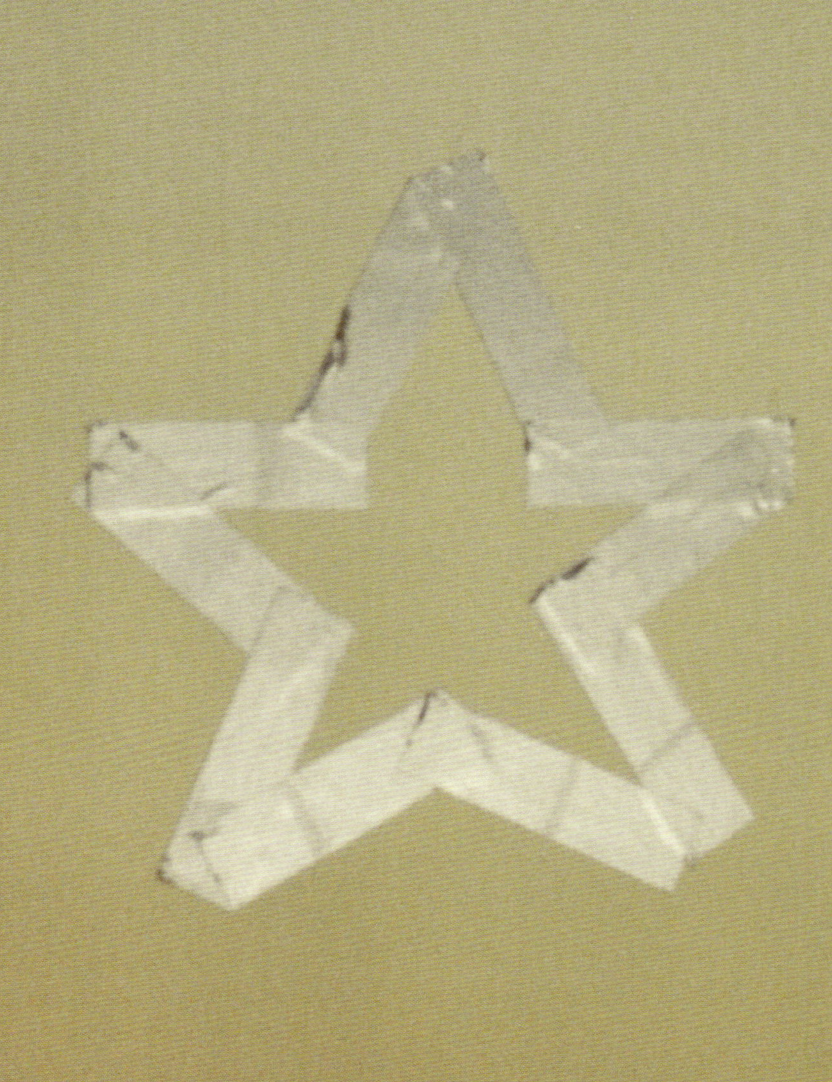

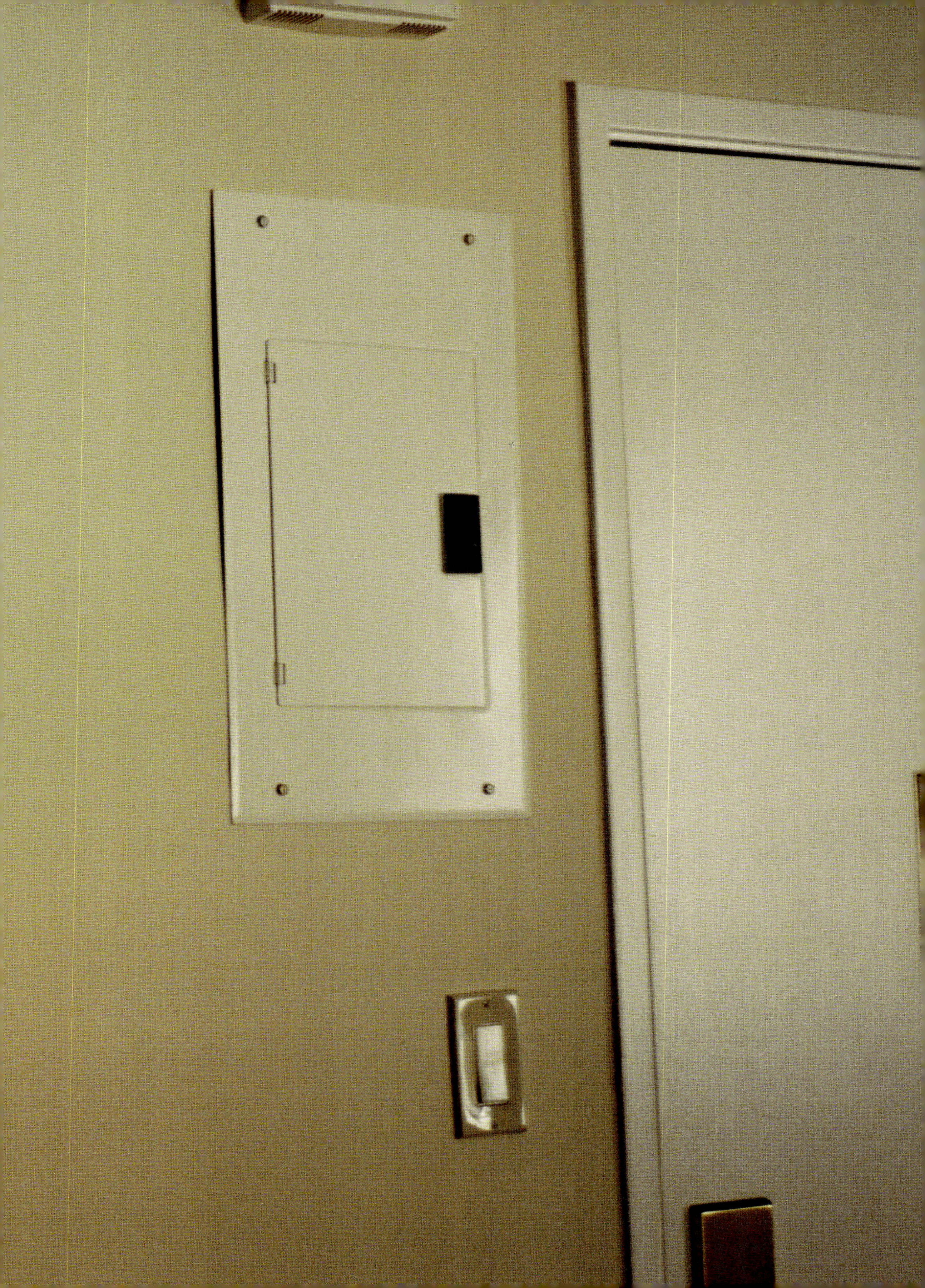

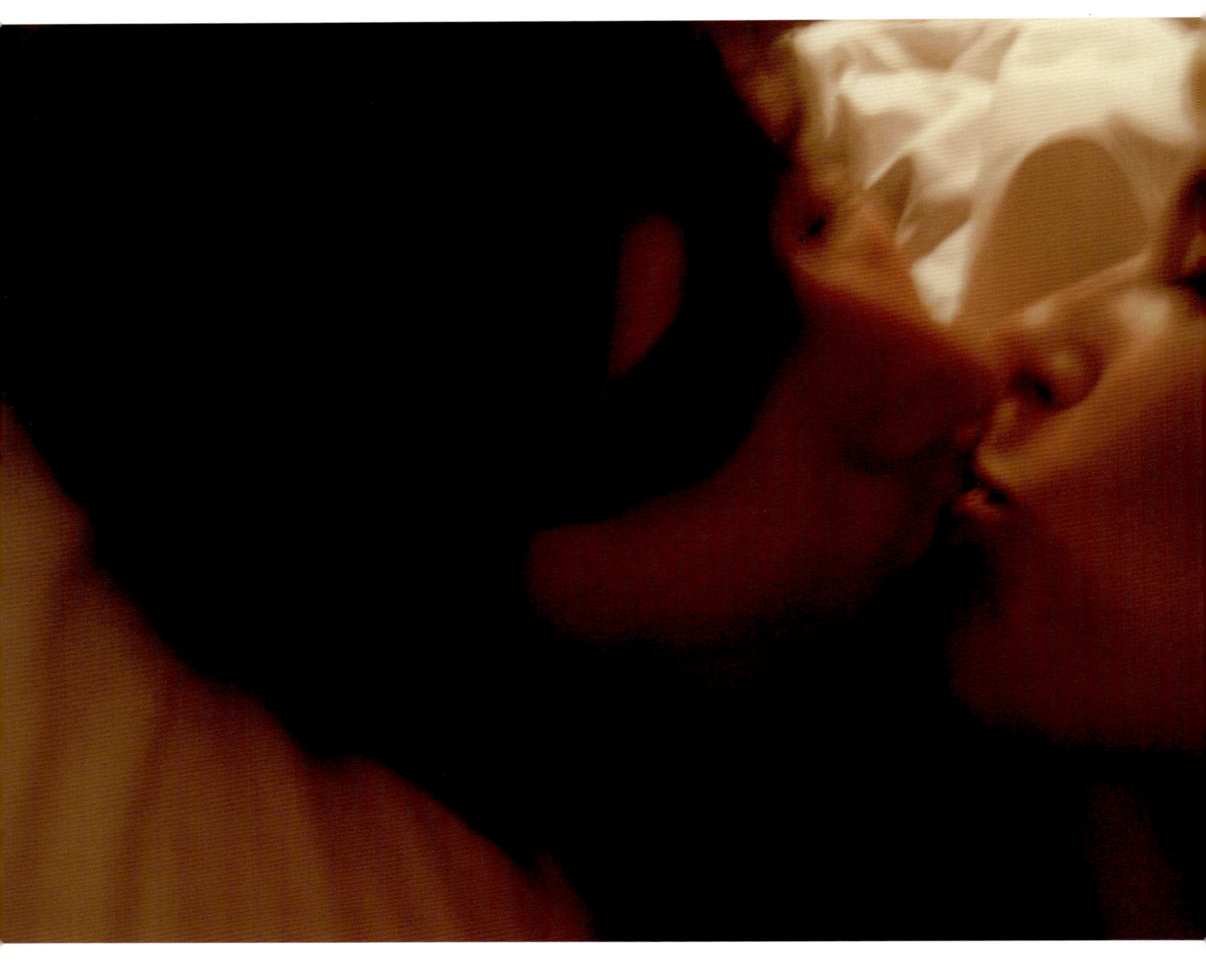

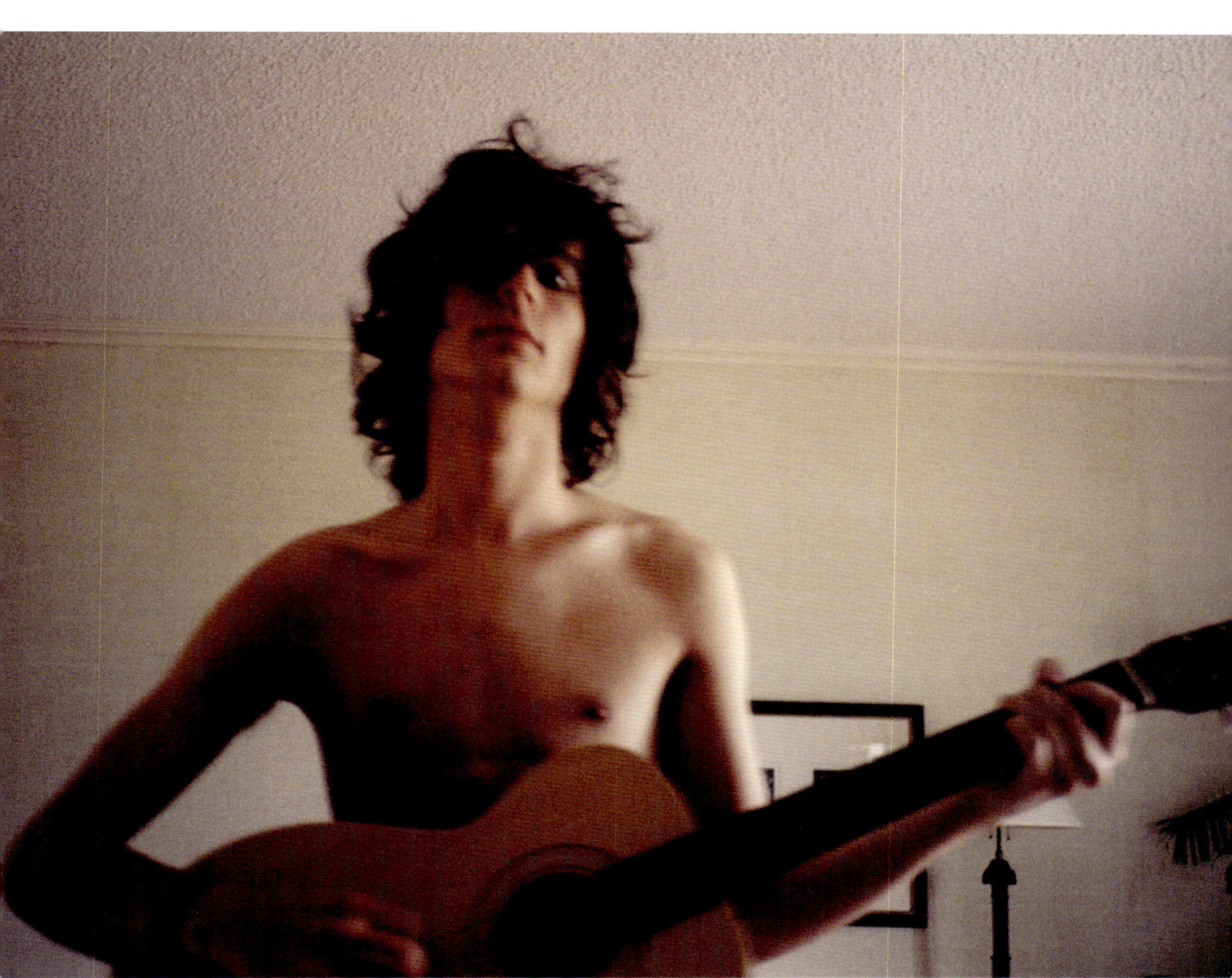

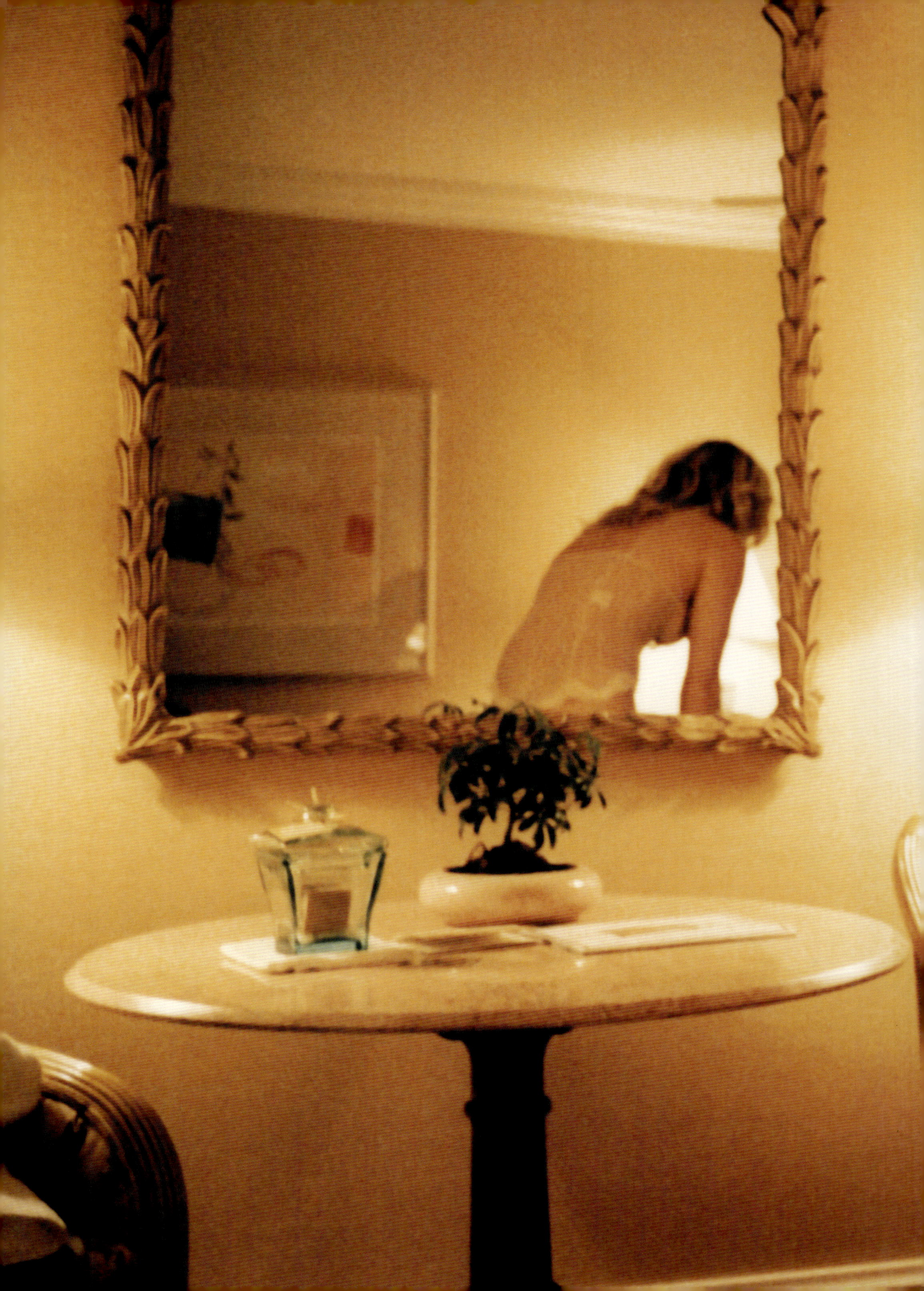

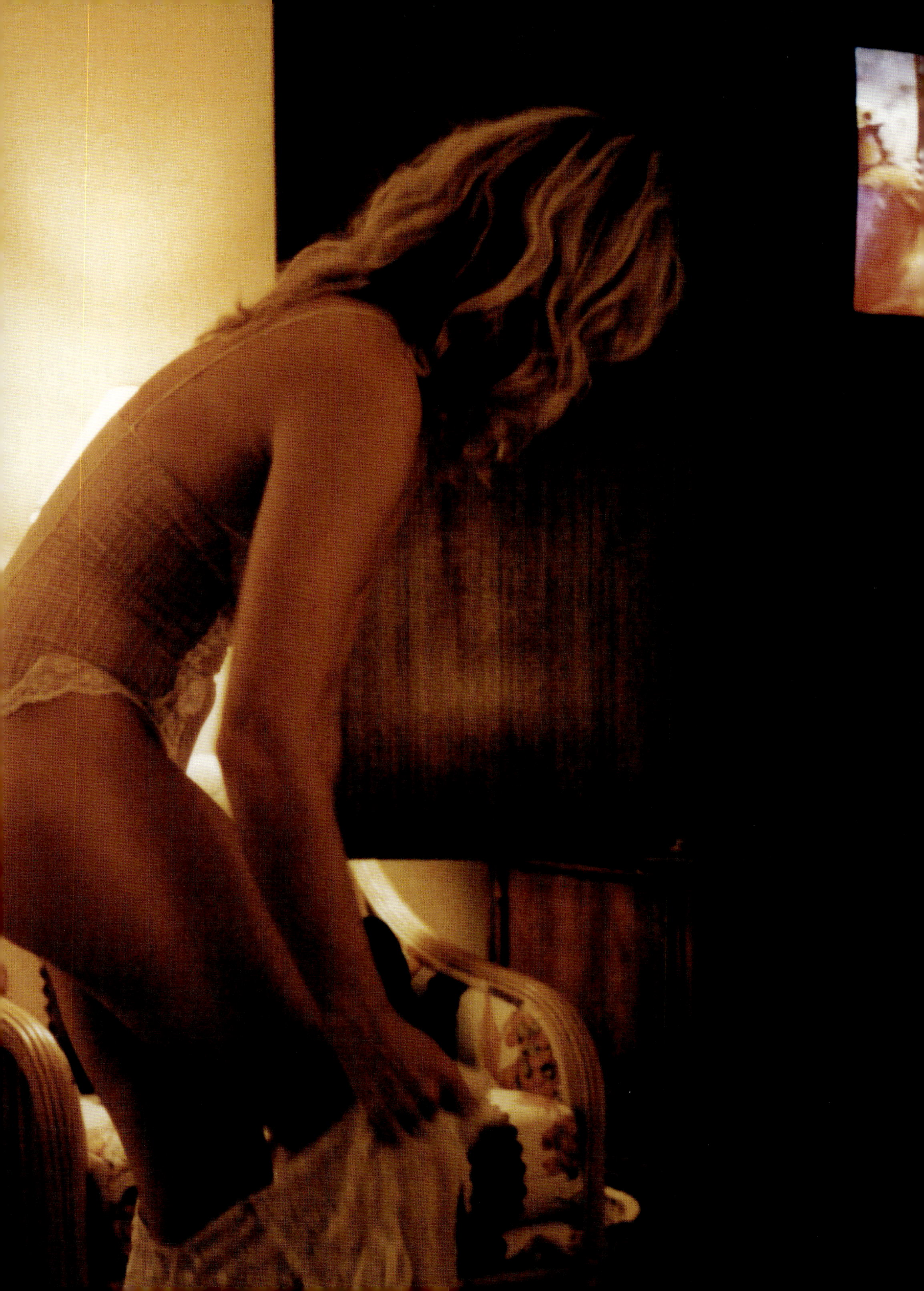

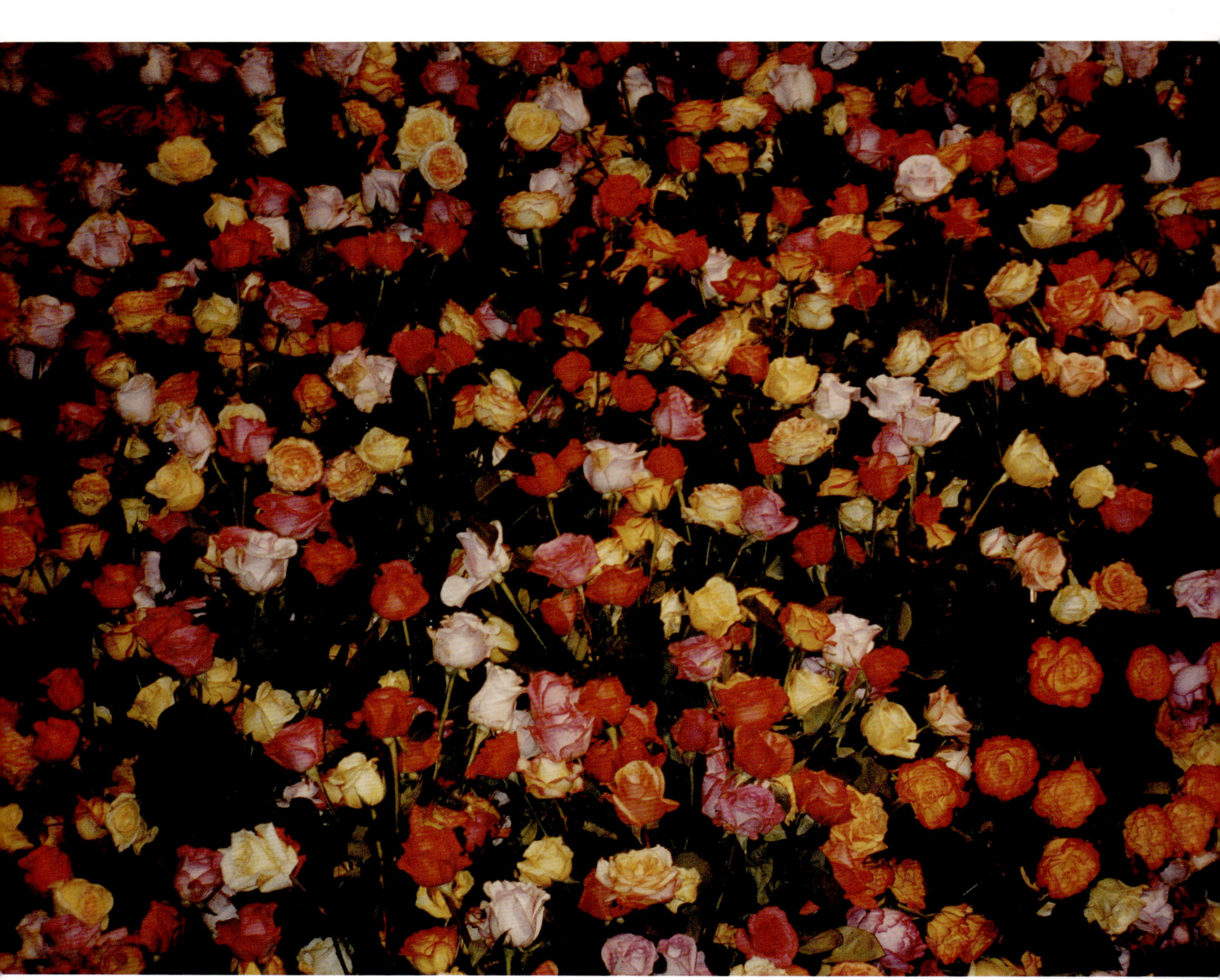

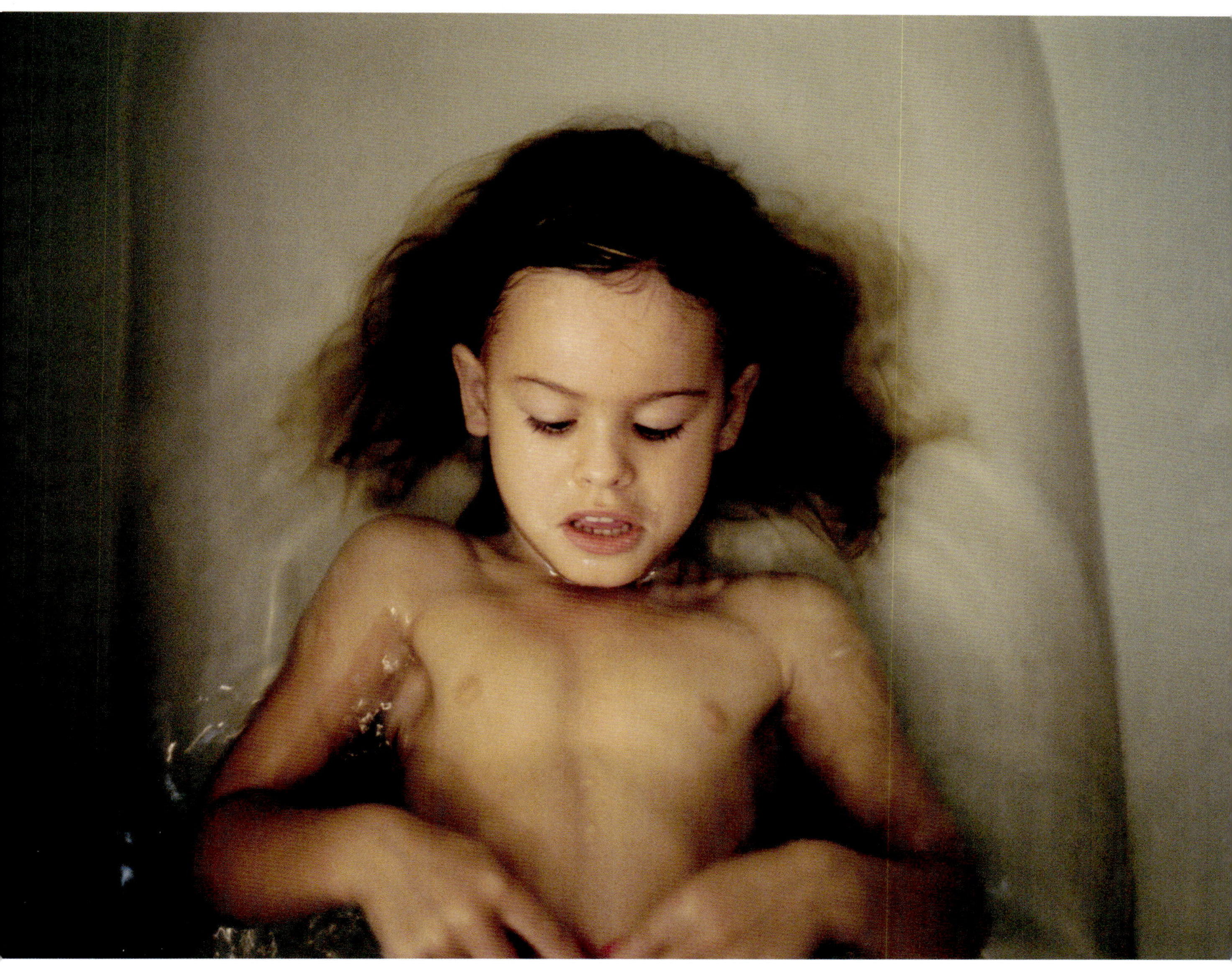

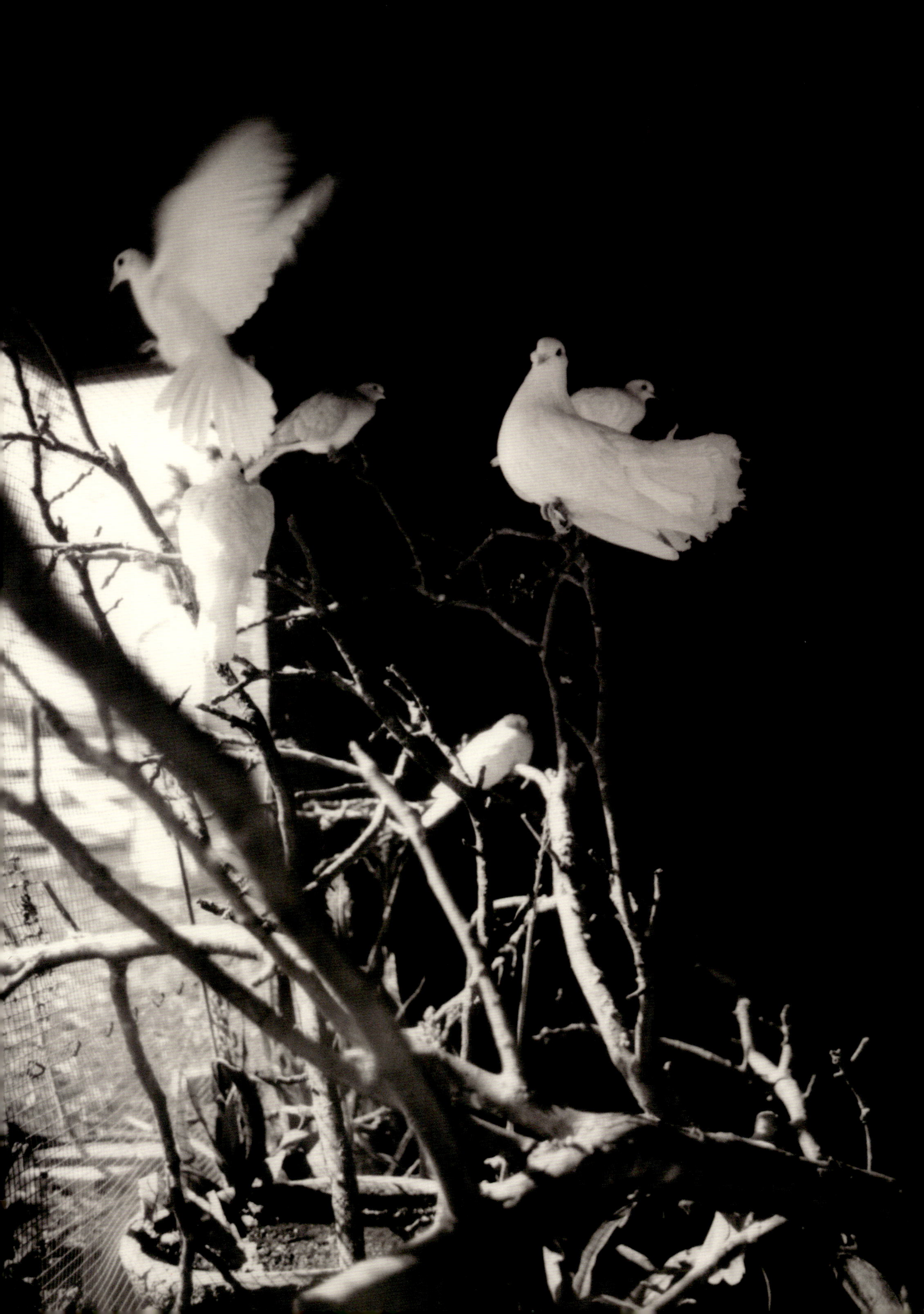

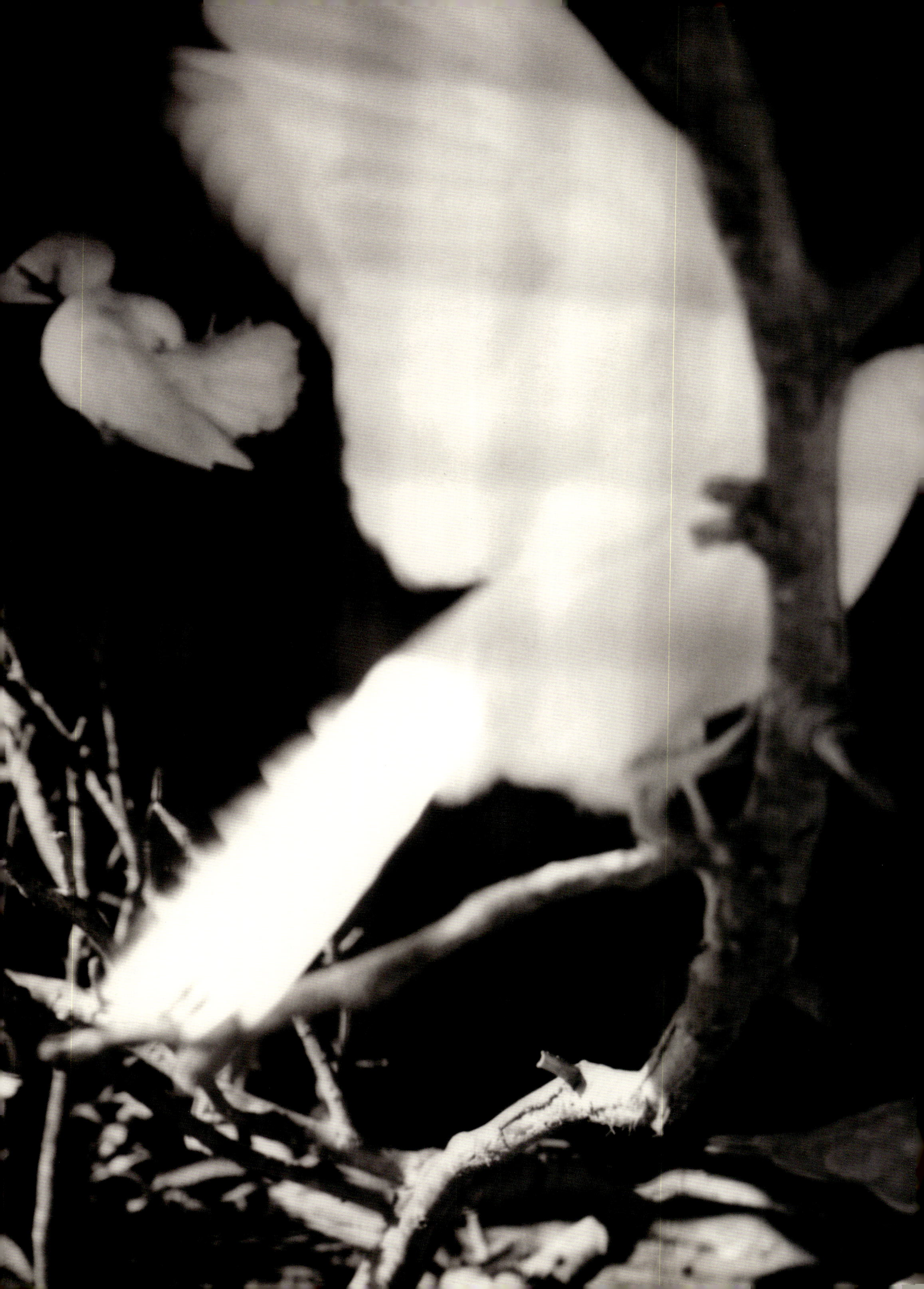

I first met Amanda in the summer of 1999, the summer before I moved to New York City. It was a hot quintessentially English July: Wimbledon and strawberries, people spilling onto the streets from pubs, Pimm's glasses firmly in hand. I had been aware of Amanda since I was quite young, when photographs of her were constantly peppering the English tabloids. A pouty blond Catholic school girl, going out with this one or that one, always in a Chanel miniskirt, high as the sky, with an air of irrepressible naughtiness spilling off the page. She was only thirteen when all of this salacious attention began, though to a minor degree she courted it, in so much as we court dangerous things when we are young and don't know any better. She was wrapped up and boxed, placed on a shelf where she simply didn't belong: a beautiful teenage creature whose voice was drowned out by the clamoring projections of others.

The Amanda that I know bears no relation to the Amanda in the headlines. She was almost shy, irrefutably funny, and hid her vulnerability beneath a rather tough exterior that for years has served as her armor. Our friendship began with the gaucheness of a teenage crush. Endless blushing lunches, walks in Holland Park, gossip, swapping books that touched us, phone calls long into the night, filled with cigarettes and secrets. It is important when viewing this book to know a little bit about where Amanda came from and how far she has come. What I love about these photographs is their utter candor and lack of pretense. They are unabashed, raw and real. We are graciously invited into Amanda's world without fanfare or pomp and left to make our own conclusions. The photographs are tender and sly like a love affair, a silent testament to her own skin shedding. While many of her subjects are well known, this is far from a book on celebrity. Instead we feel we have stolen upon something, the heartthrob napping, baseball, boots, birthdays and bruises, courtship and karaoke, the girl scout eating a lollipop with childish relish. Snatches of other people's lives, their highs and lows, solitude, a carpet of roses. Blessed relief from a culture that is oversaturated with the fake and the posed.

What better catharsis, having been documented herself for so many years, than to be behind the camera, ever watchful, assuming the role of documentarian. Through her photography, which has become stronger and stronger, Amanda has found her passion—one that will remain with her for the rest of her life. As her friend, and captive audience, for this I am truly glad.

## Conversation with
### Sophie Dahl + Marc Jacobs

Marc Jacobs has been Amanda's great friend for the past fifteen years, and their friendship is an all-prevailing one. He is both wildly innovative and original, a huge presence in all that is considered popular culture. His voice as Amanda's friend, photography buff, and keen cultural observer is another key part of Amanda's puzzle explained—with humor, affection, and curiosity. We met at the Mercer Hotel very early one Thursday morning. —Sophie Dahl

Sophie Dahl: What's interesting about the book is that knowing Amanda's many layers, you see the different incarnations of who she's been and who she really is shine through.

Marc Jacobs: Yeah it's funny, I was at a concert with her recently, at a Strokes show in some theater in Paris, I think it was called the Zenith, and there she was waving her arms and dancing. And watching her look at the stage it sort of took me right back, and I just thought, 'she's still the same.' There was this energy and this support and there was this love...it's like the people were different. I wasn't with the same group of friends, and of course we've all grown *x* amount of years older, but there she was still with the same energy and excitement. I know Amanda in a very different way now, we've had many lengthy conversations and she's stayed with me at my home, so we've become friends in a much different way.

SD: Closer friends?

MJ: There is something about surviving all of that chaos and stuff that I think brings people together. I don't know if she'll want any of that included—but I don't care.

SD: She said the same thing, "I don't know whether Marc will want to go into the recovery stuff."

MJ: We are both very fortunate to be here today, wanting to do something to contribute to the beauty of the world as opposed to tearing down anything that we possibly could....

SD: I think that there is something so wonderful about going full circle with someone.

MJ: Well that's what I mean. To know that complete surfaceness of me, me, me, I, I, I, and who cares, let's just have fun, and then to see that you can still have fun and you can still contribute. You start from a perspective totally from the outside then go inside and out. It's really cool.

SD: I suppose it's a bit like having siblings because you know that you are part of each other's history.

MJ: I probably know more about Amanda—or I've spent more time with Amanda—than I have my own sister. I have a closer relationship with Amanda than I do any member of my family, to be honest.

SD: One of the things that I love the most about the book is how it's this documentary of what she sees as interesting. It's like what you said about watching her at the concert. Keeping those things that she loves but embracing them in a different, more creative way. What does the book say to you?

MJ: I think that it's about ego, partially, and then also a kind of generosity. It think she's saying, "I am going to share how much I have been touched by these people. I have been inspired to record and hold this moment in some way but I'd also like to share this with anyone who is interested in a little bit of my life."

SD: I thought it was a bit like stumbling on someone's personal photo album.

MJ: I personally would rather look at intimate moments. And again, I don't know if it's out of ego or generosity, or if it's both, and I think both are fine, that one decides to share their experiences with whoever is interested.

SD: I think it's a bit of both. You have to be very brave and honest to let people in like that.

MJ: It's a lot of work and it's a lot of letting go.

SD: I love that picture of the granny and the Brownie with the lollipop. What sticks out for you? Which are the ones that you love?

MJ: I like the layouts with the flowers. I love the ones of the concert, in the crowd at the Strokes show again....I guess what I respond to are the ones that say to me, "I am very much Amanda."

SD: If you could have one, which would you have?

MJ: I respond to things that are a bit clichéd. That's why I like the audience at the rock concert, and I love the Sophie Dahl. Oh no not Sophie Dahl, the Brody Dalle. You're no relation are you?

SD: I think she must be related to Béatrice Dalle because they look rather similar.

MJ: They have that same kind of punky attitude. I mean, to me those images are classic.

SD: What's not to love? You've got heartthrob boys, karaoke, and dogs shagging each other.

MJ: And beautiful girls...Sophie Dahl.

SD: Ha! Me post-heartbreak and Brody Dalle with a fuck-you smile.

MJ: And then you've got kooky old Rose McGowan.

SD: I love that picture. I also love the self-portrait of Amanda in the hotel room, I can't tell it's her.

MJ: It reminds me very much of an artist whose work I am very fond of named Lisa Yuskavage. Painterly teen girl...it has a slight *Playboy*-esque quality. And again it is that girly-ness of the picture that gives me the sense of a diary, or of being inside a girl's bedroom with pictures all over her wall. In that way the photo becomes a narrative, like a bathroom mirror with tons and tons of snapshots hung up, do you know what I mean? It opens up other stories and possibilities.

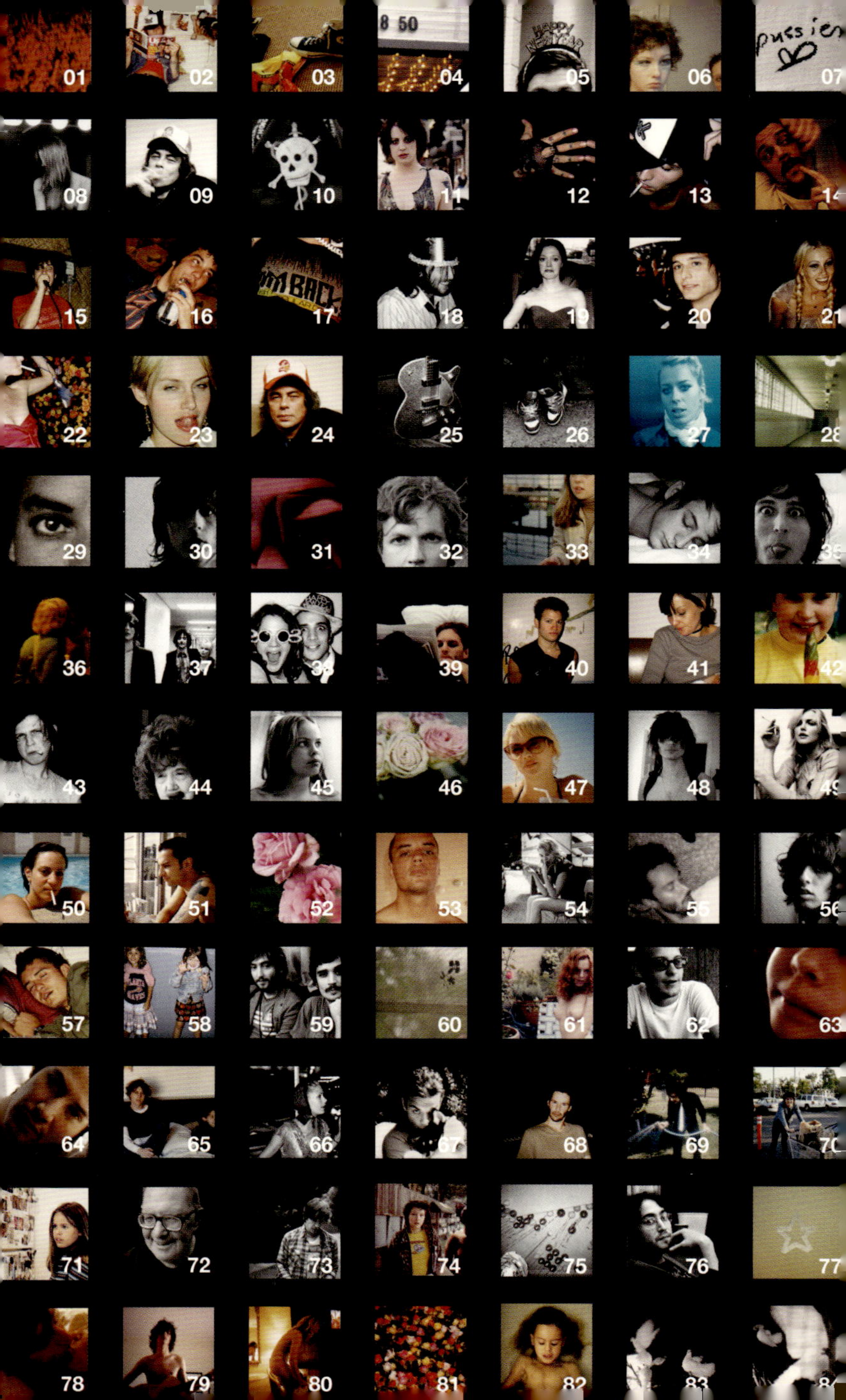
01
02
03
8 50
04
HAPPY NEW YEAR
05
06
pussies
07
08
09
10
11
12
13
14
15
16
17
18
19
20
21
22
23
24
25
26
27
28
29
30
31
32
33
34
35
36
37
38
39
40
41
42
43
44
45
46
47
48
49
50
51
52
53
54
55
56
57
58
59
60
61
62
63
64
65
66
67
68
69
70
71
72
73
74
75
76
77
78
79
80
81
82
83
84

## Index


01 Crowd
02 Nick/Bob/Zig
03 Cons
04 Matrix
05 Matt
06 Lena/Mia
07 Wall
08 Ali
09 Benicio
10 Vietnam
11 Brody
12 Hands
13 Nick
14 PJ
15 Fab
16 Albert
17 Nick
18 John
19 Rose
20 The Strokes
21 Kirsty/Paul
22 Red Dress
23 Amber
24 Benecio
25 Guitar
26 Adidas
27 Amanda
28 Interior
29 Nick K
30 Nick
31 Roses
32 Beck
33 Jenny
34 Nick
35 Nick
36 The Strokes
37 Backstage
38 Drew/Fab
39 Patrick
40 Alexander
41 Sam
42 Brownie
43 Matt
44 Funny Face Gina
45 Atlanta
46 Roses
47 Catherine
48 Nick
49 Sophie
50 Josie
51 Dave/Atlanta
52 Roses
53 Nick K
54 Annie
55 Keanu
56 Adam
57 Orlando
58 Atlanta/friend
59 Fab/Albert/John
60 Screen Door
61 Karen
62 Tobey
63 Atlanta
64 Keanu
65 The Vines
66 Tara
67 Robbie
68 Keanu/Patric
69 Albert
70 Nick
71 Atlanta/Amanda/Nick
72 Cookie Monster
73 Keanu
74 Lena/Kourtnee
75 New Years
76 Sean
77 Hotel Room
78 Amanda/Nick
79 Nick On Guitar
80 Getting Dressed
81 Roses
82 Atlanta In Tub
83 Doves
84 Doves

# Acknowledgements

Amber Valletta, Kirsty Hume, Sante D'Orazio, Emma Reeves, Richard Brown, Jason Weinberg, Francesca Sorrenti, Jillian Dempsey, everyone at Marc Jacobs (especially Jennifer Seagum and Robert Rich), The Strokes (especially Fab Morretti), Cody Smyth, Catherine Pierce, Drew Barrymore, my secret agent Carol Leflufy, John Walsh, Tracey Lynch, Andrew Richardson, Shannon Hamblin, everyone at Wiz Kid Management (Matt, Ryan, Juliet, and Esperanza), Chris Boales, John Taylor, Lena Loukes, Donald Schneider, Kent and Kath Ewing, Orlando Bloom, Vanina Sorrenti, Doraly Rosen, Brody Dalle, Patric Reeves, Jack Nicholson, Linda Atkins, everyone at the Mercer, Steven Pranica, Victoria Mahoney, Nadine Johnson, Kanya, Dennis Watson at Tapestry, Ione Skye, Raja at Coloredge, Mick Jagger, Amanda Peet, Serene Ciccora, Brent Bolthouse, Joanna Jordan, Jefferson Hack, Stephen Toner, Soraya Dayani, Terry Jones, Jill Fritzo at PMK/HBH, Holly Hein, Fleshtone LA, Pascal Dangin, Rose Cefalu, Johnny Rosza, Aleks Woroniecka, Pricilla Woolworth, the de Cadenet family, Leonie Edward Jones, Craig Cohen, Ivan Shaw, Bryan Rabin, John Thomas at Stout & Thomas, Mario Sorrenti, Mary Frey, Ciara Parks and Public Eye, Heather Sommerfield, Sophie Dahl, Marc Jacobs, Glen Luchford, Daniel Power, and Paul Jasmin. A special thank you to everyone who appears in this book.

More than ever Keanu Reeves, Nick Valensi, and Atlanta Taylor.

Book Design by Heather Sommerfield + Mary Frey
Photo Edit by Mary Frey
Prints by Raja at Coloredge
Digital Technician Heather Sommerfield
Text Edit by Jefferson Hack

Separations by Schwabscantechnik, Göttingen and Coloredge, New York

Printing and binding by Midas Printing, China

A complete catalog of powerHouse Books and Limited Editions is available upon request; please call, write, or bird-watch on our website.

10 9 8 7 6 5 4 3 2 1

Printed and bound in China



First edition, 2005

Library of Congress Cataloging-in-Publication Data:

Rare birds / photographs by Amanda de Cadenet ; a conversation with Marc Jacobs and Sophie Dahl.-- 1st ed.
p. cm.
ISBN 1-57687-266-1
1. Celebrities--Portraits. 2. Portrait photography. I. Jacobs, Marc, 1963- II. Dahl, Sophie, 1979-

TR681.F3R362 2005
779'.092--dc22 2005048912

Published in the United States by powerHouse Books,
a division of powerHouse Cultural Entertainment, Inc.
68 Charlton Street, New York, NY 10014-4601
telephone 212 604 9074
fax 212 366 5247
e-mail: rarebirds@powerHouseBooks.com
website: www.powerHouseBooks.com